Pioneers
in Every Land

Pioneers
in Every Land

E DITED BY
Bruce A. Van Orden,
D. Brent Smith, and
Everett Smith, Jr.

BOOKCRAFT
Salt Lake City, Utah

Library of Congress Catalog Card Number: 96–80168
ISBN 1–57008–306–1

First Printing, 1997

Printed in the United States of America

CONTENTS

FOREWORD

"The days of pioneering in the Church are still with us; they did not end with covered wagons and handcarts," declared President Gordon B. Hinckley, First Counselor in the First Presidency, in 1993. "The Church has been moving out across the world in a remarkable way, and each time that the gospel is introduced into a country, there are pioneers who participate in the opening of this work."[1]

President Thomas S. Monson added his observations on the same concept: "Wherever the gospel has been taught and membership in the Church flourished, there has first been a pioneer period. Silent and vocal pioneers are raised up by the Lord to prepare the base strength for the Church organization which follows. Frequently, such strength begins with one family."[2]

The Church of Jesus Christ of Latter-day Saints now has more members in countries outside the United States than in the United States.[3] The LDS Church is most assuredly a worldwide phenomenon. Obviously, for the Church to have more than half of its almost ten million members in about 160 other countries means that there are hundreds of thousands of pioneers who have helped establish the foundation of the Church in each of these places.

In 1997 The Church of Jesus Christ of Latter-day Saints is celebrating the 150th anniversary of the arrival of the Mormon pioneers in the Salt Lake Valley in 1847. Church leaders want this celebration to involve the entire world, not only Utah. The First Presidency has noted, "We pray that this pioneer sesquicentennial celebration will reflect the local story of pioneers in every nation [and] will strengthen and bless all Church members as they incorporate the celebration theme, 'Faith in Every Footstep,' into their lives." The celebration guidelines state: "Every ward and branch in our worldwide

Church is supported by faithful Saints who are committed to the restored gospel of Jesus Christ. These Saints are latter-day pioneers. Everyone who strives to stand up for what is right, keep the commandments, share the gospel, testify of Christ, and act as an example of Christian living is a pioneer."[4]

It is for the purpose of honoring our worldwide pioneers that we have compiled these biographical sketches. We desire through *Pioneers in Every Land* to contribute to the pioneer sesquicentennial celebration and to the Latter-day Saints' understanding of the diversity of pioneering experiences. We also wish to promote greater faith in all of us as we unitedly seek to spread the kingdom of God to all nations and prepare a Zion people for the return of our Lord and Master. We recall the words of Ammon, who, together with his missionary brethren, rejoiced in the knowledge that "God is mindful of every people, whatsoever land they may be in; yea, he numbereth his people, and his bowels of mercy are over all the earth" (Alma 26:37).

WHO ARE THE PIONEERS IN EVERY LAND?

The following list includes several categories of Latter-day Saint pioneers in different lands:

1. United States or Canadian expatriates who live or have lived in other countries, often isolated as members of the Latter-day Saint faith. These expatriates have variously served in the military, in diplomatic service, as businesspeople, as educators, or in humanitarian service. In scores of cases these expatriates have shared the gospel with native peoples and have been the means of establishing a legal entity for the Church in their temporary new home.

2. New members of the Church from a specific country who convert elsewhere, such as in the United States or Europe, but then return to their home country and are instrumental in building up the Church there. This phenomenon has occurred in recent years with valuable results for such places as Ghana, Nigeria, and the former Yugoslavia. Emmanuel Abu Kissi and his wife, Benedicta Elizabeth Banfo, in Ghana and Krešimir Ćosić in the former Yugoslavia are examples of this pioneer type; their stories appear in this book.

3. Missionaries who labor diligently to establish the foundation of the Church in a country or region during the first five or so years after it is opened for proselyting. These missionaries include couples, young elders, and young sisters.

4. Converts made within the first five or so years of proselyting in a country or region. Occasionally some of the influential pioneers are men or women who later leave the Church or its activity, but who help establish the Church in the new country while they remain in it. But the pioneers who have the greatest impact are those who are in for the long haul and who, over the period of the next few decades, create solidarity for the Church and the gospel in their region. Rhee Honam and his wife, Youn Soon Park, from South Korea fit into this category, as do Masao and Kisako Watabe in Japan and Milton and Irene Soares in northeastern Brazil. Pornchai Juntratip, the first Thai patriarch, came into the Church about seven years after missionary work recommenced in modern Thailand and at a time when the Church in that strongly Buddhist country was very much in its infancy.

5. New immigrants to a country who bring the precious restored gospel with them at the time of their immigration. These individuals often request that the Church send representatives to care for them and their spiritual needs and to baptize their interested family members or friends. This was especially the case with the immigrant German Latter-day Saints in Argentina and Brazil.

6. Men and women who in times past were sent by Church leaders in Salt Lake City to colonize places far away from the center stakes of Zion. The two most noteworthy examples are the southern Alberta colonies in Canada and the Chihuahua colonies in northern Mexico, both created as refuges during the antipolygamy era. We have included in this book the story of President Charles O. Card, the prophet's designated leader in the Alberta colony.

7. Individuals who build up or help consolidate the Church in a country or region following a major crisis such as war or revolution or after many years of the Church's being essentially absent from the country. This has been the case again and again in Mexico after periods of revolution, in European countries after the two world wars, and today in Vietnam. Hermann Mössner, who played a major role in rebuilding the Church in post-World War II southern Germany, and Arwell Pierce, who helped bring dissident central Mexican Saints back into the fold, are examples whose stories are recounted.

8. Church members who jump into the public arena in their home communities or nations and thus help improve the Church's image in that area. These people make substantial and impressive

contributions in business, politics, public service, and education. Milton Soares in Brazil and Emmanuel Kissi in Ghana are examples here.

9. Local Church leaders who have to fight against severe odds in holding the Church organization and membership together under periods of government tyranny where they live. Such pioneer experiences have been notable in East Germany and other countries associated with the former Soviet bloc and are represented here in the account of Wolfgang Zander.

10. Individuals who converted in the old country and emigrated to the western United States and who went back again, sometimes repeatedly, to their native land or continent to bring the message of the restored gospel. Often these same people demonstrated cultural traits from their home countries that enriched the whole fabric of Mormonism. These pioneers have been examples of faith and devotion to immigrants from their country and to other Church members. We have included the stories of Elder Anthon H. Lund, the Apostle from Scandinavia, and Giuseppi Taranto, converted in Boston in 1843, who returned twice as a missionary to his native Italy.

11. Individuals from a particular minority race, culture, or creed who are pioneer members within a dominant Church society. Ketan Patel, a convert in the United States from a Hindu cultural and religious heritage, is an example in this volume.

12. Men and women who labor diligently to promote family history and temple work before temples and family history centers are commonplace where they live and following the establishment of such facilities in their area.

Regional histories such as *Building Zion: The Latter-day Saints in Europe,*[5] *Unto the Islands of the Sea,*[6] *Historia del Mormonismo en Mexico,*[7] and *Mormons in Mexico*[8] identify a number of such pioneers and their contributions. *Tongan Saints: Legacy of Faith*[9] goes much further in specifically telling the story of pioneers.

With *Pioneers in Every Land,* we are eager to celebrate a variety of international pioneers. These noble souls come from widely diverse continents and cultures. We desire in these sketches to cover a broad gamut of contributing pioneers, including rank-and-file members. The pioneers of the international Church come in all races and colors. Indeed, we estimate that by the year 2010 there will be more people of color in the Church than white people. Certainly by that time there will be more people in the Church who speak Spanish than who speak English.

To further highlight these points, we quote Howard W. Hunter, fourteenth President of the Church:

> I take as a theme a passage from the Book of Mormon referring to the Lord's relationship to the children of men throughout the earth in which it is stated: "And he inviteth them all to come unto him and partake of his goodness; and he denieth none that come unto him, black and white, bond and free, male and female; and he remembereth the heathen; and all are alike unto God, both Jew and Gentile" (2 Nephi 26:33).
>
> From this statement it is clear that all men are invited to come unto him and all are alike unto him. Race makes no difference; color makes no difference; nationality makes no difference.
>
> The brotherhood of man is literal. We are all of one blood and the literal spirit offspring of our eternal Heavenly Father. Before we came to earth we belonged to his eternal family. We associated and knew each other there. Our common paternity makes us not only literal sons and daughters of eternal parentage, but literal brothers and sisters as well. This is a fundamental teaching of The Church of Jesus Christ of Latter-day Saints. . . .
>
> The Church, being the kingdom of God on earth, has a mission to all nations. [Quotes Matthew 28:19–20.] These words from the lips of the Master know no national boundaries; they are not limited to any race or culture. One nation is not favored above another. The admonition is clear—"teach *all* nations." . . .
>
> As members of the Lord's church, we need to lift our vision beyond personal prejudices. We need to discover the supreme truth that indeed our Father is no respecter of persons. Sometimes we unduly offend brothers and sisters of other nations by assigning exclusiveness to one nationality of people over another.[10]

Pioneers coming from every nation, kindred, tongue, and people have differences, of course. Their cultural traditions are vastly different. Each convert will have to make a conscious decision upon embracing the restored gospel which cultural attributes from his country or region should be laid aside in deference to gospel standards and which cultural traditions should be retained as rich, uplifting, and consistent with the gospel. Cultural diversity among Latter-day Saints should be maintained, not abandoned. For example, most Saints throughout the world do not need to learn to speak English, and there is no need to adopt cultural attributes of the Wasatch Front or the United States.

In assembling the sketches contained in this volume, we note that pioneers in every land have several traits in common. These include an unwavering devotion to building the kingdom of God; willingness to sacrifice daily in doing the Lord's work and helping fellow Saints as well as others; the ability to express love according to their own culture; personal humility in giving God the credit for whatever good has taken place through their efforts and service; the willingness to assist newcomers in the faith and the rising generation in understanding gospel principles and overcoming difficult trials; an eagerness to make solemn covenants in the house of the Lord and to participate in regional and general conferences, often traveling great distances to do so; and the consecration of efforts to help strengthen the Church in their own area, doing whatever it takes.

BRUCE A. VAN ORDEN
D. BRENT SMITH
EVERETT SMITH, JR.

Notes

1. Gordon B. Hinckley, quoted in Gerry Avant and John L. Hart, "Many Are Still Blazing Gospel Trails," *Church News*, 24 July 1993, p. 6.

2. Thomas S. Monson, quoted in ibid.

3. See Jay M. Todd, "More Members Now Outside U.S. Than in U.S.," *Ensign* 26 (March 1996): 76–77; John L. Hart, "Over Half LDS Now Outside U.S.," *Church News*, 2 March 1996, pp. 3, 6.

4. "Sesquicentennial Legacy to Be Observed," *Church News*, 22 April 1995, p. 7.

5. By Bruce A. Van Orden, Deseret Book, 1996.

6. By R. Lanier Britsch, Deseret Book, 1986.

7. By Agricol Lozano Herrera, Editorial Zarahemla, 1983.

8. By F. LaMond Tullis, Utah State University Press, 1987.

9. Translated and edited by Eric B. Shumway, Institute for Polynesian Studies, 1991.

10. Howard W. Hunter, " 'All Are Alike Unto God,' " *1979 Devotional Speeches of the Year* (Provo: Brigham Young University Press, 1980), pp. 32, 33, 35.

PORNCHAI JUNTRATIP:
FIRST THAI PATRIARCH

by Nathan C. Draper

I first became familiar with Brother Pornchai Juntratip some-time in 1989 during my mission in Thailand. I saw him translate for a member of the Seventy who was speaking at a Bangkok district conference. I do not recall the details of the meeting, but I distinctly remember this blind man standing confidently next to the speaker, translating meticulously into Thai for the Thai congregation. Though I had never met Pornchai, I was very impressed with him. He had a unique wisdom about him.

It wasn't until the organization of the Bangkok Thailand Stake in 1995 that I met Pornchai and became personally acquainted with him. I happened to be visiting Bangkok during this historic occasion, and was fortunate to attend his Sunday School class at his ward the following week. After listening to the lesson he taught, I knew that he was an extraordinary man.

Later that same year, I again found myself in Thailand. During this time I was blessed to spend many hours talking with Pornchai, and through our conversations and common interests, we became good friends. Early in 1996, I interviewed Pornchai several times to learn of his experiences as a Thai Latter-day Saint pioneer.

I have also enlisted the help of David N. Phelps, who served as a missionary in Thailand, was later a counselor in the Thailand Bangkok Mission presidency, and at this writing works in scripture translation in the Church's Translation Department. Brother Phelps's close, personal observations of Pornchai and Elder Neal A. Maxwell in 1995 at the time of the creation of Thailand's first stake provide an invaluable addition to the story.

Unless otherwise stated, all quotations in this account come from my interviews with Pornchai or from briefs that he wrote for this sketch. In Thailand it is customary to use one's first name as the formal name. Thus, I call my subject Pornchai (or Brother Pornchai) throughout this story.

CHILDHOOD

Though he is unsure of the exact day, Pornchai Juntratip was born sometime during the first week of January 1947 in Bangkok, Thailand. He was raised in a bicultural environment, with his mother following Chinese religious traditions and his father practicing Thai-style Buddhism. Pornchai also learned about Buddhism at his Thai grade school, but was exposed to Chinese traditions and rites at home. "My maternal grandfather was an immigrant from China, passing on the Chinese traditions to my mother. My mother performed various Chinese rites at home on days such as Ancestor Day, Spring Day, the Moon Festival, and New Year's Day."

Pornchai's father worked for a local bank, but had a small taxi business on the side. His mother ran her own beauty shop at their home. The family's lifestyle was better than that of many Thai people; they enjoyed many comforts of life. Pornchai's first exposure to Christianity was when his father attended Assumption College, a Christian school in Bangkok. "My father would bring home Christian literature and books, which I looked at with a child's curiosity. Though I knew very little of Christ when I began studying with the elders, I had seen Christian pictures before. I also recall watching three movies as a young boy. I was nine or ten when I saw the first CinemaScope picture, called *The Robe*. I had also seen *The Ten Commandments* and *Ben-Hur*.

"My childhood life was rather comfortable and uneventful until both of my parents died tragically in July 1961." Pornchai's immediate family, which now consisted of himself and two younger brothers, were entrusted into the care of a senior relative.

The loss of both parents in 1961 was not the only trial he would face. At age fourteen Pornchai also began losing his vision. His sight was lost gradually yet rapidly, caused by retinal detachment. Between the ages of fifteen and nineteen he could still see dimly, but by age twenty-six he had no sight at all.

These two trials marked a major turning point in Pornchai's life. "Because of my waning sight, I had to quit school and remained homebound for eight years. About 1969, I was pronounced legally blind by my doctor. I then decided to learn English Braille. Books in Thai Braille were scarce, so I decided to learn English.

"I wanted to attend the school for the blind in Bangkok, but I was too old to be admitted. I did, however, attend on Saturdays and Sundays to learn Braille. Reading by Braille came quite fast for me, and I felt comfortable with it in about one week. About a month later I completed a copy of *Reader's Digest* in Braille.

"In 1970 I began my correspondence study with the Hadley School for the Blind, in Illinois, U.S.A. After four years of study, I was awarded a high school certificate from this school."

It was during these correspondence classes that Pornchai discovered his love of writing. He also developed an exceptional facility for the English language. At this time, Pornchai became a fan of the BBC World Service, listening regularly at night on his shortwave radio. During these years this radio program had an annual short story contest, asking for submissions no longer than two thousand words. Pornchai gave it a try, submitting his first story, entitled "Courage," about a young man losing his sight and how he coped with this challenge. The story's title not only hinted of its content, but reflected Pornchai's character in dealing with his own trials. "Using a Braille typewriter I had obtained from Hadley College, I would first write my stories in Braille, then use a standard typewriter to print the stories I would send to the BBC. I did this entirely by myself and was quite skeptical about the appearance of the first story I submitted. To my surprise, my first story was accepted and broadcast over the BBC World Service. I received nineteen pounds for my story."

This success was a great boost of confidence for Pornchai. He continued to write and submitted three more stories in the following three years. All three stories were accepted and broadcast.

CONVERSION STORY

In July of 1975 Pornchai Juntratip felt he needed to leave his home in Samutprakan (near Bangkok) to go to a more peaceful setting so that he could concentrate on his writing. His brother arranged for him to stay with his sister-in-law's family in Lampang, a small, quiet city located in the northern region of Thailand. It was here that his life would again change dramatically.

Soon after his arrival Pornchai was sitting alone on the front porch eating lunch. Though he did not see them coming, two full-time missionaries on bicycles saw Pornchai and stopped to talk. "They said they were representatives of The Church of Jesus Christ of Latter-day Saints, and asked if they could talk with me. I said yes."

The elders told Pornchai about Joseph Smith and the First Vision. "I thought it was a strange story," remembers Pornchai. "I had never heard it before. I didn't think Joseph Smith was bad, but thought he was someone who had done good, who tried to find truth by asking God.

"The elders asked if they could come back again, and I said sure. Before they left they asked if the three of us could kneel and pray. As we prayed I felt something softly rising. It was not a strong feeling, just a soft rising feeling."

During their first visit, the missionaries were not aware that Brother Pornchai was blind. He remembers the elders telling him later that they wondered why he moved so strangely. "They did not know that I was blind." On the second visit the elders learned of his blindness, and they soon found him a Braille Book of Mormon and a Braille copy of Talmage's *The Articles of Faith*, both in English. "If I remember correctly, pages eight and nine [of *The Articles of Faith*] captivated me. It said something like this: 'If what Joseph Smith claims is false, then the whole Church of Jesus Christ of Latter-day Saints would lie on a fragile foundation. But if what he claims is true, then there could be no doubt that the Church's phenomenal growth was because it was true.' This statement was a witness to me. It made sense."

Over the next three or four months, Brother Pornchai prayed, and read the Book of Mormon. "The Book of Mormon was quite difficult for me to read in Braille. The words were very difficult, but it gave me much to ponder."

Pornchai also began attending church. After the elders showed him the way a couple of times, he would walk about three miles to the church using his walking cane. "Sometimes the elders would pick me up to go to the church. I would sit on the back of one elder's bicycle."

On December 6, 1975, Brother Pornchai was baptized a member of the Church. "My conversion was not a dramatic event. It was more like water flowing in, a little at a time. Through faith in Jesus Christ, my testimony was gradually growing."

BLESSING THE CHURCH WITH TALENTS

"Shortly after I was baptized, I went to Chiang Mai for a district conference. Because the mission president did not speak Thai, his assistants, two American elders, translated for him. As I listened to the translation, I noticed some minor mistakes. Following the meeting, as I talked with the missionaries, I mentioned to them the minor mistakes in the translation that had taken place. Three months later, as another district conference was approaching, the local missionary district leader came to me and asked if I would translate for the mission president. I said I would!"

In the summer of 1976 a new mission president arrived in Thailand. President Harvey D. Brown presided over his first district conference in the Chiang Mai District with Brother Pornchai as his translator. This was the beginning of a very significant relationship. "President Brown, his wife, Mary Lee, and I became very close. They were very kind to me and helped me in many ways. They and Elder Jacob de Jager [of the Seventy] were those who helped me go to study at BYU-Hawaii."

CHALLENGES AND MIRACLES IN OBTAINING COLLEGE DEGREES

Despite some major obstacles, Pornchai made all the necessary arrangements to begin study at Brigham Young University—Hawaii Campus. Pornchai relates two miracles in his life that allowed him to pursue his studies. "Late in November 1979 I went to the American embassy in Bangkok to obtain my visa. It was during the time that the embassy would receive only fifty applications each working day due to the overwhelming number of applicants who tried to enter the United States. I remember arriving at the embassy very early in the morning, and I waited patiently during the ordeal. Finally, with the help of the American missionaries who accompanied me, and with my own ability to answer all questions in fluent English, I found myself standing in front of the consul, with all of my necessary documents ready. Then the stern-voiced official snapped out his last question: 'What will you do after you have finished your graduate study?' Without any hesitation I replied, 'It's up to my future, sir.' Indeed, I just wanted to be honest. I did not have anything left here in Thailand. I no longer had a family, as my two brothers had recently said they no longer wanted me. The consul, however, interpreted my answer to mean that I was among those who were trying hard to get into America and stay there permanently. Thus, he denied my visa by simply saying that he needed a document from BYU-Hawaii stating that the campus had a program for blind students. I was stunned and opened my mouth to argue with him, but I felt the hand grip of my missionary friend on my arm. I left the embassy in despair.

"Back at my little lodging, I knelt down and prayed to Heavenly Father, asking for his help and guidance. Eventually, the answer came. I took out my portable typewriter and wrote a polite letter to the consul, explaining to him my circumstances and the reason I wanted to go to study at BYU-Hawaii. The next day the two missionaries came to see me, and I asked them to take my letter to the consul. It was the Tuesday before Thanksgiving in 1979. Before noon, the missionaries returned with great news. My missionary friend put my passport into my hand and said, 'The consul did not ask any questions. He read your letter and then stamped the visa.'

"I believe that the spirit of Thanksgiving also helped me obtain the visa. I had almost no money, only a letter explaining how I would work and support myself. Had it not been the week of Thanksgiving, I may have never received the necessary visa to go."

Soon after this blessing, Pornchai received another needed blessing. "Due to my financial circumstances, I wrote a letter to the general manager of Pan American Airlines requesting a special discount ticket that would get me to Hawaii anytime before school began. The missionaries took the letter to the Pan Am office for me. To my great delight and gratitude, during a monthly gathering with the missionaries and President Brown, the missionaries presented me with a free ticket, compliments of Pan Am Airlines."

Pornchai's visa and financial situation were not the only obstacles he faced in getting his education. His younger brothers were in a state of disbelief that Pornchai was going to go to the United States for a college education. "They couldn't believe that there was such a school as BYU-Hawaii, a school that would take a blind student who they had never met, and who had no money. My brothers felt this was impossible and that I would cause them future financial problems by leaving for this imaginary school. They were afraid I was going to cause them serious problems, so they disowned me."

On December 16, 1979, Pornchai left for BYU-Hawaii to begin working on a bachelor's degree, something that seemed impossible to him a few years earlier. Having already scored very high on the Michigan English Test for college entrance, Pornchai was able to go straight into regular classes without additional English training.

To support himself while in school, Pornchai worked for Dr. Kenneth Baldridge as a transcriber. At this time, Dr. Baldridge was working on a program called "Oral History of the Church in the Pacific." "This was a very spiritual and testimony-building experience," says Brother Pornchai.

After four years of study, Pornchai obtained a B.A. in English and a minor in Spanish. "I was very blessed to attend BYU-Hawaii, but I do not want to make my experience there sound like I was anyone especially unusual. I had many weaknesses and was foolish in many ways. I was the only blind student on campus, and one of three disabled persons during my years there. But thanks to many good friends and great teachers, I made it."

His next step was to attend Brigham Young University in Provo, Utah, to begin working toward a master's degree. In January of 1984, he began graduate school in Provo. After two years, Pornchai completed a master's degree in English literature. Pornchai's four years at BYU-Hawaii and two years at BYU-Provo provided invaluable experience for the work he would soon be doing.

RETURNING HOME

"I returned to Bangkok in June 1986. I wanted to teach English at a college in Thailand, but things didn't work out. I had two big problems: One, I had no connections, and two, I was blind.

"I did interview at some colleges but nobody wanted to hire me. I think they were not sure how to accommodate a blind person. So, in the meantime, I began giving English lessons at my home. This lasted about six months."

It was not long until Pornchai was asked to work on translating Church materials, a job he could do in his home. This became his major source of income and a career that he works at to this day. Pornchai's first project was the Church's seminary manuals. These books alone accounted for about three thousand pages of translation. Other Church manuals were also translated. To date, Pornchai's translations total about five thousand pages.

A highlight of Pornchai's translation work came in 1991 when he accompanied a group of six Thai members to Salt Lake City to complete translation work on the temple ordinances. Brother Pornchai speaks of his preparation for this work: "[My] experience [at BYU] was very important in my preparation to translate many Church materials and the temple ordinances. By my second year at BYU-Hawaii, I think I had attended the temple endowment more than 150 times. I had the endowment memorized."

COURTSHIP AND MARRIAGE

"When I returned to Thailand in 1986 I lived with my aunt, who helped me rebuild my relationship with my brother who had since become an engineer. My brother agreed to let me live with him at his home in the Bangna District, on the east side of Bangkok. Thus, in 1987 I moved from the Bangkhen area to Bangna."

In the summer of 1988 Brother Pornchai met Sister Kwanjai Muangsub, a kind sister attending the local branch. She soon began picking him up every week to go to church. "The location of my new home made it especially difficult to walk to church, as I would have had to cross Bangna-Trad Road, a major highway that is difficult for even the sighted to cross. Through the kindness and sacrifices of Sister Kwanjai, I was able to attend the branch. My service to her in return was English lessons."

Sister Kwanjai had joined the Church in 1980 and served a mission in Thailand from 1982 to 1983 under President Floyd Hogan. Her service to Pornchai during 1988 and 1989 resulted in a growing and soon-to-be eternal relationship.

During 1989 Pornchai and Kwanjai began making plans for marriage. Both were working to save money for their future and were not planning to marry until 1991. However, in May of 1990, under the direction of mission president Anan Eldredge, the first large group of Thai Latter-day Saints were scheduled to travel to the Philippines to receive endowments and be sealed in the Manila temple. Pornchai and Kwanjai changed their plans and went as participants in this historic event.

Before the trip, however, they were met with an additional challenge. Pornchai explains: "About one month before our sealing in the Manila temple, my wife [then fiancée] was diagnosed with a tumor in her abdomen. Having known about our trip to the temple, the doctor—a very kind woman—assured my wife that she would be able to make the trip about three weeks after the operation. It was a major operation that lasted several hours. Fortunately, the operation was successful. On May 5, 1990, my wife and I boarded the plane along with a large group of other Thai members and arrived at the Manila temple safely the same day. The next day we were married and sealed, with both President Harvey D. Brown and my wife's mission president, Floyd Hogan, present."

Pornchai explained that neither of them knew that these two important people would be attending their sealing. "We did not know it at the time, but my wife's mission president, President Hogan, was the Manila temple president, and President Brown, a key influence in my life, just happened to be there that day. They and their wives attended our sealing. They represented our parents because neither of our parents could attend. It was as though we had parents there."

Pornchai and his wife were soon blessed again after returning from the temple. "When we returned home, we went to my wife's doctor for advice about having a child. The doctor said it would be best not to think about this matter for at least six months. After six months, and after a thorough examination, the doctor said we could think about having a child. The following month, and to our surprise, my wife was expecting our first child.

Pornchai Juntratip and his wife,
Kwanjai Muangsub.

"The following months were both trying and exciting, yet with the help of her sister and her sister's husband, and of Church members, we got through all problems and trials. Although we had prayed for a pretty baby girl, the Lord blessed us with a chubby-looking baby boy who looked very much like his father and mother blended. We named him Pituporn, meaning patriarchal blessing. Such was another miracle in our lives, and we know that without intervention from above, it could not be like this."

THE CALL FROM A MEMBER OF THE TWELVE

On June 18, 1995, after twenty-seven years of proselytizing in Thailand, and under the authority of Elder Neal A. Maxwell of the Quorum of the Twelve Apostles, the Bangkok Thailand Stake was established. With this came a special call to Brother Pornchai. He was called as stake patriarch, the first Thai patriarch in the history of the Church. The Thai members would now receive patriarchal blessings in their native language.

"I felt very surprised. I had no idea that it could happen to me. I thought, 'How could I ever do this?' As for training, I heard about training and thought that someone would come to me and work with me, but that did not happen. I received some articles and written words of instruction from some Apostles. I received this in December 1995. Elder Maxwell did give me some counsel when he interviewed me and called me. He said I would feel exhausted after giving a blessing, which really happened. My lower body went very numb."

Patriarch Pornchai gave his first blessing in late January 1996. He currently gives two blessings per week, on Sundays, after his church meetings. Because his home is not adequately quiet and private, Patriarch Pornchai gives all his blessings at the church building he attends.

SENTIMENTS

"I believe that the teachings of the Church, such as the Word of Wisdom and the law of chastity, can help people, especially young people. I wish more young people would turn away from materialism and modernism to religion and also listen to their parents.

"I want my boy to be a missionary. It will be best for him. We are trying to raise him up in a home environment with love, under-standing, and patience."

"I want to work for the rest of my life. I wasted fifteen years when I was young. I want to teach and write. I want to do anything that will make my life worthwhile. I want to be like the old man that becomes strong at the end of life."

Pornchai's current translation project is working on the first revision of the Thai Book of Mormon. He works at home while tak-ing care of his young son. In the future he hopes to use his educa-tion more directly by writing a book. His wife sells food at a nearby factory. Their son will begin school soon. They attend the Bangna Ward.

ADDENDUM: BROTHER PORNCHAI'S CALL AS A PATRIARCH

by David N. Phelps

A milestone in the history of the Church in Thailand was reached during the weekend of June 17–18, 1995. With Elder Neal A. Maxwell of the Quorum of the Twelve Apostles presiding, the Church's first stake in Thailand was created. There were many inspiring moments during those two days as the Spirit was felt in abundance by all those involved in this historic event.

Among the most tangible of these spiritual rewards was the calling of Brother Pornchai as the first Thai patriarch in the history of the Church. The process of his call is not only interesting but also instructive as regards the inspiring manner in which priesthood leaders receive revelatory guidance in extending calls to serve.

During the morning of June 17, Elder Maxwell began the process of interviewing approximately thirty brethren who were prospective stake priesthood leaders. Also in attendance were Elder K.Y. Tai of the Asia Area Presidency, and Troy L. Corriveau, presi-dent of the Thailand Bangkok Mission. I was there acting as Elder Maxwell's interpreter.

Before any candidates were invited into the interview room, one of the matters discussed by Elder Maxwell was the calling of a stake patriarch. He emphasized the importance of this calling, stressing the high spiritual qualifications required for the sacred work of a patriarch. Elder Maxwell also stressed that if there were no members of the new stake properly prepared to receive the calling of a patriarch, it was not essential that that particular calling be extended at that time but could be done at a later date. Several names were discussed, including that of Pornchai Juntratip. Brief information was provided to Elder Maxwell regarding each of these individuals, including a comment indicating that Brother Pornchai was blind. Following those comments, there was no further discussion regarding a stake patriarch. The first candidate on the list of prospective stake priesthood leaders was invited into the room to be interviewed by Elder Maxwell.

Several hours and many candidates later, Elder Maxwell spoke again about a stake patriarch. Inasmuch as the interviews during the preceding hours had all focused on the calling of a stake president, it seemed as if that cadence had been interrupted out of spiritual necessity. Elder Maxwell did not dwell long on the subject at that juncture, saying only that he felt moved to have an interview with "the blind brother," whose long Thai name he unfortunately could not remember. He asked that we assist him by scheduling an interview with Brother Pornchai prior to the general session of the conference on Sunday morning, in which the Thailand Bangkok Stake would be created.

The following morning of June 18 was filled with excitement as members and missionaries gathered in anticipation of one of the most important Church events to ever take place in Thailand. Among the throngs of Church members arriving early for this special conference were Brother Pornchai and his family. He was led to the designated room to meet with Elder Maxwell.

In the warm style typical of Elder Maxwell, he graciously welcomed Brother Pornchai to join him inside the room. Due to Brother Pornchai's outstanding English ability, it was not necessary to have anyone else participate in this remarkable interview.

With a few minutes remaining until the start of the conference session, the door of the interview room opened. Brother Pornchai came out first and was joined by his wife, who escorted him to their seats in the large meeting room. Elder Maxwell then walked over and spoke to me. His words sounded with apostolic insight and power. "Today, the Lord will call Brother Pornchai as the first patriarch of the Bangkok Stake. Brother Pornchai may not have any earthly vision, but his spiritual vision is very profound." As the meeting was nearly ready to begin, the sense of excitement was now even greater.

With Elder Maxwell presiding, the conference session began. Following the opening song, prayer, and other formalities, Elder Maxwell rose to the podium to take care of the historic business for which he had returned to Bangkok. First, he dissolved the Bangkok District and the branches it comprised. He then proposed the creation of the Thailand Bangkok Stake, to comprise five wards and three branches. This action was unanimously sustained.

With a spiritually electrifying feeling in the air, Elder Maxwell continued to present the names of those who had been called to positions of service. To the surprise of many, the first calling announced by Elder Maxwell was that of stake patriarch. As Brother Pornchai sat with his family in the congregation, Elder Maxwell invited him to stand. With tender words, Elder Maxwell announced to the congregation that Brother Pornchai Juntratip had been called of the Lord to serve as the first patriarch of the Bangkok Stake. The moist eyes and smiling countenances of nearly all assembled were ample evidence of the inspired nature of Brother Pornchai's call. Before moving on, Elder Maxwell invited Brother Pornchai to come to the front and take his designated place on the stand.

As Brother Pornchai was led to the front of the room, an Apostle's powerful words once again inspired testimonies of the divine nature of a sacred call. "Brother Pornchai may have no earthly vision, but his spiritual vision is very profound." Numerous patriarchal blessings have now been bestowed under the hands of the only Thai patriarch in the Church.

KREŠIMIR ĆOSIĆ OF YUGOSLAVIA: BASKETBALL SUPERSTAR, GOSPEL HERO

by Kahlile Mehr

In the early 1970s the communist veil over Eastern Europe remained inscrutable and forbidding to any influence from the West, much less the incursion of any religious belief. While The Church of Jesus Christ of Latter-day Saints had briefly enjoyed recognition in East Germany, Hungary, and Czechoslovakia earlier in the century, its presence was virtually obliterated after World War II by a political system that fostered a godless society. It was a circumstance that defied nations and armies but not the gospel light in the soul of a single individual who saw past the moment. In 1972 a tall, lanky native son of Yugoslavia returned to his homeland imbued with the enthusiasm and hope of a newfound faith.

Krešimir Ćosić played basketball in a country that was basketball crazy and he played it better than anyone else. A national hero in Yugoslavia, he opted to play college basketball at Brigham Young University (BYU), in Provo, Utah. He returned home for the summer from his junior year as a newly baptized member of the LDS Church—at age twenty-three, the presiding elder in a country where he was, at the time, its only faithful member.

In brief, the events leading up to this circumstance began at the 1968 Olympics in Mexico City, where Ćosić played on a Yugoslavian team that garnered a silver medal. Unbeknown to Ćosić, a Finnish player who had previously played at BYU was there to scout him out. Vako Vajno befriended Ćosić and was excited to learn that the Croatian wanted to play for a school in the United States. Vajno raved about this potential recruit to BYU coach Stan Watts, who then undertook a successful recruiting effort.[1]

In late 1969 the young player arrived at BYU—unruly, fun-loving, undisciplined, standing 6 feet 11 inches tall, and wearing a size

14 sneaker. He was totally unprepared for the environment of a campus where religion mattered, and was even more appalled to learn that even though he was an Olympic star he could not play during his freshman year. Despondent, he at one point, abruptly and without telling anyone, packed up and headed for the airport. Only a vigilant BYU sports staff caught him before his departure and convinced him to stay.[2] Patience was a quality Ćosić would need to cultivate for his life's work.

At this troubled juncture he confided in a friend that in spite of this episode, he knew he was not going home. He explained that even before coming to Provo, he had seen himself in a dream playing ball between the mountains and a lake. His confidant was Christina Nibley, girlfriend of Ćosić's roommate, Zdravko Minček, a tennis player at BYU. Christina said that her father had also dreamed dreams such as his. Ćosić began to question her about her beliefs and eventually accepted an invitation to be taught by Christina's father, BYU professor Hugh Nibley. After his sophomore year, 1970–71, Ćosić played with the Yugoslav team. When he returned to school in the fall he immediately went to Professor Nibley and requested baptism. When asked why, Ćosić said that he could think of a hundred reasons why not and only one why, "Because it is true." He provided more detail to the Truman Madsen family, who had befriended him: "I read the Book of Mormon. It was true. I was baptized."[3]

More than two decades later he told the BYU student body in 1993 that even though he was raised an atheist and his life and career in Europe were everything a youth entering manhood could dream of, he was still drawn somehow—in a way he did not fully understand—to this college in the mountains of America. "It was not easy in the beginning. . . . I had to give up some habits: smoking cigarettes for what seemed to me to be a never-ending diet of chocolate brownies. . . . Likewise, I gave up drinking alcohol for what I still believe is the Mormon soul food—ice cream. . . . Within my heart, there began to burn familiarities—feelings I had known as a child, the comfort and peace of eternal truths. . . . Suddenly, I was overcome by a sense of loss for the valuable time I had allowed to escape from me in coming to understand sacred and important principles. . . . And my desire to know more became unquenchable."[4]

The conversion took many on the BYU sports staff by surprise.

The flamboyant Ćosić had never seemed to be at all disposed toward religion. When Floyd Johnson, a member of the sports staff, heard the rumor that he was baptized, he replied, "That guy will never be baptized, and if he is, the water will never stop boiling." In a conversation with Johnson's colleague, Rod Kimball, Ćosić asked, "What you do if I tell you that I be Mormon?" Rod replied, "Kresh, if you ever get to be a Mormon I'll apostatize." Ćosić responded, "Rod, one thing we Mormons don't like is man who say he do something and then not do it." When the event was confirmed and Johnson learned the ordinance had been performed by Hugh Nibley, he wondered how the smartest man at BYU had been so dumb as to baptize Ćosić.[5]

He eventually achieved national attention as a player and great popularity on campus. He was simply one of a kind: "He galloped like a camel, he jumped like a gazelle, shot eighteen-foot hook shots, made length of the court passes, led the fast break, passed like a man with a third eye, shot double-pump layups, all the time smiling that familiar and contagious Ćosić smile. Kresh played basketball like it was really a game. None before or since ever played the game with more outward enthusiasm for the sheer joy of

Krešimir Ćosić playing basketball for the BYU Cougars.

it like Krešimir Ćosić."[6] He was the first foreign player to ever earn All-America honors.

Ćosić devoted equal zest and intensity in serving his church. He had no intention of hiding his conversion but rather began making plans to inform everyone in his native land of it. Even then he was well on his way to becoming not *a* national hero but *the* national hero; a combination of Babe Ruth, Larry Bird, and Muhammad Ali all wrapped into one.[7] This prominence gave him the "podium" he desired to deliver an ever-greater message than basketball prowess to his fellow countrymen.

He arranged to have two films produced of BYU basketball games with special halftime features inserted: for one, the 1964 World's Fair film produced by the Church, *Man's Search for Happiness*; and for the second, *Meet the Mormons*. Ćosić personally narrated the halftime shows in Serbo-Croatian.[8]

The intentions of the young enthusiast received support from the highest echelons of Church leadership. In two private conferences during the spring of 1972, Elder Gordon B. Hinckley discussed plans to establish the Church in Yugoslavia with Ćosić and Neil D. Schaerrer, the incoming president of the Austria Vienna Mission.[9] Elder Hinckley set Ćosić apart as a missionary.[10]

During the summer of 1972, Elder Ćosić returned to his hometown of Zadar, a town at the time of about seventy thousand inhabitants, located halfway down the Adriatic Coast of Yugoslavia. Concurrently, Elder Hinckley implemented another plan conceived earlier that year. Many people in Zadar spoke Italian. Hugh Nibley's son Paul was serving in the Italy North Mission. Acting on a request from Ćosić for the assistance of his mentor's son, Elder Hinckley called President Dan Jorgenson of the Italy North Mission and directed him to send Paul Nibley over into Yugoslavia.[11]

Elder Nibley and his companion, Elder Gail McOmber, spent almost two months, from May to June 1972, in Zadar and vicinity engaged in a variety of proselyting activities.[12] They taught discussions in Italian to Ćosić's friends and neighbors. They showed the basketball films several times at a nightclub where Ćosić's friends played in the band. They would show up before closing time, encourage people to stay, and then show the films after hours. They also took a film to the island where Ćosić's grandparents lived. They played it on a bedsheet hung in the air. So many came that some had to watch it backwards from the other side of the sheet. As a result, one of Ćosić's friends, Vladimir Peric, was converted, and Ćosić baptized him in the Adriatic Sea.

The missionaries left and Ćosić headed for the Yugoslavian Olympic basketball training camp in the resort center of Kranjska Gora, located in the northwest corner of the country, just south of the Austrian border. Ćosić phoned President Schaerrer to come and visit. The president, his wife, and assistants to the president, Chad Turner and Ruediger Tillmann, crossed the border and took in a supply of the tract *Meet the Mormons*. They decided to proceed with all their energy to legally establish the Church in Yugoslavia as soon as possible.[13]

Ćosić led his team to a bronze medal at the Munich Olympic Games and then returned home. In early September 1972, the Schaerrers and missionary assistants travelled down the coast to Zadar. Ćosić's name was literally their passport. Elder Tillmann, who was driving, failed to communicate in German with the heavily armed border guards. He finally said, "Krešimir Ćosić! Basketball!" and they waved the car through. When they reached Zadar he stopped a passerby and said, "Krešimir Ćosić!" Within fifteen minutes Ćosić was there to greet them.[14]

On September 17, they held a sacrament and testimony meeting, the first ever held in Yugoslavia. Three members were there, Ćosić having baptized the daughter of his coach just prior to the arrival of the group from Vienna. The members and three investigators listened to the encouragement of their visitors with Ćosić interpreting. Great hopes for the future were expressed and felt on this occasion, hopes that were not destined to be fulfilled immediately. The next day the visitors and Ćosić consulted with Milan Vladovic, an attorney in Zadar. He stated that door-to-door proselyting was prohibited. Though pessimistic about the outcome, he outlined the procedure for obtaining recognition and agreed to file a petition with the Department of Religious Affairs.[15]

Ćosić then returned to BYU for his senior year. His success on the court led to professional contract offers that would have earned him millions, but he opted to return home, manage the Zadar basketball program, and play on the Yugoslav national team. When asked why he returned, he responded, "It was the right thing to do. I would have enjoyed playing in the NBA, and maybe I did lose something by not doing so. But I don't regret it. I regret when I do something wrong. But I never regret when I do something right."[16]

His decision reflected not only love for his native land but also his continuing commitment to establish his new church there.

In the years to follow he made Yugoslavia a basketball power-house at world and European championships, first as a player and later as a coach. At the same time he served as the country's presiding elder. His religion was an irritant to communist leaders, but his popularity and talent on the court made them withhold action.[17]

From 1973 to 1975 he remained in Zadar. Doug Richards, a fellow player from BYU, joined him during the 1974–75 basketball season and assisted not only with the sport but also with teaching the gospel. Richards noted that Ćosić took advantage of every opportunity "to help the light of the gospel seep through the iron curtain." Richards's fiancée, Kerry, spent six weeks there as well. Remembering the experience, she said, "Not only were we different because of our observance of the Word of Wisdom and the law of chastity, but we were noticed because we were happy." The couple were able to answer questions about the Church because many Yugoslavs had some knowledge of English. The Zadar team became the national champions and played in the All-Europe tournament, taking third place.[18]

Ćosić's proselyting methods were often unique, not unlike his style of basketball. He asked Floyd Johnson at BYU for all the old T-shirts printed with "Brigham Young" on them. When kids followed him around and asked for a shirt like his, he would pull out a card with the Articles of Faith on it and say, "If you will memorize what's on the card, I will give you a T-shirt just like mine."[19]

Ćosić's friends from all over the country visited him in Zadar. The missionary effort was punctuated only occasionally by conversions as the task proved more daunting than any challenge on the court. Some of Krešimir's longtime friends joined—Mladen Dunatov, Mišo and Ankica Ostarčević. The Ostarčevićs were baptized in the Adriatic at two in the morning to avoid attracting any unwanted attention. They were the first couple to join the Church in Yugoslavia and remain active, one of the few to ever do so for decades. The fledgling branch met in homes and rented a house for a short time in 1974. Most Yugoslavs, however, showed little interest in Ćosić's religion and regarded his conversion an insignificant blemish on his ever-growing status as a national hero.[20]

Attempts to obtain legal recognition proved futile. In October 1974, David M. Kennedy, a special representative of the First

Presidency, visited Beograd to seek recognition for the Church as a precursor to permitting regular missionary work in the country. Elder Kennedy had previously held prominent positions in the U.S. government under Richard Nixon. He had high government contacts around the world. President Spencer W. Kimball called Elder Kennedy with the explicit purpose of getting the Church into countries where it as yet had no presence. On the tail of Kennedy's visit, President Schaerrer made a series of official visits to Ljubljana, Zagreb, Zadar, and other small cities in between. He contacted attorneys, language specialists, printing companies, and the Seventh-Day Adventist and Jehovah's Witnesses churches to get a feeling for the manner in which to proceed.[21]

The Church began to program the training of missionaries in Serbo-Croatian at the Language Training Mission in Provo, Utah. A group of missionaries assigned to Austria arrived there in February 1975. Their assignment was changed to Yugoslavia. They studied two languages—first German, then Serbo-Croatian.[22] They proceeded to Austria in May. Yugoslav visas were never granted. The group either taught Yugoslav emigrés in Austria or were reassigned to proselyte Austrians. A second group of Yugoslav missionaries arrived in August 1975. Ćosić crossed the border to visit and assist the missionaries, but no one of these two groups was ever permitted to cross over the other way.

By 1975 there were six Church members in Zadar. They needed seven to petition for recognition in that city. They invited a Church member from Trieste to stay in Zadar for a few months. They received the requested status.[23] The impact of this decision was only local and never extended to the entire country. The Church continued to hope for a change of circumstances, for in early 1977 it sent two more contingents of Yugoslav missionaries to Austria in order to replace those who were soon to head home.

Reflecting on the limited success of his efforts to establish the Church, Ćosić noted in 1993, "It was here [BYU] that I began to learn patience, that God's time is not our time. . . . This lesson prepared me well for my return home to be the presiding elder in the former Yugoslavia."[24] Pitted against an anti-religious government and a disinterested people, he never gave up hope.

In 1975, Ćosić was drawn away from Zadar by other responsibilities. During 1975 and 1976 he spent his obligatory time in the military and then focused on preparing for the 1976 Olympics in

Montreal. There he assisted his team to obtain the silver medal, adding further to his national stature. Gone from Zadar, he could not continue to foster the Church there. With Ćosić absent and the missionaries still sitting on the other side of the border, the Church in Yugoslavia remained high-centered for the while.

In 1977 Ćosić took up residence in Ljubljana, a city in northern Yugoslavia close to the Austrian border. He suggested to President Kimball that missionaries enter Yugoslavia without white shirt and tie.[25] President Kimball agreed. While his policy was to always enter by "the front door," he was hoping to find that the door was only shut and not locked.[26] Missionaries were instructed to dress casually and then were sent into Yugoslavia in the role of students studying the language and culture. They would not openly proselyte but were to answer the questions of the curious. While it was an unusual tactic for the missionaries to pose as students, the impelling desire of a prophet to pursue any effort to take the gospel to all nations and the urging of a devoted subordinate led to an atypical missionary experience.

At first, missionaries visited the country for only short periods. In early 1978 the time was extended to the full term of their missions.[27] They had to leave every three months to renew their visas, but this could be done without too much problem at the border. Elders Kirk Barrus and Michael Meyer left Austria for Zadar on February 1, 1978, the first missionaries to be in Yugoslavia full-time. Four more soon followed.[28]

Sending young missionaries into a communist society was a risk. Missionaries could either succeed in building a membership that would make the Church a fait accompli, or antagonize civil authorities who would become ever more obdurate in their opposition. The effort was not publicized within the Church, much less without. It was a mission with little prospect of success and with real dangers to those involved. President Kimball was willing to take the risk with the stature and support of Ćosić as the only insurance. Missionaries were sent to Zadar and Zagreb in Croatia and to Beograd, the capital city of Serbia as well as of Yugoslavia as a whole.

To test the boundary of religious tolerance the missionaries had to be innovative and circumspect in their approaches. One missionary, a musician, played the piano in a lounge and gave piano lessons. Missionaries joined pickup games of soccer and basketball and ate at student restaurants, seeking to develop friendships with youth. They got to know shopkeepers, merchants at the market-place, bank tellers, postal workers, or anyone else they came in contact with during the normal course of a day. They enrolled in language classes to meet fellow students as well as study the lan-guage. They even served as den leaders and physical education teachers. The most pervasive technique, however, was street con-tacting, or engaging passersby in casual conversation with the hope of turning the conversation to religion. For instance, they would ask for directions. People would notice their accent and talk with them. They would likewise strike up conversations on trains and buses. Krešimir's name served as an icebreaker. His identity as a Church member was well known. The discussion of religion was legal as long as the missionaries only answered questions.[29]

Meanwhile, a project initiated by Ćosić in 1974 finally came to fruition—translating the Book of Mormon into Serbo-Croatian. He employed a Catholic priest, financing the project with his tithing money. The priest was in a car accident and as a result could devote nearly his full time to the project. Ćosić saw this as an unex-pected but effective way of getting the job done. Members and mis-sionaries helped edit the book as it neared completion. After nearly five years the book finally came out to assist the missionary work in late 1979.[30]

Continuing to play on the Yugoslav national team, Ćosić would

Six hundred copies of the first Serbo-Croatian translation of the Book of Mormon were stored in a missionary apartment in Zagreb.

visit missionaries and members whenever he was in town. The missionaries in Beograd would see him every several weeks. For example, on Sunday he might show up at seven in the morning and say, "We have church now; you give talk; you give prayer," and the service would proceed. Considered the best player on the national team, he attracted crowds as he walked along the street. Because it was illegal for a foreigner to baptize or perform any religious ordinances, Ćosić did all the baptisms and confirmations. His influence was again attenuated during 1978 through 1980 while he played professional basketball in Italy.[31]

In 1980 he played for Yugoslavia at the Moscow Olympics and was awarded most valuable player honors in a gold medal effort. Rather than basking in the glory alone, Ćosić took the gold medal to BYU, asked for his old coach, Stan Watts, and athletic director, Pete Witbeck, and handed them the medal in recognition for their service to him as an aspiring young player a decade earlier.[32] Then Ćosić returned to Yugoslavia to reside in Zagreb, capital of Croatia. At the time there were about thirty Yugoslavian members on Church rolls but only a handful were active.[33] Administratively, the heart of the mission was now Zagreb, with Krešimir Ćosić presiding.

The missionary force in Yugoslavia had reached fourteen by September 1980 when, in an unexpected development, two missionaries were expelled from the country for being teachers of religion. They were given forty-eight hours to leave. Other expulsions followed. Because of the expulsions, the flow of missionaries from the States was stopped. In 1981, the Church decided to temporarily replace young missionaries with older couple missionaries. Though common in later years, the concept of couples serving missions was relatively novel at the time. Their public profile was less conspicuous than that of the younger missionaries. The couples would be the only outside Church representatives in Yugoslavia for five years.[34]

In November 1981, Ćosić married Ljerka Kobasic. The reception was held at the Hotel Esplanda, the premier hotel in Zagreb. It was the social event of the year. There were 150 guests, including dignitaries from the government. Surprising to many guests, no liquor was served, unheard of at a wedding and a topic of controversy in the press afterwards.[35] It was, of course, no surprise to those who knew the substance of Ćosić's belief.

The key to obtaining legal recognition was to secure title to a facility in which to hold Church meetings. The problem was that the Church needed a legal address to be recognized; and an approved place of assembly could only be owned or rented by an officially recognized church. Nevertheless, Ivan Valek, a friend of Ćosić who was baptized in 1981 and an architect, was instrumental in obtaining the second floor of an apartment building located on Svačićev Trg in downtown Zagreb. During 1984 the facility was renovated. Missionary work and branch activities proceeded as normal until September 17, 1985, when notification was received that in two weeks Elder Thomas S. Monson of the Quorum of the Twelve Apostles would arrive in Zagreb to dedicate the building and, more important, to dedicate the land of Yugoslavia for missionary work.[36]

The year 1985 was a defining moment in the history of communist Europe. Mikhael Gorbachev came to power, auguring an era of unprecedented reform in the communist system. The Freiberg temple was dedicated in East Germany, a symbol of religious liberty in a world long bereft of such freedom. Ezra Taft Benson, obdurate opponent of communist ideology, became President of the Church in time to witness the crumbling of a system he had long opposed. In Yugoslavia the harbinger of change was the visit of Elder Monson, culminating thirteen years of effort by Ćosić and others to finally turn the key that would permanently unlock the long-shut door.

Wednesday evening, October 30, 1985, at a session just prior to the dedication of the chapel, Elder Monson brought words of greeting from President Spencer W. Kimball. It is perhaps fitting that the President whose vision sent the missionaries into Yugoslavia in 1978 should live to know of the momentous proceedings in that land. At the next session, Elder Monson dedicated the chapel. Ćosić arranged to have government officials present and a camera crew to record the event. He also provided much of the simultaneous interpretation during the talks.

The session on Thursday, October 31, to dedicate Yugoslavia for missionary work was much smaller, as it was during working hours. Elder Monson arose and explained the purpose of dedicating a nation and the sacred nature of the event. Further explaining that dedications are normally performed outdoors, he requested the windows be opened, symbolic of blessing the entire country. He intoned many promises, some of which soon began to be fulfilled.

Krešimir Ćosić (left) with friend and convert Ivan Valek (center) and Jeffrey Moore (right), a missionary who helped open up missionary work in Slovania.

Among these was that the missionaries might go forward with their work unhindered and with success.[37]

Only a week after the dedication, Radmila Ranović, a member living in Beograd, was set apart as a district missionary. She and the couple missionaries had their hands full teaching new investigators. Some people even came to the missionary couple's apartment on their own asking questions. During the winter of 1985–86 they were teaching discussions every single night.[38]

Though there were still sloughs as well as peaks, proselyting in Yugoslavia had entered a new age. Yugoslavs began in greater numbers to take seriously the gospel message. Sensing a dissipation of anti-religious resolve, the Church again sent young missionaries into Yugoslavia in July 1986. In a six-month period there were fifteen baptisms, an unprecedented success.[39] This activity did not go unnoticed by the civil authorities, who abruptly expelled the missionaries after a few months for exceeding their privilege as tourists. In short order the same missionaries went in as students and enrolled in language classes at the University of Zagreb.[40]

Elder Russell M. Nelson, an Apostle; Hans B. Ringger, Europe

Area President; Spencer J. Condie, Austria Vienna Mission president; and Krešimir Ćosić visited top officials in Croatia and Serbia in April 1987 to smooth out the situation with missionary expulsions. They received assurances that there would be no future problems. From the Church perspective, permission had now been granted to prose-lyte, if not in all Yugoslavia, at least in Croatia.[41] When missionaries entered Croatia in the summer of 1987 they did so as missionaries.[42]

Ćosić retired from playing to begin coaching the Yugoslav national team in 1985. In 1986 the team won the bronze medal in the World Basketball Championships, keeping alive Yugoslavia's twenty-three-year-old streak of finishing in the top three of these championships. They missed the finals by only a single point, drop-ping a 91–90 decision to the Soviet Union.[43] In 1987 Ćosić accepted a coaching position in Greece.[44] For most of fifteen years he had been the bedrock of the Church in Yugoslavia, a figure that could not be dismissed or silenced by authorities, a constant shepherd over a flock surrounded by wolves. His patience had finally borne the desired fruit.

In 1991, the political demise of Yugoslavia erupted in a civil war between Croats and Serbs in Croatia. After offering service to his newly independent homeland, Ćosić was appointed in Septem-ber 1992 as the Croatian deputy ambassador to the United States to develop relationships with America to help his country grow eco-nomically and become more secure. A person without a political past, he rose to a position of high political import. Ćosić did not take much credit for the appointment. As he explained to the stu-dent body at BYU, "I qualified for my assignment because after Croatia became an independent state, most—if not all—of the diplomats belonged to the previous regime, or to different nationali-ties in the former Yugoslavia. Fortunately for me, there was not much competition for any top jobs. The problem wasn't that we had five individuals for one post. Rather, we had five posts for one good individual."[45] And he was not entirely unprepared for the job. As noted by Truman Madsen concerning his student days at BYU, he was not just a "jock," he was brilliant and studied political and historical topics as if he were "on fire."[46]

A year after his assignment, cancer was discovered in his body. He took it with the same good humor that had sustained him throughout his life, speaking only of how nice it was to have more time with his wife and three children. He also used the time to

Krešimir Ćosić (back row, third from the left) with
Yugoslavian missionaries at a zone conference in Graz, Austria, 1979.

work on his family history, frequenting the Washington Temple in behalf of his ancestors. At the same time he enjoyed the peace he found there, having lacked that chance to live near a temple most of his life.[47]

Krešimir Ćosić died May 25, 1995, at the age of forty-six. Ten thousand people paid their respects when he was interred among other national heroes at the national cemetery in Zagreb. More significant from an eternal perspective, during the month of his death, twenty-seven Croatian converts visited the LDS temple in Frankfurt, Germany, to perform work for themselves and their ancestors.[48] He had his flaws, his Croatian nationalism and authoritarian disposition sometimes grating on others.[49] Still, it was Ćosić and his unflinching faith that took the gospel across the threshold of the communist realm when communism was still the ideological adversary to the free world.

Notes

1. Glen Tuckett, speech at the memorial service for Ćosić, May 31, 1995, audiotape (Marriott International Audio-Visual Operations Department); Carri P. Jenkins, "Krešimir Ćosić Moves from Basketball to Diplomatic Courts," *BYU Today*, November 1992, p. 10.

2. Phyllis Nibley, telephone interview by Kahlile Mehr (all interviews by Kahlile Mehr unless otherwise noted), November 24, 1995. Also the source for most of the next paragraph.

3. Truman Madsen, speech at the memorial service for Ćosić, May 31, 1995.

4. Krešimir Ćosić, speech at Brigham Young University, October 24, 1993, typescript in possession of the author, pp. 1–2.

5. Floyd Johnson, *Touchdowns, Tipoffs and Testimonies: A Look at the Spiritual Side of BYU Athletics* (Orem, Utah: Alba Publishing, 1989), pp. 15–16.

6. Tuckett.

7. Tuckett.

8. Paul Nibley, telephone interview, November 22, 1995, notes in possession of the author.

9. "Yugoslavian History," in Austria Vienna Mission Manuscript History, LR 10876, series 2, v. 3. 1968–1977, LDS Church Archives.

10. Phyllis Nibley.

11. Paul Nibley. Source for most of the next paragraph as well.

12. Jay G. Burrup, "Church History in Italy," *1996 Directory* (Ogden: John R. Halliday Italy Milan Mission Organization), unpaged.

13. "Yugoslavian History."

14. Ruediger Tillmann, interview, March 9, 1991, Draper, Utah, notes in possession of the author.

15. Austria Vienna Mission Manuscript History, September 16–19, 1972, LR 10872, series 2, v. 3. 1968–1977, LDS Church Archives; also "Yugoslavian History." Sources for the next paragraph as well.

16. Jenkins, p. 10.

17. Lee Davidson, "Ćosić Was a True Man of Principle," *Deseret News*, June 3, 1995, p. A-9.

18. Mildred Austin, "The Zadar Mormons," *Monday Magazine*, September 22, 1975, pp. 7–8.

19. Johnson, p. 18.

20. William T. Black, *Mormon Athletes* (Salt Lake City: Deseret Book, 1980), pp. 29–30; Dick Davis and Duane Hiatt, "Krešimir Ćosić—Basketball and Baptism," *New Era*, February 1974, pp. 8–13; Ankica Ostarčević, telephone interview, February 23, 1996, notes in possession of the author; and Mišo Ostarčević, interview, February 28, 1995, Salt Lake City, Utah, notes in possession of the author.

21. Austria Vienna Mission Manuscript History, Report for 1974–1975, in v. 3. 1968–1977.

22. Jeff Anderson, telephone interview, February 21, 1996, notes in possession of the author.

23. Ankica Ostarčević.

24. Ćosić, p. 7.

25. Spencer J. Condie, oral history by Jim Allen, March 15–22, 1989, Provo, Utah, tape 3, audiotape in possession of the interviewer.

26. Martin Berkeley Hickman, *David Matthew Kennedy: Banker, Statesman, Churchman* (Salt Lake City: Deseret Book Co., 1987), p. 342.

27. Kurt Bestor, telephone interview, November 20, 1995.

28. Austria Vienna Mission, Historical reports, LR 10876, series 3, February 1, February 11, and April 26, 1978, LDS Church Archives.

29. Kurt Bestor, interview, October 18, 1995, Provo, Utah, notes in possession of the author; Everett Smith, interview, June 22, 1995, Kingston, Ontario, notes in possession of the author; Charles Lamb, "Early Missionaries in Yugoslavia," manuscript, unpaged and undated, copy in possession of the author; and Radmila Ranović, oral history, interviewed by Matthew K. Heiss, Provo, Utah, 1988, typescript, MS 200/847, pp. 35–36, LDS Church Archives.

30. Ranović, oral history, p. 43.

31. Bestor, October 18 and November 20; also Smith.

32. Tuckett.

33. Ranović, oral history, pp. 38–39.

34. Edwin Morrell, telephone interview, November 20, 1995, notes in possession of the author; also Austria Vienna Mission, September 22, 1980, and January 20, 1981.

35. John and Arlene Irwin, "Remembering Krešimir Ćosić," *Morgan County News*, June 2, 1995.

36. William G. and Barbara T. Williams, dedicatory conference program and notes, October 30–31, 1985, typescript, copy in possession of the author, p. 10.

37. Williams, pp. 5, 16–17.

38. Ranović, "Missionary Reunion," typescript of speech given at the Yugoslavian Missionary Reunion, October 28, 1995, Sandy, Utah, in possession of the author, p. 8.

39. Spencer J. Condie, interview, August 5, 1991, Frankfurt, Germany, notes in possession of the author; also Condie, tape 2.

40. Kirk Teske, telephone interview, February 20, 1996, notes in possession of the author. Source of next two paragraphs as well.

41. Arlene B. Darger, *Europe Area Historical Report, August 15, 1986–August 15, 1989*, bound typescript, copy in possession of the author, p. 410.

42. Kevin Field, telephone interview, February 21, 1996.

43. "Y.'s Ćosić Again in Limelight; Coaches Yugoslavian Team," *Church News*, July 27, 1986, p. 11.

44. Condie, tape 2.

45. Ćosić, p. 5.

46. Truman Madsen, speech at the memorial service for Ćosić, May 31, 1995.

47. Davidson.

48. Ed Haroldsen, "Ćosić Still Missed by Those He Served," *Provo Daily Herald*, April 30, 1996, text from Internet download in possession of the author.

49. Kenneth Dudley Reber, oral history, interviewed by Matthew K. Heiss, Salt Lake City, Utah, 1994, typescript, copy in possession of the interviewee, p. 50; also Bestor, November 20, and Ranović, "Missionary Reunion," p. 9.

CHARLES O. CARD:
PIONEER TO CANADA

by Dennis A. Wright

O n a cold and rainy June day in 1887, a small group of Latter-day Saints huddled at the 49th parallel separating the United States and Canada. They had traveled seven hundred difficult miles under the leadership of Charles O. Card in response to counsel from President John Taylor to "seek refuge under the British flag." Canada would be their new home where they could live free from the persecutions sweeping through Cache Valley, their Utah home.

Little did Card know that from his first efforts a stone would roll forth to carry the LDS Church throughout a new and largely unsettled nation. In years following the original colonization many more Saints would join his settlement. Farms, ranches, industries, meetinghouses, and finally a holy temple would firmly establish the Church and the gospel in Canada. From this humble beginning, descendants of these early pioneers would spread across the face of Canada, sharing their faith and providing Church leadership wherever they went.

But in 1887 the Saints were just cold and fearful. Sensing their hesitation, Charles O. Card stepped forward and waved his hat in the air. He shouted, "Hurrah, hurrah, hurrah for Canada." His vision raised the spirits of the pioneer company, and they courageously moved ahead to claim their Canadian destiny.

"MUCH INFESTED WITH SPOTTERS"

The Edmunds Act passed by the U.S. Congress in 1882 made the practice of plural marriage illegal. Persons found cohabitating were prosecuted to the full extent of the law. With a spirit of righteous indignation, the federal government provided marshals with

Charles O. Card

the power to track down all "cohabs" and end this "Mormon problem."[1]

With great zeal and aided by Church apostates and others serving as "spotters," marshals pursued Mormon leaders as common criminals. Even while the Church used all legal means possible to challenge the law, many of the ecclesiastical leaders were forced into hiding to avoid harassment and arrest. Charles O. Card, president of the Cache Stake in northern Utah, was driven "underground"[2] to avoid arrest and imprisonment.

Soon after addressing his stake members in March 1886, President Card was forced into hiding. He successfully evaded the marshals for a short while, but he was soon discovered and arrested while having breakfast at one of his homes. Of this, a plural wife recorded: "That summer, 1886, Charlie had planned to take all his family up the canyon, but in July while eating breakfast at Aunt Sarah's [another plural wife] the deputies surrounded the house. . . . He dashed out the back door and there were men there. He drew his pistol and the deputy drew his. . . . He saw the danger of the children and told the man so. The deputy said for him to put down his pistol, and Charlie said he would when he put his away. One of the men spoke up and said, 'Put up your pistol. If Charlie Card said he'd put his up, he will.' So, Charlie went in and ate just as long as he could while the deputies waited."[3]

Federal marshals transported Card by train to the nearest jail, where he would await trial. There was a heavy guard on the train because stake members threatened to free their leader. Tension was high as the train pulled out of the station, but with the train moving, the nervous guards soon relaxed and allowed Charles to move about the coach. Seizing this opportunity, Card leaped off the moving train and ran for a small pony grazing nearby. The members of the stake cheered as their president, feet dragging on the ground, galloped for safety.[4] Waving their rifles in the air, the marshals loudly demanded that the train stop, but the conductor refused, informing them, "Gentlemen, you are at liberty to follow Mr. Card, but this train does not stop between stations."[5]

President Card had escaped for the time being, but he was now a fugitive and knew that the marshals would not rest until he had been recaptured. Charles described Logan, Utah, as being "much [in]fested with . . . spotters" and recognized that his home was no longer safe.[6] The Apostle Moses Thatcher, who lived in Logan, was organizing a colony in Mexico and asked Card to join him. Card accepted the invitation and began preparations for the trek southward. Feeling that he had to first complete his responsibility as stake president, he sought out Church President John Taylor, who was also in hiding, to ask if he might be permitted to flee to Mexico. With prophetic insight President Taylor responded that he felt impressed to send Charles to the British Northwest, where the prophet was confident that the Saints could find refuge under the British flag.[7]

"IN COLUMBIA WE ARE FREE"

On September 10, 1886, Charles O. Card was set apart for a mission of exploration by Elder Francis M. Lyman of the Twelve. Four days later he traveled by wagon to American Falls, Idaho, with his friend James W. Hendricks, an experienced frontiersman. There they joined another friend, Bishop Isaac Zundell, who had considerable experience with Native Americans.

Boarding the train in American Falls, they rode the Oregon Short Line three hundred miles to Huntington, Oregon. Changing trains, they rode another four hundred miles north to Spokane in Washington Territory. Arriving on Sunday, September 19, they found Spokane to be a growing frontier town with thriving shops and saloons operating without regard for the Sabbath. Weary from their journey, they spent the next two days at the Keystone Hotel.

At one A.M. on the second day, they were awakened by heavy footsteps on the stairs outside their door. Charles Card recorded: "We heard some one come up stairs and hold a conversation at the head of the stairs which was within a few feet of our room but Bro. Jas. W. Hendricks and myself went to sleep again being very weary and had lost so much sleep during the past week. But Bro. Z remained awake and heard the party speak of the renegade

Mormons and demanded admittance into our room but was refused by the Land Lord until daylight. Bro. Zundel came to my bed side and related the above and I told him [to] go back to bed and listen further which he did but could only hear parties whispering and could not understand what they said."8

Exercising faith, the missionaries knelt in prayer and asked that their pursuers fall fast asleep and sleep long enough to allow the elders to pack their provisions and escape. One at a time they crept down the stairs to their horses and made their way along the river-bank, praying again and again that they would be protected.

They escaped without discovery, but soon Brother Zundell fell ill and travel was slowed to allow for his recovery. Local miners were interested in the travelers and teased Brother Zundell about being with "too many women" in Spokane. Accepting this teasing enabled the elders to pass without being recognized as Mormons. The road north was not well marked, making travel confusing and often difficult. Frontier hospitality provided the missionaries with meals and lodging. Ranchers, miners, and local Indians all treated them with kindness. On September 29 they arrived at the British Custom House to pay the required duty on their pack goods before entering British Columbia at the south end of the Okanagan Valley. Card reported, "As we passed the stone monument that designates the line, I took of[f] my hat, swung it around and shouted **in Col-lumbia We are free.**"9

"CURSED BY THE GRAND MONOPOLY"

Sunday, October 3, found President Card and his party camped near Osoyoos Lake in southern British Columbia. He described his Sabbath as follows: "To day we remain where we camped last night to rest. . . . Our prayer is constantly [']Father direct us by revelation that we may seek the right place.['] . . . [We] invoked the blessings of God upon us in seeking a haven of rest for the persecuted and imprisoned. . . . We concluded we would hold a meeting to day at 1 P.M. . . . Probably this is the first meeting . . . here under the authority of the Melchezedek Priesthood in the Latter days."10 It was a moment of testimony and faith as the missionaries shared their hope and vision for the future, confessing that they were on God's errand.

The party continued north, finding the land rich but unsuited for agriculture because of limited irrigation possibilities. Card observed that the land that was suitable was "cursed by the grand monopoly"[11] of large cattle ranches. Somewhat discouraged, they continued their search, finding the land more arid and mountainous as they traveled north. During this difficult part of the journey, they met a mountain man who was to provide information crucial to their mission. "At noon to day we met an old mountaineer from Montana who gave us some information in regard to the country East of the Rockies. His name is Mcdonald. I understand there is a mtn Peak named after him. This information comes as we need and we all feel to acknowledge the hand of the Lord in it."[12]

Following the advice of the mountaineer they continued north toward Kamloops, where they could catch a train across the Rockies to Alberta. On October 14, 1886, Card and his party sold their horses and boarded the train bound for Calgary, Alberta.

"THE LEAST SIGNS OF FROST"

The train carried them across the Selkirk and Rocky Mountain ranges, bringing them to Calgary, Alberta, during a severe snowstorm. In spite of the discouraging weather, the missionaries prepared themselves to travel south in search of the mostly uninhabited prairies described by the mountain man. For five days they drove through wind, snow, and sleet looking for a site suitable for their settlement.

As they traveled southward, they noted that the land appeared rich and well watered. On October 22 they passed through the village of Macleod and drove until they reached the junction of the Kooteney and Belly Rivers. Here Card reported "the least signs of frost we have beheld since we landed in Alberta."[13] This was significant because they were worried about the severity of the Canadian weather.

On Sunday, October 24, their team became lame and they decided to rest the horses until noon. President Card and Bishop Zundell knelt in prayer and dedicated the land as a gathering place for the Saints. Card's wife Zina Young Williams said of that event: "They camped on the banks of Lee's Creek . . . and in the early morning . . . with their heads bowed in reverent inspiration they knelt before the Lord and asked his blessing to rest upon them for a decision that would meet all the requirements that were asked. His spirit was with them in gret [sic] abundance . . . and [Card] turned to them and said 'Brethren, this is the place.' "[14]

The return trip to Utah was more direct than the exploration journey through British Columbia and Alberta. Traveling south through Montana they reached the railhead at Dillon on November 4. Fearing that he may be recognized as he drew near his home, Charles shaved his beard to change his appearance and offered a prayer that he might pass unrecognized by both friends and enemies. Card was successful and rejoiced at meeting his family at sundown on Wednesday, November 17. He had been away over two months and had much to report about the success of his mission. He had found a place of refuge in the open prairies of southern Alberta.

"I Resolved to Go If I Went Alone"

Card was welcomed with great enthusiasm by the Cache Valley Saints. The news of his mission spread quickly, and many families were anxious to know of the location for the new settlement. Card had great expectations but was soon met with the reality that few families desired to leave their Logan homes. His efforts were further frustrated when Church officials decided that they would not issue mission calls to settle in Alberta. This left Card with only a handful of families that were willing to leave Utah for the new land.

Faced with this disappointment, Card wrote: "Today seemed a very lonesome day my spirits were much oppressed. Many of the brethren that had promised to go North with me to aid in forming a settlement in Alberta . . . I learned thought of going [elsewhere]. . . . Although I had reported some 41 names It seemed I would not get 10 to accompany me, Though I resolved to go If I went alone. This with other dark clouds of a financial nature pressing upon me with Prospects of close pursuit by the Marshals & spotter I felt much oppressed in spirits."[15]

"Lee's Creek Was the Best Location"

President Card selected a small group of friends and left Logan, Utah, for Alberta on March 23, 1887. His objective was to prepare for the spring pioneer company that would arrive a few weeks later. He was again forced to travel in disguise, as the federal marshals were in pursuit. He shaved his beard, cut his hair short, and purchased a pipe and a heavy maple cane to complete his disguise. While traveling in the dark of night they missed a corner and ran their carriage off a four-foot embankment. Soon the confusion of the wreck drew a crowd and the marshals were there to investigate. Card assumed a thick Irish accent and was able to continue on his way without arrest.

Heavy snow and driving rain left the roads in Montana in poor condition and slowed travel. It was not until April 16, 1887, that they finally reached the Canadian border. After reporting to the Royal Canadian Mounted Police office for an entry permit, they traveled north looking for the site selected the previous fall.

President Card instructed members of his party to visit the local government offices and pay the required duties. After meeting with several local ranchers, the men were disappointed that no land was for sale. Tension grew as the party became frustrated with their lack of success. On the Sabbath, tempers flared during a sacrament meeting held at camp. Card reported: "We held a sacrament meeting. I opened by Prayer and called Bp. T.X. Smith and Elder Neils Monsen to administer the sacrament. The Latter declined saying he had feelings against Prest Ricks for some remarks he had made a day or two previously. I told them that now was an opportune time to settle the matter, Bro R. who had grieved Bro M. Unintentionally, asked for his forgiveness & in turn he asked Bro R's. Then I arose and stated that if I had offended any of our party & begged their pardon."[16]

After considerable discussion the brethren were able to resolve their differences, and all were able to partake of the sacrament emblems feeling again the brotherhood of their mission.

The next day they explored the Lee's Creek area and located several pieces of land suitable for settlement and available for sale. The brethren celebrated with a hearty dinner of trout caught in the local creek. That evening, on April 26, they voted unanimously that "Lees Creek was the best location" for the settlement.[17]

"EXILES FOR OUR RELIGION"

Shortly after President Card and his advance party left Logan, the pioneer company organized their affairs and completed necessary preparations for the eight-hundred-mile trip through Idaho and Montana to Alberta. The mood of the company was upbeat, but they were well aware of the challenge ahead as they referred to their destination as the "land of desolation." Jonathan Layne's feelings were representative: "On April 3rd, Sunday, I started out . . . stopped and looked back on the peaceful home of Cache Valley. . . . I am an exile, going, I know not where. Well, it was a clear day but there were large drops of water on my cheeks for sometime, but I saw this would not do to be standing here looking back, so I turned my face northward, braced up and pulled my cap over my face and drove on."[18]

With determination and great courage, the pioneer party traveled north through eastern Idaho toward the mining camps of Montana. The endless miles of sagebrush were complicated by the spring rain and sleet, making the journey most difficult. The animals soon grew lame, and it was necessary to cover their hooves with burlap and tar to protect them from the wet and muddy conditions. Wagon covers were pulled tight to protect the travelers from the blowing sleet and rain.[19]

On May 3 Charles O. Card left Lee's Creek and traveled south to meet the pioneer company in Montana. On Monday, May 9, he met the first members of the pioneer company near Carterville, Montana. Leaving the first group, he traveled farther south, greeting other members of the company along the way until he joined his wife Zina on Thursday. "I can assure the future perusers of my Journal that this was a happy meeting for me to meet a faithful wife and sons who had toiled through a month of cold stormy weather over Mountains, hills and black plains & snow capped Mountains. I found this little Spartan like Band in good spirits for they had leaned on the Lord. I returned about 2 miles with the company & we camped for the night and after returning gratitude to God rested in peace."[20]

For the next month Card led the pioneer company north in difficult conditions caused by the spring thaw and rising river levels. The party struggled to cross swollen streams and was at times forced to build boats to carry wagons and goods safely across. On Wednesday, June 1, the pioneer company began the last leg of the journey. It was raining as they approached the boundary line between Canada and the United States. Card describes the crossing with this journal entry: "We crossed the Boundery line between the Brittish possessions and the United States, halted and gave three cheers for our liberty as exiles for our religion."[21]

Another in the party described the historical event with greater detail: "It was June 1st at 10:30 a.m. when President Card stopped his team, now always in the lead since leaving Helena. Mrs. Card was assisted by him to alight or rather to climb out over the wagon wheel. They stood by a pile of stones. He waved his hat and shouted something we none could hear but all understood. Wagons were drawn up while smiling occupants alighted and gave their salutes—shouts of 'Hurrah for Canada!' 'Three cheers for Canada!' 'Canada or bust!' Laughter and gladness on every side! Each selected a stone which was added to the fast growing mound marking the boundary. They had reached the new home land. They were nearing the end of the trail."[22]

That evening the rain continued to fall as the pioneer company established their first camp in their new Canadian home. When they awoke the next morning, they found four inches of new snow. Young Wilford Woolf's comment, part of the account quoted below, is representative:

> On nearing the location in the rain with nothing in sight except one covered wagon box setting on the ground, Wilford Woolf, aged four, gazed all around and said, "Ma, you said we'd be home tonight."
>
> "Yes," she answered, "this will be home from now on."
>
> "But Ma," the question came with quivering lips and tearful eyes, "where's all the houses?"[23]

THE FIRST DOMINION DAY

Charles O. Card faced the reality of establishing a permanent Canadian settlement as the Fourth of July approached. Were the pioneers to celebrate the United States Independence Day, or were they now Canadians who celebrated the birth of their new nation on the first of July? The group decided they were Canadians, and the first of July became a day of celebration, setting the stage forevermore for Canada's Mormons. A bowery was built, a play area was cleared, nearby settlers were invited, and a general feast was planned. There were races, contests of skill and strength, and displays of wildflowers and fresh fruit. The general air of the day was upbeat and positive as Card took a first significant step in establishing a Canadian identity.

Other firsts soon challenged the pioneer leader. Town lots needed to be surveyed and cabins built. The cabins were all similar in construction and design: square, built of logs covered with rough sawn lumber, with tar-paper roofs covered with sod. The pioneers plastered and whitewashed the inside walls and covered the rough lumber floors with rag rugs. Wooden cases became dressers and shelving, tallow candles and coal-oil lamps provided light, and woodstoves were used for heat and cooking. The cabins were warm and comfortable but lacked the finishing touches of their former Utah homes.

While the Saints were generally well accepted as neighbors by nearby Canadian settlers, Brother Card was still faced with many community challenges as the settlement grew. There was some opposition to a colony, as many of the original settlers felt the Saints should scatter rather than live together. Ranchers were upset with the new farmers, and arguments developed over timber and grazing rights. Not only did Card have to solve these problems according to the laws of a new land, but he had to maintain good public relations with the community. In such matters Charles demonstrated his genius for solving the most difficult problems.

MEETING THE CANADIAN PRIME MINISTER

Charles O. Card determined to meet the political and legal challenges by obtaining the support of the Canadian government. On October 30, 1888, Card and two Apostles, John W. Taylor and Francis M. Lyman, boarded a train to Ottawa, the national capital, to meet with Canadian authorities concerning the legal status of the settlement and the Mormons' access to adjacent land and resources. It was also determined to lay before the Canadian government the Church's teachings regarding plural marriage, hoping for their tolerance in this matter. On Thursday, November 8, the delegation arrived in Ottawa, optimistic that their case would be well received.

Included in the matters presented before the Canadian government were the following: (1) approval for a town site; (2) land for a church site; (3) timber rights; (4) water rights; (5) stone quarry rights; (6) free custom duty for settlers to come; (7) ferry access across the St. Marys River; (8) weekly mail service; and (9) government assistance with immigrant transportation costs. The final petition was for government acceptance of the practice of plural marriage in Canada.

The first meetings with government officials were positive, and the petitions were welcomed as appropriate for discussion. It was recommended that the delegation meet with Prime Minister John A. MacDonald. Card described this significant meeting:

> We done a little writing & shopping and preparing to meet "Sir John" at 1:30 which we did to the minute. When we arrived at the waiting room of the interior department we were ushered into the presence of His honor (E. Dewdney, Min. Int,) and were then escorted by him to the Office of the Premier Sir John and after the formalities were over and we were all seated. The Rt Hon Sir asked, "Gentlemen, what is your business?" When Apostle F.M. Lyman related what we presented to the Minister of the Interior the day before when the Minister stated he had all the subjects in form for the several Departments to which they applied to which Sir John stated they would be attended to at an early date.[24]

Elder John W. Taylor then spoke for a considerable time about the actions of the United States regarding their treatment of the Church. He asked the prime minister to consider providing refuge for the Saints who were fleeing such persecution. As the Apostle spoke, the rest of the delegation prayed that God would soften Sir John's heart.

Card then responded to Sir John's questions about the growth of the settlement. Apostle Lyman added that continued growth would depend on the government's attitude toward plural marriage. Sir John asked the delegation to put their requests in writing, as he felt it was a complex matter that needed more consideration. Card said of the meeting, "We felt well satisfied with the manner in which Sir John received us."[25]

The ultimate effect of the visit fell far short of the optimistic expectations. The Saints would be sold the land they desired at the current market price. The other issues, including timber, water, and stone, were to be handled according to the existing laws and practices. No exceptions were to be granted for the Saints. In the matter of plural marriage, the government of Canada would not tolerate the practice and considered it contrary to the laws and morals of the country. While the delegation was disappointed with the final results, Card accepted the decisions and acted to sustain his new government by establishing the settlement in keeping with the laws of the land and respecting the Canadian government ban on plural marriages. Hence, he instructed the Mormon men in Cardston to obey the law and live with only one wife. In less than two years, the subject became moot as President Wilford Woodruff, acting under revelation, ended the practice of plural marriage with the September 1890 Manifesto.

In accepting the decision of the Canadian government, Card again acted with vision that helped forge a Canadian identity for the Saints. As citizens of the United States, they had emigrated to Canada. This was to be their home and their destiny as they became Canadian citizens. In doing this they enabled the Church to take root in a new land. It was Charles O. Card who seemed to understand best the opportunity they had to build more than just another Church settlement. They were among the first to accept an international identity for the Church and appreciate the opportunities it offered.

"I Opened a Store in My Granary"

Soon after returning from Ottawa, President Card opened the first store in the settlement. His intent was to develop a cooperative from the small shop.[26] The idea was based on the Utah model that he had presided over in Cache Valley. On June 19, 1890, Card made application to local government agencies for recognition as a cooperative. The community responded with resistance, fearing that local merchants would be harmed by the Mormon cooperative. Card was able to gain the support of several prominent businessmen, and the cooperative was approved. The Cardston Company Ltd. was born.

Soon the cooperative expanded to include a cheese factory that encouraged farmers to increase their herds and earn a profit on milk products. A flour mill followed and was an immediate financial success. Other enterprises of the cooperative included a sawmill, hardware store, coal mine, ice business, and a boot and shoe factory. This effort had a stabilizing effect on the economy of the settlement and enabled continued growth.

"Come Along with Your Capital"

As Charles O. Card attempted to purchase more land, he found it difficult because the government would not allow the Church to purchase property in large blocks. Furthermore, the purchases required cash payment. After seeking the assistance of the Church's First Presidency, he was provided with the necessary capital to purchase land needed by the expanding settlement. Card was able to obtain sufficient land by purchasing every other section, thus circumventing the large block purchases prohibited by the government. With the First Presidency's investment in land, the settlement, now called Cardston, became more economically appealing to Utah Saints.

A major challenge to the development of agriculture was the lack of irrigation. Brother Card proposed that a large canal be built to serve as a water source for the growing number of farms. In 1894 the Pioneer Canal was built to enable agricultural production to expand. The Cardston irrigation project attracted considerable interest throughout western Canada, and Card became respected as an expert in this field.

In 1897 local businessmen proposed constructing a large canal, through the entire section of country. Brother Card felt that this business opportunity would greatly accelerate development and immigration because Utah was experiencing an economic depression in the 1890s. The proposal provided inexpensive land and employment opportunities that increased immigration to Card's settlement. To make the move even more appealing, businessmen allowed the immigrants to work for their land by building the canal, resulting in mortgage-free land with full water rights. Card placed advertisements in Utah newspapers announcing the opportunity. Soon new settlers were arriving in an increasing number to take advantage of the land and employment. The original purpose of providing a refuge for those practicing plural marriage had been replaced by the economic attraction of the new and growing settlement.

Construction began on the canal in 1898. Immediately it was evident that more men and teams were needed. Card's enthusiastic advertisement in the *Deseret News* encouraged even more to immigrate: "200 Teams Wanted to Work on Canal. . . . An industrious able-bodied man with a good team can earn a good farm, town lot and cottage in one year. . . . We invite shoemakers, watchmakers, blacksmiths, carpenters, bakers, tailors, cooks, and laundrymen, all trades are necessary to make our towns and hamlets a success.

Come along with your capital and build our flouring mills, sugar factories, electric railways and electric lights, and to aid to establish other industries in a healthy country. Don't forget to secure a good farm adjacent to one of the grandest irrigation systems of modern times."[27]

PRESIDENT OF THE ALBERTA STAKE

The rapid growth of the community resulted in the organization of several Church units. During a trip to Salt Lake City, Card proposed the organization of the Alberta Stake. He was granted immediate approval and set apart as the stake president. Returning to Canada, Card called a quarterly conference, where the Apostle John W. Taylor organized the stake. Card reports that "a good spirit prevailed & the Elders all felt well that spoke & the good spirit prevailed throughout all of our meetings."[28]

As stake president, Charles O. Card was known for his practical advice as well as his spiritual insights. His sermons were often filled with references to livestock care, business hints, proper care of dairy herds, and horticulture. During his seven years as stake president, he provided both temporal and spiritual leadership to thousands of Saints scattered over a large area. He served faithfully until his health began failing in 1902. At this time he was released as president and called as the first patriarch of the Alberta Stake.

"A TEMPLE TO THE NAME OF ISRAEL'S GOD"

In 1888 President Card had escorted a group of visiting Church authorities around the new settlement. After stopping the carriage on a hill overlooking the humble homes beside Lee's Creek, Elder Francis M. Lyman spoke to the group. Nellis Todd Taylor, wife of the Apostle John W. Taylor, recounted what was said to Card and those assembled:

> President Francis M. Lyman, the senior Apostle, informed those present that they had been invited to come on "this morning trip that they might participate in the sacred service of dedicating that land to the habitation of the Saints." He then moved forward until impressed to stop, taking his place facing the east. He said to Apostle John W. Taylor: "You will please stand at my

right, your wife Nellie next, President Charles O. Card at my left, his wife Zina Y. next, Bishop John A. Wolf and wife (Mary Hyde) facing me." Thus was a perfect circle formed by seven men and women. At this point he called upon Apostle John W. Taylor to be mouth in the dedicatory prayer. The outpouring of the Spirit of the Lord during the conference the previous day had warmed the hearts of all present but now the Spirit was of a pentecostal nature, accompanied by a divine light. Everything seemed hushed as those present listened to the inspirational words of the prayer. Then there came a pause: "I now speak by the power of prophecy and say that upon this very spot shall be erected a Temple to the name of Israel's God and nations shall come from far and near and praise His high and holy name."[29]

Charles O. Card never lived to see this prophecy fulfilled; the announcement of the Alberta Temple did not come until 1912. But when it came time to select the temple site, Church President Joseph F. Smith said, upon seeing pictures of the hill where the prayer was given, "I feel strongly impressed that this is the one."[30]

A FINAL FAREWELL MESSAGE

Charles O. Card's health grew worse after his release as stake president in 1902. He decided to live out the remainder of his life with his extended family in Logan, Utah. He passed away in 1906.

Prior to his departure from Canada, Card addressed his fellow workers in the Alberta Stake. An excerpt from that address captures the spirit of Charles Ora Card, whose faith and vision enabled thousands of Latter-day Saints to shout "Hurrah, hurrah, hurrah, for Canada."

Several of my brethren and sisters were pioneers with me in this land and we have stood shoulder to shoulder in building up of the Quorums and organizations in the various wards of this stake of Zion. In this they have been one with me and we have been one with the Lord in striving to obey the mandates of his servants and carrying out his will in this land. . . .

Our labors here together have been labors of love and in common interest of the Kingdom of God. . . . I thank you one and all for the support given me and I trust that in continuance

of your labors that you may be united and grow together until
we have many stakes of Zion, many towns, cities and villages,
which was the impression given to me by the Lord when I first
arrived here. Even before the putting in of the first little garden
the Lord showed to me that there would be many towns and
settlements besides the one of Cardston, and to this end my
course has been bent, as well as that of my brethren and sisters
who have labored with me. . . .

I feel to acknowledge the hand of the Lord that he has preserved this land for the latter-day Saints to occupy and extend
his work, which is in accordance with my first prayer in the
dedication of this land.[31]

Epilogue

Charles O. Card's settlement continued to grow. During the pioneer years seventeen separate settlements were established in the
southern Alberta area. Most of these continued as strongholds for
the Church's faithful. The twentieth century brought significant
changes to the agricultural communities of western Canada. These
resulted in many of the descendants of the early Latter-day Saint
pioneers leaving their southern Alberta homes for schooling and
employment throughout Canada. Significantly, these Canadians
chose for the most part not to seek employment in the United
States. They took with them their faith, and soon Church units were
growing in every province. These faithful pioneer descendants
served as Church leaders in promoting missionary growth and the
establishment of wards and stakes. The pioneer heritage of Charles
O. Card continued in the lives of these faithful Saints who moved
the Church from a small southern Alberta settlement to an important part of the national Canadian mosaic.

Notes

1. See James B. Allen and Glen M. Leonard, *The Story of the Latter-day
Saints* 2d ed. (Salt Lake City: Deseret Book Co., 1992), pp. 402–7.

2. The term *underground* was commonly used by the Saints in Utah to
describe the condition of hiding from federal officials to avoid arrest.

3. Lavinia Rigby Card, "History of Lavinia C. Rigby Card," unpublished typescript of an autobiography in the possession of Stirling Card, Logan, Utah.

4. Zina Williams Card, handwritten account of Charles Card's arrest and escape in Logan, manuscript in possession of Ms. J. Card, Lethbridge, Alberta.

5. Sterling Williams, "Temple History—Beginnings of Cardston," typescript narrative based on Card's journals, 1886–1891, manuscript on file in the Cardston temple vaults, Cardston, Alberta.

6. Charles Ora Card, *The Diaries of Charles Ora Card: The Canadian Years, 1886–1903*, ed. Donald G. Godfrey and Brigham Y. Card (Salt Lake City: University of Utah Press, 1993), p. 39.

7. Jane E. Woolf Bates, "Charles Ora Card: Pioneer Leader, Founder and Builder," typewritten manuscript on file in the Glenbow Foundation Library, Calgary, Alberta, p. 3.

8. *Diaries of Charles Ora Card*, p. 10.

9. Ibid., p. 12; emphasis in original.

10. Ibid., pp. 13, 14.

11. Ibid., p. 16.

12. Ibid., p. 15.

13. Ibid., p. 18.

14. Zina Williams Card, "An Incident in the Settling of Canada," manuscript in possession of Ms. J. Card, Lethbridge, Alberta.

15. *Diaries of Charles Ora Card*, p. 35.

16. Ibid., pp. 51–52.

17. Ibid., p. 52.

18. Jonathan Ellis Layne, "Writings and History of Jonathan E. Layne," typewritten manuscript in Special Collections, Brigham Young University, Provo, Utah.

19. See Jane E. Woolf Bates, "Founding of Cardston and Vicinity," typewritten manuscript in Special Collections, University of British Columbia, Vancouver, British Columbia.

20. *Diaries of Charles Ora Card*, p. 55.

21. Ibid., p. 57.

22. Jane E. Woolf Bates, quoted in an interview for the *Lethbridge Herald*, 19 June 1937, special issue commemorating the fiftieth anniversary of the arrival of the Card party, Special Collections, University of British Columbia, Vancouver, British Columbia.

23. Jane E. Woolf Bates, "Founding of Cardston and Vicinity."

24. *Diaries of Charles Ora Card*, pp. 66–67.

25. Ibid., p. 67.

26. Ibid., p. 71.

27. *Deseret News*, 10 January 1898.

28. *Diaries of Charles Ora Card,* p. 295.

29. Nellis T. Taylor, "Prophetic Gift Made Manifest," in N. B. Lundwall, comp., *Temples of the Most High,* Collector's Edition (Salt Lake City: Bookcraft, 1993), p. 165.

30. Quoted in Lundwall, *Temples of the Most High,* p. 166.

31. "Charles Ora Card's Farewell Message to his Co-Workers," *Logan Journal,* 11 September 1906. Copy located in Clarice Card Godfrey papers, Harold B. Lee Library, Special Collections, Brigham Young University, Provo, Utah.

Rhee Honam:
Hallmarks of a Korean Pioneer

by Spencer J. Palmer

Torrential rains inflicted devastating damage throughout South Korea in July 1966. Due to rising flood waters, many people lost their homes, shelters along the banks of the Han River were swept away, major bridges were weakened and seriously impaired, and roads leading in and out of Seoul became practically impassable. There was widespread loss of personal property.

I was serving as president of the Korean Mission of the Church in Seoul at the time. Our headquarters property at Chongun Dong was nearly engulfed in water, and the missionaries spent hours together shoveling mud in knee-deep water to save the facilities. But I became particularly alarmed when we received a radio report that the outlying area of Suyuri was suffering especially frightful destruction. That was where my first counselor in the mission presidency, President Rhee Honam, had only recently finished building a modest fifteen-pyong (540 square feet) house. President and Sister Rhee (surnames are typically listed first in the Korean culture) had struggled long and hard to save money to make the initial down payment on their new home. It was located far out of town and had been built on the edge of rice paddies in a countryside setting where land was relatively inexpensive in price—but it was their pride and joy.[1]

My wife and I were most concerned for the safety and well-being of the Rhee family. Intent on giving them encouragement and consolation, several of us mission-home missionaries brought out the "Green Camel"—our four-wheel-drive, high-off-the-ground van —and set out for Suyuri in a relentless rainstorm. After a rather arduous drive through chuckholes and the mud that was stranding a good number of people, carts, trucks, and cars, we finally reached the road leading to President Rhee's neighborhood. We parked the van and walked the rest of the way.

Since all electrical power was out, the area was dark. We practically groped our way along the unfamiliar paths leading to President Rhee's house. As I assessed the damage in the area, I wondered if I would be able to say or do anything that would effectively lift the spirits of these victimized first-generation Latter-day Saints.

But then we experienced something strange. As we neared the outer front gate to the Rhee property, we heard singing. The song was a familiar Church hymn. I had heard Koreans sing this song many times in Church meetings, always with great fervor, like a rousing battle cry. But this night at Suyuri the lyrics reached our ears in tones of tenderness and devotion, more like a prayer than a battle cry: *"Songdo-dura, turyo wolgot opta, osodul nagaja. Modun'-got ch'al daeri!"* Translated into English: "Come, come, ye Saints, no toil nor labor fear; but with joy wend your way." And the chorus: "All is well!"

I looked through a crack in the wooden gate and was totally overwhelmed by what I saw. There was the president, his wife, and several of their children seated in a circle on a floor, surrounding a small table with a lighted candle in the center. They were reverently singing this robust anthem of the early Mormon pioneers! We were all deeply moved.

Water was pouring down from the edges of the roof; water had risen so high in nearby rice paddies that one of the corner foundations of the house had collapsed. The outhouse in the front yard was damaged. Inside, the basement was filled with a foot of water that had soaked the burning coal *yontan* briquettes designed to provide heat for the floors of the house. Water leaking from the ceilings was being caught in pans and buckets strategically placed on the floors. Several pieces of furniture were soaked, and there were water spots on the walls.

I called out: "What is going on, President Rhee? What are you doing?" I shall never forget his enthusiastic and positive reply. "We are singing the songs of Zion, President. We are thanking the Lord and praising him for our many blessings. Tonight more than at any other time, we are grateful for our precious testimonies of the restored gospel of Jesus Christ and for our membership in the Lord's true church."

We were amazed. We were humbled and inspired. The Rhee family that night was neither discouraged nor afraid. They were calm and full of faith. In them that night I could see that the intrepid spirit of the Mormon pioneers was still alive. The candlelight reminded me of this family's beginnings in the Church, a gospel light that was small and flickering at first but after more than a decade of membership had now grown into radiant, persuasive, and powerful faith. Like pioneers of earlier times in America, they also were fighting a good fight. They were enduring and overcoming many hardships in helping establish the kingdom of God in Korea.

BOYHOOD OF RHEE HONAM

Rhee Honam, a first-generation Korean convert to The Church of Jesus Christ of Latter-day Saints, was born in Shimonoseki, Japan, on February 28, 1934, the third child and second son of five boys and three girls. During the years of Japanese colonial rule in Korea, his father had become a member of the Korean minority in Japan, finding work in a cement factory. His father was burned badly during World War II in an Allied bombing raid on the city. His uncle was killed by Allied bombs.

Honam lived in Japan for eleven years. He was taught by his Japanese teachers to hate the Americans, who were a cruel people who started the Second World War by so severely choking the Japanese economically that they were forced to bomb Pearl Harbor. As a boy living in Japan, he feared the high-flying American B-29 bombers but was particularly afraid of the fast, low-flying Grumman fighter planes. Honam and his friends looked upon American air power with awe and fearful curiosity. On a few occasions, however, rather than run for the air-raid shelter, they doused their white shirts with red ink and lay down in the open streets pretending they were dead so the fighter planes would pass them by.

When the Americans occupied Japan in 1945 at the end of the war, most Japanese were very cautious about coming out of their homes to personally meet them. But Honam and his young friends were filled with curiosity to see these tall, red-faced foreigners and to receive C rations and other goodies at their hands. Even before the end of the war, Honam admired the integrity of the Americans because the propaganda pamphlets that they air-dropped gave the numbers not only of Japanese casualties but also of American casualties. He thought they did not really have to reveal this kind of information.

CONVERSION

Honam returned to his Korean homeland in 1946 and attended high school, where he studied English. After the beginning of the Korean War, he joined a volunteer military corps and on one occasion was assigned as an interpreter in a serious Korean-American dispute. The American officer in charge of the investigation was Lieutenant Calvin R. Beck of Tooele, Utah, a member of The Church of Jesus Christ of Latter-day Saints. Honam was deeply impressed with the respectful and kindly behavior of this American GI and asked him about his religious background. Lieutenant Beck replied that he was a Mormon. Honam looked up the word in a Korean dictionary, which indicated that this was a small polygamous sect in the United States.

The lieutenant and his young Korean interpreter became good friends, and in time Honam was invited to attend a Latter-day Saint MIA meeting in Seoul. "I was surprised and touched by what I experienced that night," Honam recalls. "Lieutenant Beck introduced me to the members as Brother Rhee, and everyone addressed me in that way. I had never heard that before. I wondered, How could these Americans call me their brother? But I could tell they were sincere, and I was deeply touched."

That was the beginning of intensive gospel study that culminated in Rhee Honam's baptism by Alan Potts, an American Latter-day Saint serviceman, on September 5, 1954. He was confirmed a member of the Church by Elder Harold B. Lee of the Council of the Twelve Apostles, who was visiting Korea on assignment from the First Presidency to decide whether to open Korea as a mission field of the Church. On that occasion Elder Lee strongly admonished Brother Rhee to stay close to the Lord, share his testimony often with other new members, and endure to the end. There were fewer than a dozen new Korean members scattered throughout the peninsula when Rhee Honam was baptized in Seoul.

At first, new Korean members in Seoul could attend Church meetings at only one location—the U.S. Eighth Army base, if accompanied by an American soldier. The first full-time American proselyting missionaries arrived from Japan in 1954 and began teaching the gospel and organizing small convert groups in several locations in Seoul.

In August 1955 Joseph Fielding Smith, President of the Quorum of the Twelve Apostles, dedicated Korea for the preaching of the gospel. During his visit, President Smith ordained Rhee Honam to the office of priest in the Aaronic Priesthood and strongly emphasized that he must always be submissive to the Lord and be willing to answer calls that would be given him in the future.

MARRIAGE

While he was serving as president of the East (Tongbu) Branch, Honam met Park Youn Soon, who later became his wife. One Sunday at church, Dr. Kim Ho Jik, the distinguished Korean Latter-day Saint leader who had been converted while attending Cornell University in the United States, said: "Honam, I think you need to get married as soon as possible."

Brother Rhee was impressed by this comment, interpreting it to mean that Dr. Kim was worried about developing strong priesthood leadership in Korea. Sometime later Elder Gordon B. Hinckley visited Korea to conduct a Church conference at Kyŏnggi Commercial High School. After the last session Sister Marjorie Hinckley, Elder Hinckley's wife, mentioned Youn Soon to Brother Rhee. Sister Hinckley lavishly praised Sister Park's personal qualities and simply remarked, "That's the girl that I have in mind for you." This comment had a serious effect on Rhee Honam. It motivated him to approach Sister Park during the following weeks.

First he assigned Sister Park to give several talks in church so that he could decide what kind of testimony she had. She bore strong testimony, and Honam thought, *Amazing. She has great faith!* He learned that she was born in Manchuria and was two years old when her family returned to Korea. She was raised in Seoul. She was a beautiful Korean sister who was talented and successful in her work at Ewha University. But the final persuading experience was the manner in which she presented her tithes and offerings to him, the branch president.

Honam recounts: "One day there was a knock on my office door. It was Sister Park Youn Soon. She said, 'These are my fast offerings,' as she held up a bag of rice. She had brought the rice in a bag she had made herself. It was beautifully sewn, with her name on it. I was very surprised. Sister Park was just a student with no income, yet every month she would bring in her fast offerings in an ornately made, hand-stitched bag."

Honam has other memories of Sister Park. "During the winter months the church seats were cold and hard, so the members sat on cushions to keep warm. The cushions became very dirty from use. One day when I came in for a meeting, I noticed that all the cushions had been washed, pressed, and mended. The doer of the deed remained anonymous, but I knew it must have been Sister Park. I was very impressed with Sister Park's faithfulness. It should not be too surprising that I later asked her to be my wife."

President Rhee decided the best approach would be to have an interview with Sister Park during which he would make a formal request for marriage. She was patiently waiting at the appointed hour outside his office. She was very innocent, naively waiting. President Rhee said to her, "Sister Park, I think I'm going to walk with you for a little while, if that is all right with you." So they walked together for a short while, and Honam proposed. "I'm going to say something now, but you need not answer this question. You can wait a week. Please listen." Then he said, "I want to marry you." Of course, this was a sudden surprise to her. He hadn't been very tactful. She didn't say anything. Later she admitted that she was embarrassed. Sister Park explains that she was so surprised she couldn't say anything.

One week passed without any verbal reply from Sister Park. So President Rhee did not ask her if she accepted his proposal. No one said, "I love you." Both understood, and in their own Korean way they felt joined heart to heart.

Brother Rhee and Sister Park were married in the Sam Chong chapel by mission president Gail E. Carr on December 21, 1963. There were a few Christmas decorations in the room, mainly red, purple, and blue paper streamers dangling from the ceiling. After the brief ceremony, a photographer took a formal picture with his old-fashioned powder-explosion camera. Several of the streamers caught fire. Honam immediately jumped up and pulled the burning papers to the floor and stamped out the flames. There was smoke and excitement for a time, but the happy wedding festivities continued.

"WE WILL PROVE THEM HEREWITH"

As with so many first-generation Korean converts, it was not easy for Rhee Honam to remain constantly active and faithful in carrying out his duties in the infant Church, to answer the many calls to serve the Lord and yet, on the other hand, meet the demands of Korean society and his family. But it was precisely because of these difficult experiences that Rhee Honam gained greater understanding of what it meant to be a trustworthy priesthood leader in "the land of the morning calm," which is the meaning of the word *Korea.*

A marker in the spiritual growth of Brother Rhee involved a call in January 1964 from mission president Gail E. Carr to accompany him to Pusan to serve as his interpreter during a Church conference. Rhee Honam was the district president at the time, and the mission president needed him. President Rhee had been taught that a faithful Latter-day Saint never turns down a Church assignment, so he agreed to go. As usual, he taught his classes at Tuksong High School on Saturday and then met President Carr at the Seoul train station to take the all-night ride to Pusan.

After meetings and business all day Sunday, he caught the night train for the return to Seoul. He knew he would have to be at school early Monday morning because he was assigned to administer important high school entrance examinations, an enormous event in the life of prospective high school students throughout all of Korea.

Since Brother Rhee was both hungry and tired Sunday night, he bought some apples and boiled eggs on the train. Rather than eat by himself, he shared this food with people who sat or stood nearby. He arrived in Seoul at 6:30 A.M. Monday morning and set out to go directly to school. He had followed this routine many times before. His wife was familiar with the routine and had asked President Rhee's sister to stay with her on Saturday and Sunday nights to keep her company.

He was standing on a platform outside the Seoul station waiting for a *hapsong*, a jeep-like minibus, to take him to school when suddenly another such vehicle pulled up in front of him, parked illegally, and started recruiting passengers. The driver called out: "I'm taking passengers to Chegi-dong. Get in, we're on our way immediately!" Chegi-dong was where the Rhees lived.

President Rhee recalls: "All of a sudden something told me, get on that bus! You must go home before you go to school." So he did. When he arrived at the outer gate of his home and knocked, no one answered. He shouted, and no one answered. Becoming uneasy, he went to the landlord's house nearby, and together they went to his home with a passkey. The minute they opened the door they could smell the deadly fumes of escaping *yontan* gas. Apparently all night this lethal carbon-monoxide gas had escaped into the room through a crack in the floor. His wife and sister asleep looked as if they were dead.

President Rhee immediately carried his unconscious wife and sister to a neighborhood medical clinic and solicited the help of a female doctor. The doctor said there was little chance that Sister Rhee and her sister-in-law could be saved. "I cannot help you. Take them quickly to St. Paul's Hospital, where they may be in a better position to help."

President Rhee was frantic. It instantly came to his mind that he was now a holder of the holy priesthood of God and that if they could receive a priesthood blessing, the Lord could heal them both. He telephoned the nearest missionary, Elder Michael Nichols (who years later became a mission president in Korea), to come quickly and assist in the blessing.

When Honam and Elder Nichols entered the emergency room to bless his wife, he was startled to see that the attending doctor was one of the people with whom he had shared his apples and eggs on the train the night before. The man recognized him, and from that time on he took special personal interest in his wife's condition. He told President Rhee that this may have been the worst case of *yontan* poisoning he had ever handled and that he could not give him much hope. They gave Youn Soon and her sister-in-law priesthood blessings, after which President Rhee spent much of the day in the privacy of a dark corner of a hospital room, kneeling on the cold cement floor praying earnestly for the Lord to spare the life of his beloved wife and sister.

Since prospects seemed so discouraging, Honam asked his mother to collect all the money she could find and make it available to pay for funeral expenses. Nuns from this Catholic hospital came to the bedside and began singing requiem songs. His wife and sister remained in a coma for three days and nights, but on the afternoon of the third day Sister Rhee began to show signs of regaining consciousness. In sheer ecstasy President Rhee repeatedly and profusely thanked his new friend, the doctor. But the physician said: "Don't be so excited. I fear she has brain damage. We must make further tests." After three more hours of tests, he guardedly reported that she did not seem to have any brain damage. Thankfully, President Rhee's wife and his sister both had a complete recovery.

Rhee Honam and Park Youn Soon had been married on December 21, 1963. This accident of carbon-monoxide poisoning took place only one month later, on January 27, 1964. They were a newly married young couple, and he felt sorry to have to leave her alone for two days and two nights on a weekend. But the Lord had called him to carry out an important Church assignment. Honam felt certain that this was an extraordinary instance of the fulfillment of the divine promise: "I, the Lord, am bound when ye do what I say; but when ye do not what I say, ye have no promise" (D&C 82:10).

Brother Rhee says that he has many times asked himself these questions: "What would have happened if I had refused to answer the call to go to Pusan? Would we both be dead? What would have happened if I had not shared my apples with the doctor on the train? What difference did it make that the *hapsong* driver pushed his car into place right in front of me at the train station and took me with dispatch to my home in Chegi-dong? What difference did it make that I had great faith in the Lord and in his holy priesthood for the healing of the sick?"

He has reached these conclusions. "It made all the difference in the world! I know for sure that my wife and I were honored for our dedication. I shall always be thankful to Heavenly Father for that. This experience helped prepare me to be more faithful in keeping the oath and covenant of the priesthood. It taught me what true discipleship means. It is a lesson I have repeatedly passed on to other Koreans as they have been called to serve in positions of responsibility in the Lord's church."

LABORING IN THE KINGDOM

Rhee Honam was one of a select number of outstanding Korean men and women, mostly high school and college students, who laid the preliminary foundations of the Church in Korea in the 1950s and 1960s and who have remained faithful in making significant contributions since those years.

Brother Rhee, along with other early Korean converts, was an authentic Mormon pioneer. He was among the first Korean converts to the Church. He encouraged and assisted the earliest Latter-day Saint servicemen in their efforts to establish the gospel among the Korean people. He was invaluable as a companion and interpreter for the first foreign proselyting missionaries from Japan and the United States. In time he became a trusted counselor for mission presidents and supervising General Authorities. And in all these years of service he was invariably cheerful, dependable, and energetic. He loved the members of the Church. He understood the importance of the gospel in their lives. He was a leader full of Christlike faith.

In 1965, when I began my service as mission president in Korea, Rhee Honam was called to serve as first counselor in the mission presidency, the first Korean to be so called. This was one result of a policy to release foreigners and install Koreans in branch, district, and mission positions whenever possible. President Rhee was very helpful in abetting this process of turning the leadership of the Korean mission over to Korean members of the Church.

In 1967 President and Sister Rhee were invited to Salt Lake City to attend the sessions of the annual April general conference of the Church and to deliver the first copies of the newly published Korean edition of the Book of Mormon to Church President David

Rhee Honam and his wife, Park Youn Soon, with their family.

O. McKay and Asia Area supervisor Elder Gordon B. Hinckley. This was their first visit to America and to Church headquarters. It was a wonderful spiritual experience for the Rhees because, among other privileges, they were sealed together as husband and wife for time and all eternity in the Salt Lake Temple by Elder Hinckley. Brother Rhee expressed the importance of this event:

> To be very honest with you, we did not know how to pre-pare to receive temple blessings. We were sealed in the Salt Lake Temple, and years later all our other children were sealed to us: Brian (Byung Youl), Kyung Hae, Kyung Un, and Kate (Kyung Ji). Out of those experiences the temple has become our fulness of joy in our lives.
>
> Whenever we have lived near a temple, whether in Seoul, Salt Lake City, Washington, D.C., or in Provo, we have gone to the temple each week without fail. When we visit the temple we visit the celestial kingdom. Returning into the presence of our Heavenly Father is no longer a strange or vague thing. It is a living experience. It's so beautiful. Especially since we lost our oldest daughter, Kyung Hae, in a car accident in Provo, we know that going through the veil is entering the presence of God and the enactment of having of our beloved daughter with us forever.

Brother Rhee received another profound and inspirational blessing—a patriarchal blessing—under the hands of Church patri-arch Eldred G. Smith on April 7, 1967, during his visit to Salt Lake City. Included were the following promises: "Obstacles and barriers have been removed from thy pathway, in advance, to enable thee to receive of thy blessings and to assist thee in fulfilling thy mission upon the earth. The Lord shall continue to be mindful of thee and shall bless thy efforts in serving others and in generously using thy time, thy talents, and thy means in advancing the work of the Lord upon the earth. He shall reward thee richly for thy efforts therein. His providing care shall be over thee that thou and thy household shall not be in need for the necessities of life. Thou shalt have means sufficient to accomplish the duties and responsibilities required of thee. Thou shalt be given assistance from others both in and out of thy family." This patriarchal blessing gave Brother Rhee great motivation and desire to serve others and remain faithful.

The contributions of Rhee Honam in the establishment and development of The Church of Jesus Christ of Latter-day Saints in Korea have been many. In 1973 Spencer W. Kimball, President of the Council of the Twelve Apostles, organized the first stake on the Asian continent, the Seoul Korea Stake. Rhee Honam was called to serve as the first president of the Seoul stake, with Kim Chang Sun as his first counselor and Choi Wook Hwan as his second counselor. President Kimball took President Rhee aside in the Chosen Hotel and told him that he must realize a vision of the greatness of the Lord's work. He told President Rhee that one day the gospel must be carried to North Korea and other Chinese areas of northeast Asia. He advised President Rhee that it would be well for him to study the Chinese language so as to be prepared to further participate.

Being assigned as the first stake president of a newly established and inexperienced membership was a unique challenge because the Saints expected so much, in accordance with Korean cultural tradition. It seemed to President Rhee that they expected the stake president to be an almost perfect leader. President Rhee not only prayed fervently for divine guidance but also frequently challenged the bishops, branch presidents, and other leaders that they must follow the example of Nephi to get their own personal Liahona and learn to be led by the Holy Ghost in all their righteous endeavors (see 1 Nephi 16). President Rhee felt that if everyone took this course, the leaders and members would be in tune with the stake presidency. There would then be no murmuring or disharmony. All would live together in a unity of faith.

From 1972 to 1978 Rhee Honam served as area administrator of seminaries and institutes of religion in the Church Educational System (CES) in Korea. He was released in 1978 to serve as president of the Korea Pusan Mission, and after his return from that assignment in 1981 he resumed the directorship of CES until 1985.

Brother Frank D. Day, a CES administrator from Church headquarters, set the program in motion in Korea by calling Brother Rhee to establish CES study classes throughout the country. Brother Rhee explains:

> I first learned about the program from Brother Day, and I knew that it would strengthen the members in Korea. I was honored and pleased to be called to set up the Church Education System there. Since the program was established in Korea,

*Stake president Rhee Honam with Elder Gordon B. Hinckley
at a news conference in Seoul, Korea, in 1975.*

hundreds of brothers and sisters have been able to take advantage of the program and benefit from the teachings. I would say that almost one hundred percent of those local Koreans serving missions have gone through the seminary and institute program. This program helps these young brothers and sisters gain the desire to serve the Lord. And upon returning home, these brothers and sisters are a valuable resource, serving diligently in their home wards. A true testimony comes, not only from listening here and there, but from a systematic study of the scriptures. I know that the seminary program is inspired, and I am thankful for the blessings that it has brought to the Korean people.[2]

Between 1978 and 1981, Rhee Honam served as president of the Pusan mission. Illustrative of varied challenges facing him, his wife, and the missionaries at that time in this far-flung mission, which included all the South Kyŏngsang and South Chŏlla provinces and adjacent southern islands, was the historic social upheaval of May 1980 known as the Kwangju Uprising. Kwangju was the name of the city.

In May of 1980 residents of Kwangju, mainly students at first, demonstrated against the takeover of the government by the Korean military, and they were met with violent mistreatment. President Rhee had twenty-two missionaries serving in the city at the time. The upheaval was so sudden that the mission president had no way of immediately contacting his missionaries. The army had surrounded the area and had cut off all lines of communication. No one could leave or enter the city.

President Rhee attempted to enter Kwangju but was prevented from doing so. He regarded the situation as "a desperate time." As news of fighting spread throughout Korea and into the outside world, President Rhee kept in close contact by phone with Elder Yoshihiko Kikuchi, the Church area administrator over Korea and Japan, headquartered in Tokyo. He called President Rhee regularly, as did many parents of missionaries in the United States and Korea. But President Rhee had no information. He simply did not know whether his missionaries were dead or alive. As President Rhee relates the experience, "I was blessed to have very righteous and obedient missionaries." They did what they had been taught they should do in times of grave emergency; that is, go immediately to the U.S. embassy or to the U.S. Kwangju Air Force Base. Consequently, all the missionaries were taken by airplane to safety at the U.S. Osan Air Force Base near Seoul.

Immediately after the Korean army withdrew from Kwangju, President Rhee called Kwangju stake president Pak Byung Kyu to inform him that he would arrange for relief food supplies to be sent to the Korean Saints in the area. President Pak replied: "President Rhee, I appreciate your concern, but the Saints are doing just fine. While there is a great shortage of food and other things, we are fine. All this year we have talked about family preparedness and food storage. Some of our Saints have faithfully followed the counsel of the Church leaders and have plenty to share with all the members here." Again, out of this experience, President Rhee Honam saw the importance of following the advice and teachings of the General Authorities of the Church.[3]

Between 1981 and 1985 Elder Rhee was called to serve as a Regional Representative of the Twelve. In this position he served nine stakes in the Seoul area.

In April of 1981 Korean members of the Church were thrilled to receive an official announcement from President Spencer W. Kimball of the intended construction of the Seoul Korea Temple. The teachings of Confucius regarding the three bonds and the five moral principles of human relationships include the importance of filial piety among family members. Koreans already believed that they should do anything possible to please their ancestors. So it was a source of great satisfaction for Korean members to learn that through temple ordinances the living can be sealed to their dead ancestors and that family members can be sealed to one another for time and all eternity. This doctrine fit traditional Korean beliefs.

President Kimball asked a group of Korean leaders, including Rhee Honam, attending general conference in Salt Lake whether the Korean members would be able to come up with their local share of the cost of the temple. The group, which was headed by Elder In Sang Han, later called to the Seventy, responded with an enthusiastic, "For sure!" As Elder Han later reported, the commitment was more than fulfilled: "The Korean Saints were unselfish in making their contributions to the fund. The members not only fulfilled their pledge, but quadrupled their share. Many gave up their savings— savings for new homes and new rentals. I think that was the main reason why the Korea Temple was redesigned three different times. Originally it was designed to be a very simple structure—just a couple of endowment rooms and one sealing room. Then it was expanded and expanded and expanded. Finally we ended up with four endowment rooms and three sealing rooms. It's a very beautiful temple. To me it is one of the most beautiful temples in the world."[4]

Rhee Honam was particularly enthusiastic about the construction of the Seoul temple and about the prospect of performing sacred family ordinances of exaltation therein. The temple had already become a powerful force in his life. He did his part in helping raise funds for the construction of the temple, and he was called to serve as chairman of the temple dedication committee. The Seoul Korea Temple was dedicated by President Gordon B. Hinckley on December 14, 1985. Brother Rhee has often testified that the temple dedication was a major spiritual highlight in his life.

In 1986 Elder Rhee emigrated to the United States. After spending a year in the New York area, he responded to an invitation to teach the Korean language at Brigham Young University, where he has served for a decade.

Brother Rhee's Church service in Provo has included a year as a

Rhee Honam (kneeling at right) participated in the cornerstone laying ceremony for the Seoul Korea Temple on December 14, 1985, the same day of its dedication. At left are Elder William R. Bradford, Elder Howard W. Hunter, and President Gordon B. Hinckley. Elder Yoshihiko Kikuchi is at far right.

counselor in the bishopric of the Asian ward of the BYU Eleventh Stake, followed by six years as bishop of that same ward. The ethnic and national diversity of the members of this Asian ward was at first a very challenging experience because historically Koreans and Chinese had lived under Japanese rule. The new Korean bishop wondered how so many different people from so many countries of Asia could harmoniously live together. But Bishop Rhee felt the power of the gospel to bring everyone together in peace and harmony. He realized as never before that members of the Church can love one another, as Jesus has loved them. Jesus loved everyone, and if we follow him we can enjoy the great blessing of loving everyone as well.

As a member of the Church who has diligently furthered the teachings and values of the gospel of Jesus Christ during the last forty-plus years, Rhee Honam is a remarkable Mormon pioneer. Professor Mark A. Peterson, who served as a missionary in Korea in the late 1960s and later was a successor to President Rhee as president of the Korea Pusan Mission and who currently works in the Korean language program at BYU with Professor Rhee, has said: "Brother Rhee is a true pioneer. In everything he does, he is faithful and diligent. He is a wonderful colleague. As a teacher, he dedicates himself to his students; they love and respect him. He loves his students and welcomes them to his office for regular interviews, and they call on him for advice. I can see the same qualities in him now as I did when I first met him in 1965. He was a steadfast leader who laid the foundation of the Church in Korea as much as anyone else. So many of us over the years have taken Brother Rhee as a role model. His devotion and loyalty to the Church are unparalleled."

Notes

1. This sketch is based on a decades-long close association with Rhee Honam and his family. In November and December 1995 I conducted extensive interviews with Brother Rhee. All quotations are from the interviews unless otherwise noted. First-person sketches of Rhee Honam and his wife, Park Youn Soon, are also found in Spencer J. Palmer and Shirley H. Palmer, eds. and comps., *The Korean Saints: Personal Stories of Trial and Triumph, 1950–1980* (Provo, Utah: Religious Education, Brigham Young University, 1995), pp. 184–90.

2. In Palmer and Palmer, *The Korean Saints*, p. 188.

3. For further details, see Palmer and Palmer, *The Korean Saints*, pp. 188–89.

4. In Palmer and Palmer, *The Korean Saints*, p. 97.

Mormon Pioneers
in Southern Germany

by Hermann Mössner

Stuttgart was already an important focal point for our church in the last century. Swiss-German mission reports from 1898 mention five conferences (or districts) within the mission, including a Stuttgart Conference that comprised the kingdoms of Württemberg and Bavaria and included branches in Stuttgart, Heilbronn, Backnang, Saargmünd, Saarbrücken, München, and Nürnberg.

The beginnings of the Church in Stuttgart go back even further. Latter-day Saint baptisms were performed in 1881 by an Elder Schramm. According to mission records, the Stuttgart Branch in 1898 had one priest, thirty-four members, and two children under the age of eight.

My maternal grandfather, Gottlieb Schönhardt, was for me one of the great early Mormon pioneers in Stuttgart. He was baptized in April 1882 at the age of twenty-one. Born and raised in a devout Lutheran family in Hirsau in the northern Black Forest area, he married in 1886. He and his wife had nine children, including my beloved mother, Rosine Schönhardt Mössner. At that time in Germany, both Protestants and Catholics were extremely intolerant of other denominations. Ridicule and scorn were common. The closest Mormon branch was fifty kilometers away in Stuttgart. The family was unable to attend Church meetings due to financial and transportation constraints. It was a joyous occasion when the missionaries visited my grandfather's family from time to time and held meetings in their home.

Pestalozzi, the great Swiss educator (1746–1827), stated that "man only becomes civilized through participation in society," words that influenced my grandfather's decision in 1911 to leave

Translated by D. Brent Smith

the little Black Forest village. He and his family moved to Feuerbach, near Stuttgart, to live close to an organized branch and participate in Church activities.

Feuerbach at that time was a small, fast-growing industrial town with ten thousand inhabitants. World-renowned firms such as Bosch, Werner and Pfleiderer, Behr, Roser, Leitz, Kast and Ehinger, Hauf, and so on had been founded or were resident there. Stuttgart, the capital city, was an hour away by foot; it could be reached only by a very steep road. Every Sunday the now eighteen members of the extended family trekked the eight miles to the distant branch located on Alexanderstrasse, where sixty members met under the leadership of Paul Gmelin and later Alfons Müller Sr. The way home was also by foot. I participated in this weekly Sunday excursion for two years myself, pushed in a baby buggy. Grandfather loved the gospel; he bore his testimony whenever he had the opportunity. He served as a town missionary in Feuerbach and even visited the ranking Lutheran minister, a man named Kallee, who told him, "Mr. Schönhardt, I know that you are teaching the truth, but I cannot become a Mormon or I would lose my ministerial post."

In the meantime, thanks to my grandfather's missionary efforts, several families and single members were baptized. He had strong support from his son-in-law, Gottlob Rügner, from Dornstetten, near Freudenstadt, who performed his military training in Stuttgart in 1912 and married my Aunt Lina in 1914. They raised eight children in the gospel. Uncle Gottlob had been raised in a strong Lutheran home; his conversion to the Church led to great difficulties with his parents, but love eventually won out and calmed the troubled waters.

Following his return from the First World War, Uncle Gottlob began with great enthusiasm to work with Grandfather to build the foundation for an independent branch in Feuerbach. By 1924 it was accomplished; Feuerbach became an independent branch, with Gottlieb Schönhardt and Gottlob Rügner as presiding authorities. Grandfather passed away in 1931 and left a great posterity of thirty-four children and grandchildren, all members of The Church of Jesus Christ of Latter-day Saints.

Many missionaries from "Zion" served for some time on their missions with us in Feuerbach. We also sent out German missionaries into the mission field. The very first of these, already in 1921, was Gottlob Rügner, married and at that time father of three children, the youngest of which was four months old—what a sacrifice! Other missionaries from our Feuerbach Branch were my brother, Karl Mössner; Eugen Keller; and Elisabeth Rügner-Varner. Up until the present, far more than thirty missionaries have been sent out by this branch, now a ward.

My mother, Rosine, made a decision that was to have major consequences: she married a nonmember in 1912. The couple bore five children, and Mother had to take on the responsibility of raising them herself. She shirked neither work nor sore trials to raise us as members of the Church. Prayers, family home evenings, and church attendance all took place without the participation of our father; we had to find a place to pray in secret, away from his presence. Mother had to suffer many sorrows, and, together with her, we children also shed many tears. When we went to church on Sundays, we had to put up with Father's curses and unfriendly gestures, both when we left and upon our return. He hated the Church.

I will never forget my baptism at age eight in 1930. In the early evening of October 3, my mother and I left our home in Feuerbach. We met members of the branch at the railway station, and together we took the train to Ludwigsburg. From there we walked to the banks of the Neckar River at Ossweil, where the baptism took place. It was a wonderful experience. But not at all enjoyable was the reception that awaited us at home at about 10 P.M. We had our house key, but the door had been bolted from the inside; we were locked out! What had happened? Father, who had been asleep in the bedroom when we left, woke up and, observing that Mother and I had left, bolted the door from the inside. We knocked on the door and rang the bell, but there was no sign of response. Finally we heard Father cursing and stomping angrily toward the door. He opened it and then swung at our heads with a lash we used to beat rugs. This lash was a long, round piece of hardwood with many finger-thick leather strips. Blood trickled down my cheeks—what an experience for an eight-year-old! But nothing could turn Mother and her five children away from the restored gospel. Her motto was: "Let us remain true and hold on to our Lord Jesus Christ." We followed her great example of faith.

An unbridgeable chasm existed between my God-fearing, devout mother and my atheistic father. Father was industrious, providing our family with everything we stood in need of, but he was not spiritually inclined and refused all contact with anything having to do with God, the Church, and Christian living. His hatred of Mormons was boundless and blocked any chance of peaceful or harmonious living within our family. This situation remained unchanged through the time of his death in 1964. Can you understand how Father's death brought with it a certain deliverance for all of us?

The 1930 end-of-year mission records reported 396 members in the Stuttgart District, comprising eight branches: Esslingen, Feuerbach, Göppingen, Heilbronn, Ludwigsburg, Reutlingen, Stuttgart, and Tübingen. The district president at that time was Owen Jacobs. Francis Salzner had replaced Frederik Tadje as the mission president in Basel.

In 1930 the Church celebrated its hundred-year anniversary. A great jubilee celebration was held in Basel on this occasion. From June 20 to June 22, thousands of German, Austrian, and Swiss members streamed into Basel to participate in conference proceedings under the direction of European Mission president John A. Widtsoe, a member of the Council of the Twelve Apostles.

During the 1930s the branches in the Stuttgart District blossomed. At district conferences the district choir sang under the direction of Brother Hans Lang of Feuerbach. Brother Friedrich Widmar of Esslingen directed many dramatic, faith-promoting presentations that were given on Saturday evenings in connection with conferences.

Particularly responsible for the growth and strengthening of the Church in the Stuttgart area were our beloved and long-serving district president, Erwin Ruf, and his counselor, Emil Geist from Heilbronn, who later became our first patriarch upon creation of the Stuttgart Stake in 1961. Unfortunately, Brother Ruf died much too early in 1951. We will never forget the names of other families who made great contributions, such as Müller, Greiner, Zügel, Krieger, Fingerle, Stohrer, Knödler, Schaaf, Schurr, Jud, and so on.

Of course there were differences between us Mormons, considered to be members of a sect, and our neighbors. We particularly stood apart by going to church not only on Sundays, but also on workday evenings to what our neighbors called "Bible classes." As the only Mormon in a school class comprising only Lutheran students, I was often the subject of ridicule and scorn.

In our area, we as members were not subject to any hindrances or restrictions imposed by Hitler's National Socialist government—

with one sole exception. We had to take the word *Zion* out of our songbooks. Hitler was initially considered to be a model leader by our American mission presidents. They noted that he did not smoke or drink alcohol and that he often expressed his belief in divine providence in his addresses to the German people. We were counseled by our mission presidents, in accordance with the twelfth article of faith, to support the existing government and to obey the laws of the land. Church leaders from that period realized much too late that Hitler and his followers were directed by diabolical influences.

I was seventeen in September 1939 when the Second World War broke out. During one of the last few days in August, the two missionaries assigned to Feuerbach arrived on their bicycles, bathed in sweat, at the home of branch president Gottlob Rügner in Weilimdorf and informed him with tears in their eyes that they and all other missionaries had received word that they must leave Germany immediately. What had happened? The telephone had rung only hours before in the West German Mission office in Frankfurt. In the absence of mission president M. Douglas Wood, mission secretary J. Richard Barnes received the call from European Mission president Hugh B. Brown in London. President Brown told the frightened young secretary that he had just received a call from President Heber J. Grant in Salt Lake City with the order to evacuate all missionaries immediately out of Germany, Austria, and Czechoslovakia. The reason, according to President Grant, was that the German army would be invading Poland in three days.

The sudden departure of our beloved missionaries brought both pain and sorrow. Not one of us could imagine that it would take almost ten years until the missionaries would return. The outbreak of the Second World War created gaps that were difficult to fill in our branch. More and more local brethren took over the responsibilities that missionaries had often carried out.

A small tragedy took place at that time in Feuerbach. The two American missionaries had lived with a widow who had a beautiful nineteen-year-old daughter. This living situation was not in accordance with mission regulations. There was only one common bathroom and one kitchen. As was almost inevitable, the daughter fell in love with one of the two missionaries, who returned her love. Both mother and daughter were baptized, and the couple became engaged! An engagement was a commitment that one intended to marry. Now, this missionary gave his solemn word that he would make arrangements for his dear fiancée to come to Utah. The sudden departure was wrenching, with much shedding of tears. On this elder's word, this young sister forwarded her complete trousseau— linens, clothing, china, and silverware—to the home of the missionary's parents in Utah. The Second World War and this elder's broken word resulted in the severing of their engagement. The disillusionment was so great that mother and daughter fell away from the Church and the reputations of the American elders and of the branch itself were tarnished.

Due to both military inductions and forced evacuations from the cities following bombing raids, the branches lost much of their strength. During the long years of war, great service was rendered in our branches by our older brethren and also by our youth who were too young to be drafted into military service.

As a result of frequent bombings by both British and American bombers, many Sunday church services were disrupted and those attending had to flee into nearby air-raid shelters. By 1944 the bombings increased greatly. One Sunday morning the few remaining members of our branch met but were soon forced to spend many hours in an air-raid shelter. As finally the all-clear siren sounded, we crawled out of the shelter. Devastated, we stood before the ruins of what remained of the building that housed our branch. The bombers left behind great destruction and devastation. The branch quarters located on the Elsenhansstrasse in Feuerbach and on the Hauptstätterstrasse in Stuttgart and particularly those in Heilbronn and Pforzheim lay in rubble and ashes.

In the intervening period, the branch meetings were moved to alternative quarters, including individual homes. This distressing situation pushed the members closer together so that we felt great kinship with the Apostle Paul. Like him, we tried courageously to declare: "Who shall separate us from the love of Christ? shall tribulation, or distress, or persecution, or famine, or nakedness, or peril, or sword?" (Romans 8:35–39.) The accounts of distress of individual families whose fathers and sons had fallen at the war front and of the losses among the members due to air raids were painful. It was only the faith in our God and the firm hope of eternal life that gave us the strength to carry on and continue.

My home city Stuttgart was bombed heavily; almost the whole city was transformed into debris and ashes. Thousands of women and children lost their lives. Tens of thousands were seriously injured. It was during this period that I married my wife, Lore, in June 1944. Only a few weeks before, my wife received her parents' permission to be baptized, although she had already been coming to church for several years. In July 1944, four weeks after we as newlyweds had moved into a home in Stuttgart-South, it was totally destroyed in a nighttime bombing raid. We ourselves were not injured because we were able to flee into an air-raid shelter deep beneath the earth. We found a new home in Stuttgart-Weilimdorf. This home was also hit and severely damaged during an air raid. We were blessed to have parents who could take us in. It was in this uncertain and worrisome situation that I had to leave my young wife (who was soon to be a mother) on September 12, 1944, to go to war.

A little more than two months later, I was captured by British troops near Aachen, close to the Belgian border. We were moved to a collection point for prisoners in the Edingen Monastery near Brussels. Every day we stood for hours in formation for roll call in the courtyard of the monastery. As the war was still on, we could see overhead the groups of British and American bombers heading toward Germany, where they dumped their deadly cargo on the cities where our wives and children lived.

The year 1945—the terrible war was finally over! Already in 1946, the President of the Church, George Albert Smith, sent Elder Ezra Taft Benson of the Quorum of the Twelve to Germany to begin the Church's great welfare effort on behalf of those European Saints who were in need.

Following the leadership during the war period of mission presidents Friedrich Biehl, Christian Heck, and Anthon Huck, Max Zimmer of Basel was called as West German Mission president in January 1946. On June 12, 1947, Brother Jean Wunderlich, who had emigrated as a boy with his parents to Utah, returned to lead the mission with great devotion and enthusiasm. Already in May 1948, the first large mission conference after the war took place in Stuttgart-Degerloch.

But I did not myself experience these immediate postwar events, for from the end of 1944 through May 1948 I was interred as a German army prisoner of war in a prison camp in England. British troops had overrun our poorly armed infantry regiment near the city of Aachen in November 1944. Thus ended this terrible war for me. We were taken to England, where we were confined behind barbed wire in POW Camp 245 in Leeds, Yorkshire. In the beginning, without any work assignments, we spent the whole day being summoned to one roll call after another. Upon our capture, everything had been taken from us: watches, rings, and my triple combination, which was particularly painful. I therefore wrote the mission office of our church in London and received from them a Bible and a Book of Mormon. I was the only Mormon among the one thousand German prisoners of war in the camp.

At last we were given work assignments. I was assigned to a road construction crew in a new housing settlement on the outskirts of Leeds. Our meals were scant. During the evenings in our corrugated-iron huts, there was a lot of cursing and fighting; many of the prisoners had little hope or self-control. In these circumstances men certainly stood out who did not curse or complain, who hummed songs, and who folded their hands in prayer. On Sundays some devout Christians would meet in the camp chapel for worship. I preached my own faith in the restored gospel there so that some of my prison compatriots would want to know more about it.

In the intervening period, a good, faithful elder from the Leeds Branch, Brother George Camm from Horsforth, came every Saturday to our prison camp. We partook of the holy sacrament, sang the songs of Zion, and rejoiced in our brotherhood.

A special experience took place on Sunday, May 12, 1946. I was called over the loudspeaker to come to the prison gate. Surprised, I hurried to the gate. There I was met by a tall, good-looking, well-dressed man who stretched forth his hand and said to me, "My name is Hugh B. Brown, president of the British Mission." What a joy and blessing for me! The mission president had come to visit me in the prison camp during the time between two meetings of the local district conference. In a little prison hut, he laid his hands upon my head and gave me a very consoling priesthood blessing. He blessed me with the strength of faith and the necessary patience in my difficult situation and promised me a safe return to Germany to my loved ones!

No mail had arrived from home; I didn't know if my loved ones were still alive, nor did I know if my wife had given birth to a son or a daughter. Shortly before my capture on November 18, 1944, I had received a letter on the western battlefront in which my wife informed me that she was expecting a baby. Since that time my feelings had alternated between hope and anxiety.

In the prison camp in Leeds, England, four and sometimes six fellow prisoners and I sat during the evenings in one of our small huts after a hard day's work, singing the songs of Zion, praying together, and listening to my testimony of Joseph Smith and the restoration of the Church of Jesus Christ in our time. Two of my fellow prisoners wished to be baptized. What joy this brought me! The British Saints picked us up from the camp in a car and drove us to the old wooden branch meetinghouse in Bradford, Yorkshire, where I had the privilege of baptizing my German brethren.

In the meantime, President Hugh B. Brown had left England, and Selvoy Boyer had followed him as president of the British Mission. The British members loved us very much. Every Sunday a group of German prisoners would march from our camp in Butcherhill five kilometers to the town hall in Leeds, where Church meetings took place. With the letters *POW* on our backs and on the legs of our uniforms, we were often the object of public mockery and derision. Yet we were happy to be able to participate in Sunday School and sacrament meetings. I was called to be the Sunday School president in Leeds. Nobody in the branch was offended by our prisoner clothing or our poor English.

At the camp it became known that two members of the Protestant church had been converted to the Mormon church. The Catholic camp priest lodged a protest with the British camp commander. One day I was called into his office. With mixed feelings I stood before him at attention. He was not alone; next to him stood another officer—a Church of England chaplain who turned toward me in an unfriendly manner and, raising his voice, asked me: "By what authority do you baptize your fellow prisoners?" Unafraid, I looked him in the eye and responded: "With the authority of the holy priesthood I hold." His face darkened, and with a loud voice he ordered me from the commander's office: "Get out, you . . . German!" He threw me out, this dignitary of the Church of England.

Two weeks later, two more of my fellow prisoners wanted to be baptized. Again we were picked up by Church members at the camp gate. It was one week before Christmas, with the special spirit of this season in evidence. With the power and authority of the holy priesthood and in the name of Jesus Christ, I was permitted to baptize my beloved brethren. On this same evening the branch Christmas party was held. We were well prepared. For weeks we had spent the long evenings constructing small wooden toys for the

Hermann Mössner (center) with fellow prisoners of war and converts to the Church Wolfgang Krueger (far left), Willi Raschke (left), Heinz Borchert (right), and Erich Ruelicke (far right).

forty children of the Bradford Branch. The children's eyes sparkled, and their parents wept heartfelt tears.

Twenty-five years later, when I picked up my son Jürgen from his mission in the Leeds England Mission, I was able to speak to the Saints who were still meeting in the old wooden chapel in Bradford and to recall on this occasion the presents brought by the German prisoners to the children of the Bradford Branch. Some of the adults in attendance told me that they still had those toys.

At the prison camp, I was now not allowed to preach at the camp chapel on Sundays. In this way, they wanted to prevent others from joining the now five Mormons. Somehow the Missionary Department in Salt Lake City found out about this prohibition in "the cradle of democracy." One day I was told by the commander that this prohibition had been remanded. Of course I was very surprised. Twenty years later I learned the background: As the first German stake president in the former West Germany, I had the privilege of welcoming Elder Gordon B. Hinckley as a visiting authority at a stake conference in Stuttgart. In a conversation in my office, he told me that he had received the assignment in 1947 to write a letter to a British prison camp commander with the request that Mormon priesthood holders, in like manner as Catholic and Protestant clergy, be permitted to meet and preach in the prison chapel. Elder Hinckley pulled from his briefcase a copy of the letter that I had written to the Brethren in Salt Lake City twenty years previously.

There was another fruit of these labors that was harvested at that time. One of my newly baptized fellow prisoners had been assigned to work in a farmer's field. Nearby lived a couple that brought bread for the prisoners to eat. Willi, from Eberswalde near Berlin, used this opportunity to bear testimony of his new church and the wonderful gospel. The couple was touched by this testimony and joined the Church. Later they had a sweet little daughter. When I returned to England in 1974, I met this girl, who was the wife of the first bishop of the Leeds Ward, Bishop Cook.

In many ways my imprisonment in England was a great blessing. I could send a number of food packages to my loved ones in Germany, and I learned English, which allowed me on my return to Germany to be able to serve as an interpreter for several General Authorities. All four fellow prisoners who joined the Church in captivity were repatriated before me; I was not released until May 1948. Prisoners of war are always a cheap source of labor that can be taken advantage of by the victors.

My first son, Wilfrid, was born toward the end of May 1945. I was not able to find this out for a long time. Mail came through only after the restrictions for such communications to and from prisoners of war were relaxed. This took months. When I saw my first letter from home, I was beside myself with excitement. Letters were handed out at the camp gate as we returned from work. At last I held in my hand the first news from home—the sender's name on the back of the envelope, Lore Mössner, confirmed that my wife was alive! If you think that I ripped open the letter right at the camp gate and stood and read it while I was still dirty from a long day's work, you are mistaken. Full of joy, I stuck the letter in my jacket pocket. First I washed myself, changed clothes, and even polished my boots—only then was I ready. But I also wanted to find some privacy, so I hurried to the outskirts of the camp, and there, next to the barbed wire, I knelt down and thanked my Heavenly Father for this first letter from my beloved wife. Only then did I open the letter, which began with the following words: "Darling, little Wilfrid already has his first teeth; he is a lovely boy." Now I knew that I had a son, that my family was alive, and that they appeared to be living in good circumstances. Lore's letter was not the first she had written, but it was the first that I was able to receive in England.

My return home to Stuttgart in 1948 was the happiest day in my life up until that time. Wilfrid was already three years old the first time I saw him. Father, mother, and son hugged each other. My new life began. Soon after my return, I was called as Feuerbach Branch president to replace my honorable uncle, Gottlob Rügner, who had served in a selfless way in this position for eighteen years. At this time I was twenty-six years old.

I had served an apprenticeship from 1936 through 1939 in plumbing and installation of hygienic facilities. From 1939 through 1944 I had worked in the munitions industry manufacturing airplane parts. Following my return from the war and British imprisonment in 1948, I began training at the master artisan level and successfully passed the examination as a master artisan for gas, water, and heating installation. For almost forty years thereafter, I worked for the municipal utilities of the city of Stuttgart as a regional director and supervisor for one of the Stuttgart city districts. Of course, there was some degree of ridicule and scorn shown toward those who did not smoke or drink or who did not tell dirty jokes or laugh at them. But I did receive respect and esteem for my Christian way of life as a Latter-day Saint. Each one of my master artisan colleagues accepted a Book of Mormon from me. One of these colleagues became interested in the Church and invited me to visit him at his home. His wife became more interested in the Church than he did and was baptized together with all their children. Their son served a mission in England, was married in the temple, and has presided over a branch in the Stuttgart Stake. We have not given up hope that my colleague will one day also be baptized.

The Church welfare plan, begun in 1936 in the United States, brought blessings and helped rescue us in Germany from great material need. Large packages of food and clothing reached our branches in the years following the war and were distributed to the members. As Feuerbach Branch president, I personally supervised the distribution of food, clothing, and homemade quilts to individual members. The welfare shipments from Mormons in the United States were so plentiful that we could share them with our fellow

Christians by setting aside large quantities of food for the Catholic and Lutheran charity organizations to dispense. In this way we were able to demonstrate true Christian love for our fellowmen.

The end of the war and the occupation of our part of Germany by the Americans was a great blessing and help for all of Germany and especially for us as members of the Church. The Saints in East Germany under Russian occupation had a much more difficult load to bear. Many Church members fled to West Germany. As there was a great shortage of housing at that time, it was difficult for them to find a foothold. Many of them emigrated to Utah. Those who remained with us in southern Germany found help, consolation, and encouragement in the branches of the Church and fellowship with the Saints. We were blessed beyond measure by their faith and devotion to the restored gospel, and our branches blossomed as a result of their faithful service.

Soon after the reconstruction of our cities, members had the strong desire to finally own their own branch buildings. Our most ardent wish was to be able to come out of the "backyards" and to have more space and better opportunities for worship services, women's and youth meetings, and cultural and athletic activities.

In Stuttgart-North the Church secured a building site in 1952 from the widow of the city's former lord mayor. Building began in 1954, and on September 19, 1955, we were able to move into the first Church-owned branch meetinghouse in the Stuttgart District. The ceremonial turning over of keys to the building took place in the presence of high-ranking Church authorities, including Elder Spencer W. Kimball of the Quorum of the Twelve as well as West German Mission president Kenneth B. Dyer and both brethren's wives. District president Erwin Krieger and Stuttgart Branch president Walter Speidel, along with many members and friends of the tradition-rich Stuttgart Branch, were thrilled to finally have their own branch meetinghouse. Part of the construction had been performed by individual branch members. Brothers and sisters worked many evenings and Saturdays, often working up a sweat as a result of hard manual labor.

Branch president Walter Speidel, later professor of German at Brigham Young University, shared his memories: "On September 18, 1954, we laid the cornerstone of our new branch meetinghouse. It was raining very heavily this day, but we considered this rain to be a good sign and said to one another, 'What is growing should be watered.' So we were in good spirits with our dripping umbrellas. After short remarks by mission president Kenneth B. Dyer, a copper-lined box was inserted in the cornerstone before it was put in place. Inside this box we placed the standard works of the Church, the building plans for the edifice, various coins from our time, a newspaper for this date, a picture of the branch members, and a certificate with the names of branch leaders."

Building lots were also sought in Feuerbach, Esslingen, and Heilbronn for construction of future Church buildings. In Karlsruhe, the Church built its own rest home in 1955 for older members. Elder Spencer W. Kimball dedicated this building on September 7. Brother and Sister Pely and later Brother and Sister Ollenik served with great love, devotion, and diligence in caring for those living in this home. Our elderly sisters and also a few brothers were able to spend many years and in many cases the rest of their lives at home among fellow Church members. It was therefore very painful after almost twenty years of operation of this home to experience its closing and the necessary transfer of the remaining elderly brothers and sisters into homes maintained by other confessions who were not as willing to take in Mormons.

The emigration of many of our members to America subsided with the dedication in 1955 of the Swiss Temple, which could be reached in three and one-half hours from Stuttgart. Missionary efforts brought forth good fruits in our branches. Between 1955 and 1959 over two hundred missionaries labored at all times in our West German Mission, which stretched from Bielefeld in the north to Basel and Lörrach in the south, and from Saarbrücken in the west to Bertchesgaden in the east. The mission presidents of this period, Kenneth B. Dyer (1953–1957) and especially our much-beloved President Theodore M. Burton (1957–1961), spurred the great progress and quick growth of the Church of Jesus Christ in our country.

In 1957 Brother Emil Geist became president of the Stuttgart District. His first counselor was Franz Greiner, who had been branch president in Feuerbach. The second counselor was Rolf Knödler of Esslingen. Brother Paul Oppermann of Esslingen was the president of an elders quorum comprising the entire district. Although there were in Germany in the 1950s neither bishops, patriarchs, high priests, stake presidents, nor even one stake of Zion, there were numerous indications that their day would not be far from coming. Until 1959 there were only two missions in the postwar Federal Republic of Germany—the West German Mission, headquartered in Frankfurt, and the North German Mission, head-quartered in Hamburg.

For many of us it was therefore a great surprise when, on October 4, 1959, the West German Mission was split and the South German Mission was created in Stuttgart as the third mission in the Federal Republic of Germany. Over seven hundred members came together on this memorable day in the Stuttgart-Feuerbach Festhalle. Elder Marion G. Romney of the Quorum of the Twelve was the presiding official. The first mission president of the newly created South German Mission, John A. Buehner, who had with his parents emigrated from Stuttgart years before, was sustained unanimously by those present. I was sustained as first counselor in the presidency of the South German Mission, having served earlier as President Burton's counselor in the West German Mission presidency. The new mission had five districts: Stuttgart, Karlsruhe, Freiburg, München, and Nürnberg. President Buehner had to return to the United States in June 1960 for health reasons. He was followed as mission president by T. Quentin Cannon, a lawyer from Salt Lake City, who had served a mission in Germany as a young man. In Brother Cannon, we had a Church leader whose main goal was to prepare Stuttgart to become a stake of Zion, which would be a greater blessing for the members of the Church as a defense and a place of refuge. As the Lord Jesus Christ revealed to the Prophet Joseph Smith, "The gathering together upon the land of Zion, and upon her stakes, may be for a defense, and for a refuge from the storm, and from wrath when it shall be poured out without mixture upon the whole earth" (D&C 115:6).

The missionaries in the branches preached the message of the restored gospel with noteworthy success. President Alvin R. Dyer, the European Mission president in Frankfurt, kindled the flame of enthusiasm among the missionaries so that hundreds of former Catholics and Protestants in our country recognized the testimony of truth, let themselves be baptized by immersion for the forgiveness of sins, received the Holy Ghost through the laying on of hands by those with authority, and became members of The Church of Jesus Christ of Latter-day Saints, the kingdom of God on earth.

In preparation for the establishment of a stake, mission president Blythe M. Gardner, carrying out directions from the European Mission president, announced a special Stuttgart District conference

for Sunday, July 23, 1961, at the Gustav-Siegle-House on Leonhards-
platz in Stuttgart. Brother Franz Greiner was our district president at
this time. The members from the Karlsruhe, Pforzheim, and Durlach
Branches were also invited to this special conference. It thus looked
like the stake that was to be founded would have the Rhine River as
its western boundary.

On Thursday, October 26, 1961, President Henry D. Moyle, a
member of the First Presidency of the Church, under the direction
of Church President David O. McKay, created the Stuttgart Stake as
the 339th stake of the Church. Approximately 550 members met
that evening at the Lindenmuseum on Hegelplatz in Stuttgart. Also
participating in the meeting in which the stake was created were
European Mission president Alvin R. Dyer and South German Mission president Blythe M. Gardner as well as the Church's legal representative for Europe, T. Quentin Cannon. The newly organized
stake was comprised of 1,695 members. It was the first stake in the
western part of Germany (a stake had been created in Berlin in
August). I was called to be stake president, with Franz Greiner and
Hans Stohrer as counselors and Gert Gonter as stake executive secretary. Emil Geist became the stake patriarch.

The area included in the Stuttgart Stake was considerable; it
stretched from Ulm to Karlsruhe and from Heilbronn to Reutlingen.
President Moyle said in his remarks in Stuttgart that there would
soon be several stakes in Germany. By the early 1990s, sixteen
stakes had already been organized in Germany, including four
American servicemen's stakes. We are witnesses of the fulfillment of
prophetic revelations. And the growth of this work will not be
stopped. Joseph Smith, the prophet of God, declared that no power
on earth could stop this work.

Stake presidents, bishops, and branch presidents of the newly
created stakes in Germany, Switzerland, and Great Britain were
invited for the first time to the April 1962 general conference of the
Church in Salt Lake City, Utah. For outsiders, it is hard to understand what it means for us as members to visit Church headquarters
in Utah in the United States. It is the place where the prophet, seer,
and revelator and President of The Church of Jesus Christ of Latter-
day Saints lives and works; the center point of Zion; the place of
which Brigham Young, following the Saints' difficult exodus as a
modern Israel traveling over the wide expanse of America, said:
"This is the place!" For many decades we had heard of the

miraculous blossoming of the desert terrain in Utah. Now we were about to see it with our own eyes! It was hard to grasp.

A special chapter in the history of the Stuttgart Stake was the mission among the Italian guest workers. In the so-called golden 1960s, more and more Italian laborers came to Stuttgart to find work. Some of them listened to the missionaries' message and were baptized. At one time we had thirty new Italian brethren in the region around Stuttgart, so South German Mission president Blythe M. Gardner created the first Italian district in Stuttgart. It was wonderful to see how the work spread among them and how members of their families were converted to the truth. What was really a blessing was the fact that the torch of the gospel extended in this manner to Italy, establishing the foundation for preparing that country for missionary work and eventual stakes. We will never forget our Italian Brother Larcher. His brother, whom he brought into the Church, became the first stake president in Milan.

To these foreign guest workers in Germany can be added the many American members who came to Germany as soldiers or government officials or on private business, often together with their families. They were organized into their own wards and branches within the Stuttgart German Servicemen's Stake.

Also of importance to us were the countless visits of Apostles and other General Authorities in the early years of the stake, who not only preached the gospel but also made a particular effort to provide instruction with regard to all organizational and leadership questions. This instruction was further supplemented through the repeated trips of the stake presidency and bishops to Salt Lake City for the half-yearly general conference. In this manner, rewarding experience was gained that could be shared with our brothers and sisters in the stake leadership meetings.

The first two decades of growth of the Stuttgart Stake can be symbolized by the acquisition of land for and the building of the new stake center in Stuttgart-Weilimdorf. I served as stake president for ten years. At the time I was called, there were as of yet no other stake presidents in the western part of Germany who could serve as models—a stake existed only in West Berlin, which had been organized six weeks earlier. At the beginning, next to reliance upon direction from the Holy Ghost, I and my counselors had to rely on the general commandments and instructions of the Church, in particular those outlined in the Doctrine and Covenants. Handbooks

Stuttgart stake president Hermann Mössner translated for European mission president Ezra Taft Benson at the 1966 dedication of the Freiburg chapel.

and instructions were at that time mostly available only in English. Thus it was fortunate that I had learned English intensively as a prisoner of war in England. It was our goal to establish the Church in our homeland and strengthen the community of the Saints. We aimed to bring the Church in our area out of the shadows through the building of chapels and other Church buildings.

Rolf Knödler, who served as stake president for the second decade of the stake's existence, was able to build upon our experiences and further strengthen the organization, administration, and spiritual welfare of the Saints. He provided orientation and helped the bishops and other leaders master their leadership responsibilities. We will not forget the service of Helmut Müller and Josef Perle, who together served for more than twenty-six years as counselors in the Stuttgart Stake presidency. At the time President Knödler was called, the Church owned meetinghouses in Heilbronn, Karlsruhe, and Stuttgart. Due to difficult transactions relating to building permits, it often took ten years in the Stuttgart area before construction could begin after land had been acquired. This was the case with our stake center, but following several years of ongoing efforts, construction finally began. During President Knödler's administration there were important Church events, such as the first area conference for Germany that took place in Munich in 1973, presided over by the President of the Church, Harold B. Lee. Elder Spencer W. Kimball, President of the Quorum of the Twelve at that time, visited Stuttgart immediately following the Munich Area Conference, as he had in 1955 and 1962. In his address in Stuttgart, he expressed understanding of our situation and of the importance to us of being able to proceed with construction of our stake center. It has already been emphasized how important it is for the Saints in Germany to have their own meetinghouses. With major financial participation and provision of several hours of labor by our brothers and sisters, many branch houses were renovated and new chapels built in places such as Esslingen, Freiburg, Karlsruhe, Ludwigsburg, Waiblingen and Stuttgart. German and American members from all units in the stake helped for months in the construction of the new stake center in Stuttgart-Weilimdorf. Skilled artisans made special contributions, while the rest demonstrated great enthusiasm and devotion in all kinds of activities in which particular skills were not required, such as providing food for those who worked.

During the construction of the stake center, I was serving as bishop of the Feuerbach Ward. I took time out from my vocational and other Church duties to focus on the ongoing construction, organize volunteer labor from the individual wards and branches, and intervene wherever particular issues needed to be resolved. Almost as important as progress in the construction work were the growth and development associated with mutual service. Some twelve-year-old deacons, upon being told to sweep the building for the third time on their school-free Saturday, may have regretted not being able to play soccer. In any case there was far and wide no more orderly construction site. As a result, all involved developed a strong feeling of brotherhood, identity, and joy in connection with the finally successful project. When the stake center could finally be occupied in fall 1981, it really belonged to everyone.

From 1987 to 1988 my wife and I served a temple mission in the Swiss Temple. As our first son, Wilfrid, is severely handicapped, it was not easy for us to leave Stuttgart. Our daughter, Heidelinde, kindly took care of Wilfrid in the time that we were away. I was set apart by Elder Russell M. Nelson of the Quorum of the Twelve in Zurich as a temple sealer and also as a counselor to temple president Carl Ringger. Our own family had been sealed for time and all eternity in 1955 in the Swiss Temple. This experience has given us

Hermann and Lore Mössner in front of the Swiss Temple during their mission, 1987–88.

strength and courage in successfully dealing with life's adversities. It was a great spiritual experience for us to serve the Lord as temple missionaries in our beloved Swiss Temple. Our second son, Jürgen, is still working there in his twelfth year as recorder of the Swiss Temple. During the time we served, many Saints came from Spain, Portugal, and Italy to the house of the Lord. To serve them and take part in and feel of their faith and humility was both an inspiration and a blessing to us. Many tears were shed at the end of each particular week that these groups of newly converted Latter-day Saints spent at the temple. We waved for a long time at the departing buses after we had ardently sung together with them "God Be with You Till We Meet Again."

I have not forgotten the words Elder Marion G. Romney stated upon the founding of the South German Mission on October 4, 1959, before a congregation of over seven hundred in Stuttgart as I interpreted for him: "This work will go forward, either with us or without us. Many stakes of Zion will be created in Germany, and also holy temples will be built here."

I am now seventy-four years old and can testify as to the fulfilling of these prophetic words. This is God's sacred work upon the earth. Since my birth, this work has provided both substance and focus for my life, and that this may continue to be so, I pray in the sacred name of Jesus Christ.

Milton and Irene Soares:
Mormon Pioneers of
Northeastern Brazil

by Mark L. Grover

The "chapel" did not look inviting. It was a small rented room, ten by twenty feet, in a men's boardinghouse and not in a good part of town. And this was the church that Jesus Christ had restored that would cover the whole earth? The person who chose the room obviously had little experience with the tropical heat of Brazil's northeast. There should have been a large window facing the ocean to take advantage of the breeze, but this room had only a door that opened onto the street. Without the breeze, perspiration definitely played a part in the religious experience.

The contrast between new and traditional was obvious in the city of Recife, Brazil. On Sunday most citizens awoke to the sweet sound of bells pealing from several Catholic cathedrals. Walking the streets, one encountered many members of the different Protestant faiths on their way to churches with steeples, crosses, large congregations, and accomplished choirs. With these options, why go to a hot rented room and attend services with four Americans who spoke Portuguese with accents and had different customs? How could this restored Church of Jesus Christ be appealing?

Pioneers, however, are impressed not with tradition but with potential. When the Holy Spirit touched Milton and Irene Soares and witnessed to them that what these young Americans were saying was true, the size of the chapel or lack of a choir meant little to them. Because of that powerful assurance, theirs was to be a life of work and sacrifice as they did their part to build the kingdom of God. Little did they realize or expect on that hot April Sunday in 1960 that within only thirty-five years the small congregation of Americans and Brazilians would grow to over 125,000 members in northeastern Brazil, with large chapels, beautiful choirs, and the proposed construction of a holy temple. That growth is reward enough for being among the first in this vast and important region of Brazil to believe the simple message of those American missionaries.[1]

The Brazilian Northeast

Northeast Brazil is an area of stark contrasts. In few regions of the world are the beauties of nature more evident. Thousands of miles of ocean beaches blend into tropical vegetation and lush farmland of great variety and color. The Portuguese were first attracted to this region of Brazil in the early sixteenth century. Here Brazilian society had its foundation.

History has witnessed many cycles in the northeast. The lush green coastal areas proved perfect for the growing of sugarcane and other tropical crops. In the sixteenth century the region became the major producer of sugar for the entire world, and the people became rich from farming and trade. Large, wealthy plantations and the best of the world's material goods could be found in the region. But much of this wealth was paid for by Indian and African slaves, who lived in poverty and servitude under the shadow of opulence. A social structure was built during this period that favored the wealthy and left much of the rest of the society wanting for many of the basic needs of life.

As the sugar industry began to decrease and other parts of Brazil began to reap the wealth that was once the northeast's, the region was left with a society based on sharp class differences, a racial makeup primarily descended from the mixture of African and European, and an economy still dependent on the plantation. The physical beauty of the region remained and was complemented by a people who, in spite of the difficulties encountered, were kind and gentle.

Latter-day Saints in Brazil

It took time for the Mormons to get to the northeast. Missionaries were first attracted to the south, where large colonies of recently arrived German immigrants included a few Church members who had been baptized in their native land. The language of the Church in Brazil was German from the arrival of missionaries in 1928 to

1938, when governmental restrictions prohibited the speaking of any language other than Portuguese in public meetings. That prohibition resulted in a painful but necessary transition not only in language but in the population with whom the missionaries worked. By 1940 missionaries had been trained in Portuguese and were sent to the large cities of the state of São Paulo and the city of Rio de Janeiro to teach the children of immigrants from the non-German regions of Europe.

The outbreak of the Second World War slowed the progress of the Church in Brazil. In 1943 all American missionaries, with the exception of mission president William Seegmiller, were sent home. The branches struggled but did not die. With the end of the war and return of the missionaries, the Church began to expand not only in the established branches but also in other regions where missionaries had never been. Missionaries went to all the major population centers in the four southern states and to large cities in the states of Rio de Janeiro and Minas Gerais. Changes in missionary proselyting techniques introduced after the visit of President David O. McKay in 1954 resulted in significant increases in membership. Brazil was on the verge of significant Church growth. The mission was divided in 1959, and the number of missionaries sent to Brazil doubled. New cities were opened and numerous branches established.

The large cities of the northeast would appear to be logical places for the Church to expand. In 1960 Recife, the major city of the region, had a population of 780,000 and was the third-largest city in the country. Other major population centers were Fortaleza with 507,000 inhabitants and Salvador with 649,000 inhabitants. These figures were misleading, however, in terms of missionary work. The racial history of the northeast, where a high percentage of the population was descended from slaves and where considerable miscegenation took place, had resulted in a significant percentage of the population being of African descent. The Brazil census of 1950 indicated that the state of Pernambuco, of which Recife is the capital, had a 50.2 percent black or mixed population as compared to the southern state of Santa Catarina, which only had 5.2 percent. Since the gospel was not being actively preached to all peoples of the earth at that time, the numbers with whom the missionaries could work in the northeast region were significantly reduced.

The northeast, however, could not be forever neglected by the mission presidents. Every president of the Brazilian Mission took exploratory trips to the larger cities of the north and northeast, hoping to feel inspired to send missionaries into the cities. President William Grant Bangerter took a trip in 1960 to visit several of the larger cities. He felt at least three or four cities should be opened. He approached President Henry D. Moyle of the First Presidency, who suggested that President Bangerter open one city as an experiment.

President Bangerter sent four of his best missionaries into Recife to establish a branch. Elder Michael Norton from Centerville, Utah, was the district leader. The elders arrived by plane from mission headquarters in São Paulo on April 2, 1960, and immediately began working to establish a branch. The missionaries understood the historical importance of their work. They realized that if they were not successful, the Church would be taken out of the area. In a letter to his parents, Elder Norton stated this concern: "There has to be a branch in this city, because of its size and the members who are here. And there are people to be taught here. It is just a matter of time, time, time to find them. . . . The worst thing I can imagine is leaving here with nothing accomplished, so we're going to work harder and longer than ever before."[2] And work they did. There were weeks in which they averaged over seventy hours a week in pure proselyting alone.

The missionaries were able to teach many families, and some even came out to meetings. They were not, however, able to persuade any of their investigators to take the initial step and be the first members baptized in the northeast. After a frustrating month in Recife, they asked that their home wards in the United States fast and pray with them for some success.

A couple of days after the designated day of fasting, the missionaries were tracting in a beach area called Boa Viagem. They came upon a woman sitting on her front porch reading. Elder Norton wrote that her "eyes lit up" when she saw them. They made an appointment for later in the evening so they could talk with her husband, Milton, who "had no religion, because none of them answered all his questions about the mysteries." That evening they returned and gave a lesson on the Godhead, which was received less favorably than they had hoped. They also "fought through the apostasy lesson, which he couldn't quite believe, but couldn't deny."[3]

MILTON AND IRENE SOARES

Milton Soares was forty-three years old at the time the mission-aries first visited him. To say that he was an adventurer and non-conformist would be an understatement. He had seen all parts of Brazil and had worked in a variety of jobs that often placed him in perilous circumstances. The word *fear* wasn't part of his vocabu-lary. Irene Bandeira Soares, on the other hand, was tranquil and serene. Her calming influence provided a vital counterbalance to Milton's energy. Together they raised five children, who all became a major part of the foundation and bedrock of the Church in Recife and the entire northeast.

Milton did not enjoy the confines of the classroom. He loved the outdoors and the excitement of travel. At the age of seventeen he left his home in Rio de Janeiro and was out on the road. For a time he was a professional boxer and fought throughout the region. When the opportunity came to go west, he took a job working on the construction of the famous railroad between Brazil and Bolivia. This was a job filled with hard work and intrigue as they pushed the railroad through forest and swamp and over high mountains. It was an exciting and dangerous experience that fit well the person-ality and character of Milton.

While working on the railroad, Milton became a licensed pilot. When World War II began, he desired to fly fighter airplanes. That would require him to go to the United States, which he resolved to do. In 1941 he hitched a ride on a military transport to Recife in the northeast. Here Milton could easily find work as a pilot, make con-tacts with U.S. military personnel, and make enough money to get to the United States. He soon found a good job working for an Ameri-can company and began saving money. His plans were interrupted and changed forever, however, by a beautiful sixteen-year-old girl who caught his eye and captured his heart. Irene made certain that he stayed in Brazil.

Irene Bandeira Mendes da Silva was a typical product of the northeast. Her family had been farming in the area since the six-teenth century. She was a descendant of one of the founders of the region, Souza Leão, and of other early and important families. Her father worked as a farm administrator in the interior city of Moreno. The only daughter and the youngest of six children, she moved at the age of eight with her mother and five brothers to Recife so they would have the benefit of better schools. From then on her life was one of attending school in Recife and spending her vacations in the interior. Though the family was not particularly well-off financially, Irene was taught the social rules of conduct of traditional Brazilian northeastern society.

Milton and Irene met at a beach party. They dated for a few months, until school ended and Irene returned to the interior town of Palmares to be with her father. Within a week she received a letter from Milton describing his homesickness and talking of marriage. He had just accepted an excellent job as a pilot for an airline company called Panair that was based in the south, and he wanted to make sure they were engaged to be married before he left. Her family suggested he work for a time and save money, and then they would consider the situation. He, however, maintained pressure on her father, and within a year after meeting, Milton and Irene were married in a Catholic ceremony in Olinda, Pernambuco.

Due to physical problems, Milton did not stay with Panair but took a job as a flight instructor at an airplane club in Tubarão in the southern Brazilian state of Santa Catarina. The next few years were exciting as the couple began to raise a family. During this time Milton worked at several jobs, most of which were related to flying. He was able to see much of Brazil and at the same time survive accidents, plane crashes, and a variety of other interesting adventures. A serious case of asthma began to seriously hinder his work, and the small family of four, including one son and one daughter, resolved to return to the northeast where the climate was more appropriate. In Recife he was again a pilot, sometimes the personal pilot of the governor of the state of Pernambuco. After a few years he took his life savings and opened a construction company. He built homes and businesses in the beautiful beach section of Recife called Boa Viagem. It was while he was living there that the missionaries came to the city and began tracting in his neighborhood.

BAPTISM

Neither Milton nor Irene had come from particularly devout religious families. As with most Brazilians, they had gone through the traditional Catholic experiences of baptism, communion, and church marriage, but neither had strong religious beliefs or attended church often. They had their children baptized, and the two oldest,

Irajá and Irecê, had gone through communion but little else. Sunday was a day of relaxation and recreation and was really the only day that Milton could be with the family. But Irene and Milton began to worry about the training of their children and their lack of religious upbringing. They began the quest for religious truth that is common for most who eventually join the Mormon Church.

Motivated by Irene's persistence, the family began to visit the churches in the city. They studied the teachings of their own church and found too many questions that Catholicism could not answer. They attended services of the major Protestant churches, the Baptists, Presbyterians, and Seventh-Day Adventists, with the same result. They even looked outside traditional Christianity into spiritualism and the African-influenced religion called Umbanda, but were not impressed. Milton believed that if God wanted him to have a religion, He would let him know. To that point in his life God had been silent.

By the time the Mormon missionaries got to Milton, he was disillusioned and tired of the search. He had started to believe that membership in a formalized religion was not necessary. Consequently he did not make it easy on the missionaries. He questioned most of their teachings. After each visit he would study the Bible to try to disprove their statements. He actually believed little they taught, but for some reason he continued to invite them back. He went with them to meetings, but he had no intention of joining a church that met in a rented room with no local members. He would plan to tell them he didn't want them to come back but could never follow through with his intentions. The family had quickly grown to like the two young Americans and enjoyed having them in the house. This went on for almost a month with little change.

The missionaries became frustrated. Elder Michael Norton prepared a special lesson for Milton and Irene emphasizing the necessity to believe in the resurrection of Christ on the basis of the evidences available and have faith in that which is unverifiable. Milton was moved by the lesson but not completely convinced. One Sunday when the missionaries came over and interrupted his work on a shortwave radio, Milton got angry and told them to stop coming around. He told them he liked them but would not join their church. The missionaries agreed to stop visiting, but they requested Milton to give one last prayer asking God to tell him if the things they were teaching were true. If he would do this, they would leave him and his family alone. Milton promised in part just to get rid of them.

Milton was a person with an inquisitive mind. He had to have scientific proof of something or he would not accept it. Milton, however, was also an honest and sincere man. Shortly after the missionaries left he responded to their request. He closed the door to his room so that no one could see him, knelt down, and said the promised prayer. Nothing happened, so he went back to his short-wave radio.

That evening before going to sleep he took a book off his well-stocked shelf to read himself to sleep. Uncharacteristically, he opened to the middle of the book. He had chosen a book by Dale Carnegie titled *How to Stop Worrying and Start Living*. He began by reading a passage that discusses how often we use things that we don't completely understand. We don't comprehend how electricity works, but we use it. It is the same thing with God. The fact that we have never seen him does not mean that we can't believe in him. After he read this section the Spirit touched his soul as never before and the truth of the restored gospel of Jesus Christ was made manifest to him. He realized that he did not need to have a verified knowledge of everything and that what he knew and the experience of the Spirit were all that was necessary. He resolved at that moment to join The Church of Jesus Christ of Latter-day Saints. As he lay in his bed that evening, he thanked God that the search for the truth was finally over. As he had hoped, the Spirit had come to him and given him a religion. He had requested help and had received an answer. What a wonderful blessing!

The missionaries visited the next day. While the missionaries were still standing outside his door, Milton asked, "When can I get baptized?" They looked at each other in shock, not sure if he was serious. Milton finally explained what had happened the previous evening. The missionaries scheduled his baptism for the following Sunday, May 15, 1960. As they left the yard, they didn't have to open the gate; they jumped over the small wall that surrounded the house.

Irene was pleased with Milton's decision. She continued her reading of the Book of Mormon and prayed for strength to continue. She thanked Heavenly Father for the "phenomenon" that helped her husband believe in this religion. But she decided to not yet take the step of baptism and persuaded her two oldest children

also to wait. She wanted to have
a spiritual experience similar to
Milton's.

That Sunday Elder Norton
wrote: "The ice was broken. . . .
Of course there is no ice over the
warm ocean waters in Recife, but
the first true baptism to be held in
these waters represents a 'breaking of the ice' for others to enter
the same water for the same
divine purpose!"[4]

The reactions of friends and
family to Milton's baptism were as
expected. His family wasn't interested, including a brother, Moacyr, who was living with him at
the time. Moacyr was to wait five
years before joining and becoming a strong force for the Church
in all of Brazil. When Milton
informed a group of close friends

*Milton and Irene Soares at the
time of their conversion.*

that he had joined the only true church, they asked him how many
members were in the Church. "Only me," he replied. They couldn't
stop laughing. "Only you? How could a church be any good if you
are the only member?"

The branch began to grow slowly. At the end of the month a
young couple, Hélio and Mary Lúcia Leite, were baptized, and the
next week Irene and her two children were baptized along with the
rest of the Leite family, making a total of nine Brazilian members in
the branch. Milton's baptism had indeed broken the ice. Irene's
decision to be baptized was not easy to make. She genuinely liked
the missionaries and felt a strong desire to help the Church. She
saw the weakness of the Church in this area of Brazil and felt that
she could help. But she was also worried that they were joining a
religion that would not stay in the region, and then they would be
left alone without a church. But she soon decided that since her
husband had joined, it would be good for the entire family to
become members. After making the decision to join, she decided to
do all she could to strengthen the Church. She informed the mis-

sionaries that she did not yet have a strong testimony and had read the Book of Mormon but did not understand it well. It wasn't until after her baptism that the testimony she sought came.

This was a period of study and learning for the Soares family as they strived to come to an understanding of the gospel. For example, Irene was concerned about how the rented chapel looked. It was a small room with a few benches and a rented table. There wasn't even a cloth to cover the table for the sacrament. Irene sewed a beautiful sacrament tablecloth embroidered with colors and patterns that were traditional in the northeast. When she presented it to the missionary branch president, she was cautiously informed that colored cloths were not used on the sacrament table. With this lesson learned she gave the cloth to the missionary, and a white sacrament cloth was purchased for the chapel.

Soon so many baptisms took place that there was a need to move into a larger worship area. The small room with limited ventilation was abandoned, and an attractive home was rented that provided the congregation with a large chapel area and extra space for classrooms. Milton painted the house and built a pulpit for the new building. They were now assured the Church would stay in Recife.

In a few months the fledgling Recife Branch was blessed by the visit of two General Authorities—Joseph Fielding Smith, President of the Quorum of the Twelve Apostles, accompanied by his wife, Jessie Evans Smith, and A. Theodore Tuttle, of the First Council of the Seventy—who were touring missions throughout all of South America. It was an incredible blessing for these few newly baptized members to have the privilege to visit with an Apostle and future Church President. When Elder Smith descended from his plane, Irene looked into his eyes and at that moment received the testimony she had long sought. "At that moment I knew he was a man of God and that this was the true Church," she later recalled. "From that time forward my testimony has continued to grow."

Hosting these authorities at a conference was a significant event that helped the missionary work in Recife. The missionaries worked diligently to invite investigators and visitors to the conference. Over a hundred people filled a rented hall to listen to the visitors. That evening a dinner was served to the visitors in the Soareses' home and they watched the evening news on television. A local television station had just opened in Recife, and they were looking to publicize important events of the city, so the visit of the two American dignitaries was the lead story of the evening. That publicity led to many benefits over the next few years.

RAPID DEVELOPMENT

The Soareses knew their new church to be true and set about to do all they could to strengthen it. The missionaries relied on the family. Baptisms were held at 6:00 A.M. on Sunday mornings in the ocean close to their home, and the Soareses offered their home for the services. They actively participated in all the meetings and were involved in teaching and helping new members. The Relief Society regularly scheduled bazaars, so Irene spent considerable time making articles to sell. All this was in addition to Milton's running his new construction business and Irene's raising six young children. But they never complained. Irene explained: "All of this was a lot of work for us, but we wanted to do it. Even though it was difficult, we were happy."

A close relationship developed among the members as the branch grew. Entire families were baptized, which resulted in warm friendships. Milton stated: "What was very good about this period was that many good, responsible men and their families were baptized at this time. Many good women were also baptized. They became the leaders of the Church." The foundation of the Church in Recife was strengthened with the entrance of families such as Raul Barreto Lins and his wife, Olívia, as well as Marluce Almeida, Cavani Rosas, Nair Camara, and the Cisneiros family. Many of the families were financially well-off and held good positions with private companies and the government. Most of these families faithfully remained in the Church.

BRANCH PRESIDENT

In the first year of their membership, Milton and Irene had worked in various Church callings. Milton had been ordained a priest. (At this time in South America the priesthood was not given to new members for several months.) The mission president decided that the time had arrived for a local member to be called as branch president in Recife to take the place of the missionaries. On October 27, 1961, Milton was called as the first member branch president in the northeast. He was to serve in that position for four years.

To be a branch president with just over a year in the Church in a new area was exceptionally challenging. There was always a lot of work to do, but Milton enjoyed the experience, especially working with the youth. The young Church members were so attached to each other and their activities that, if possible, they would spend the entire day at the chapel talking, singing, and visiting. It became necessary for Milton to lock the doors of the church to keep them out. Their response was to climb over the wall. Their commitment was great and their friendship such that they wanted to be together all the time. Many of these young men and women became bishops, stake presidents, and auxiliary leaders when they reached adulthood.

It was also a time of persecution directed against the Church. The Brazilian nation was going through considerable turmoil. In 1961 the leftist national president was able to get legislation passed that moved the country closer to a socialist society. One of the by-products of the rhetoric of the period was a strong anti-American feeling in the country. Demonstrations were held against American influence and companies. These feelings were particularly strong in the northeast, where peasant movements and antigovernment activities nearly became violent. Missionaries were vocally abused almost daily and occasionally attacked with stones and other objects. "Go home, Yankees" was painted on the walls of the Church.

This persecution had a unifying effect on the Recife Branch. The negative publicity that was broadcast against the Church piqued the interest of some who wanted to find out who these people were. Many ended up being baptized. During these years the mission president in São Paulo decided that the numbers and strength of the Church in Recife merited the construction of a chapel.

Latter-day Saint meetinghouses at this time were built primarily by labor missionaries together with the members. As branch president during the first part of the construction, Milton skillfully organized the workload. The members' sacrifice was great, but the rewards were immensely satisfying. A beautiful chapel was constructed that continues to serve as a beacon for the Church in Recife. President Soares spent so much time supervising the project that his construction company suffered somewhat. The mission president urged him not to spend so much time, but the Soareses countered by saying that they wanted to do everything possible to further the Church in the Recife region. The branch was divided during this time, and a new branch was organized in the neighboring city of Olinda.

During this same period Milton supported his oldest son, Irajá, on two missions. Hardly any Brazilians were called at this time to serve a proselyting mission but rather were labor missionaries—that is, those few who were called. Irajá was called and went south to work on a chapel in São Paulo and learned the construction trade. After a year, mission president Wayne Beck spoke with Milton about Irajá receiving a proselyting mission call. Milton was pleased with the prospect, and Irajá was called to Chile for an additional two years. Those years of training would result in a large and important series of Church calls for Irajá. Several years later Milton's second son, Mozart, would also serve a proselyting mission in São Paulo and return to fill significant Church callings.

About this time Milton became involved with new business ventures. Because of his piloting, he had flown into various regions of the Amazon jungle and become acquainted with the Indian tribes. Along the way he had concluded that he could make a business of selling Indian pottery called *marajuazes*. He opened a shop at the new Recife airport that sold pottery and other Indian handicrafts. He also shipped items all over Brazil. Through all of this he developed a close working relationship with many Indians of the Munorucus, Guajajara, Palai, and Camelas tribes. His Indian associates came to trust him as an honest man. Over time he became acquainted with various Indian customs. He especially learned about the use of medicinal herbs. He purchased herbs from the tribes and sold them in his shop. Milton's vast knowledge of Indian customs was frequently

Milton (at left) with a fish from the Amazon River.

drawn upon by many museums and colleges that asked him for advice and assistance.

Through this line of work Milton knew the northeast and Amazon regions of the country as well as anyone. He had driven the back roads into the forest with his van especially equipped with a stove and bed. He had flown all over the region and had been able to observe things that few non-Indians have ever seen. He was not afraid of trying new things and experimented with food and drink that were not known anywhere else. The spirit of the nineteenth-century pioneer was natural in Milton Soares.

DISTRICT PRESIDENT

These activities aided Milton's Church work. When Recife grew so rapidly, the mission president concluded to open other large urban areas in the northeast. Missionaries were sent to João Pessoa in 1960, Maceió in 1966, and Campina Grande and Fortaleza in 1968. Those areas were not only remote from the Church in the south but also far from the city of Recife. Because of Milton's experience as branch president for four years, his profession, and his willingness to serve in the Church, he was called in 1966 to be the president of a newly organized district. He was charged with the responsibility of teaching new members how the Church functions. That district was certainly one of the largest in the Church at the time, spanning a distance of eight hundred miles from Fortaleza in the north to Maceió in the south.

The responsibility of the district leadership involved numerous visits to the various branches not only by Milton but by representatives of the Primary, Relief Society, and Mutual Improvement Association. Irene was called as the Relief Society district president, so the Soareses made their visits together. For the five-hundred-mile trip to Fortaleza, the leaders gathered together on Friday evening and got into Milton's van. They drove all night, taking turns at the wheel. They arrived in Fortaleza in the early morning. They cleaned up and prepared for leadership meetings that would occupy much of the day. They slept overnight in the van and stayed for the Sunday meetings. After the last meeting they drove the long hours back to Recife, where after a few hours of rest they returned to work. Most of this was done without compensation for expenses from the Church.

There was immense concern for the Church members in these remote regions of Brazil. As Milton stated: "The missionaries needed help. It was too difficult for them to have to baptize and teach the members all by themselves. They needed help from us. The chance for success was greater if we came and taught the members." It was important that members learn exactly how things worked in the Church in much the same way Milton and Irene had learned.

Their visits to these branches were greatly appreciated. There is always the potential for a feeling of isolation in remote, outlying areas of the Church. It is always difficult to maintain enthusiasm for the gospel when there are so few. Visits from leaders such as Milton and Irene were important. Keeping the members animated was not easy. Milton believed there had to be activities that would bring the members together for interaction. As a result, they organized district youth conferences that were held all over the region. Both young and old gathered to participate in the activities of the Church and to make and renew acquaintances. These pioneers in northeast Brazil helped foster feelings of love and friendship among their beloved brothers and sisters.

Also important in maintaining the faith were occasional visits to the south for regional conferences. São Paulo, where most of the conferences were held, required four days of travel by chartered bus. They would attend the conference, visit with members, and get back on the buses for four more days of travel. These trips, as hard as they were, were important morale boosters. They would see General Authorities and listen to powerful messages. But more important, they would see a region where the Church was large and strong. They would visit with many with the same ideals and beliefs as they had. They would then return to their small branches and continue to work, realizing what could happen if they maintained their faith.

Their faith, prayers, and hard work were prospered by the Lord. And Milton was to play a vital part. He remained as district president until 1971. He was called again as branch president, this time in his region of the city, Boa Viagem. He had by this time closed his construction company and gone to work as the janitor at the Recife chapel. He had made enough money that he did not need to work and was able to retire and spend time doing what he wanted. He had purchased a piece of property in an area further away from the city and built a new home.

STUPENDOUS GROWTH IN THE NORTHEAST

The day of June 8, 1978, changed the Church in northeast Brazil forever. The revelation through President Spencer W. Kimball that the priesthood was to be bestowed upon all worthy men touched every Church member in the northeast in a very personal way. Missionary work had been difficult in a region in which the percentage of Afro-Brazilians was high and in which an even higher percentage of people had mixed lineages. With the announcement, missionaries could potentially teach and baptize anyone in the region. The solid foundation of strong leaders and faithful members would be put to a test as the area began to have growth as never before experienced.

The first major administrative change occurred in July 1978 when the mission was divided and a new Brazil Recife Mission was organized with Recife as the headquarters. This meant that soon, instead of the ten or twelve missionaries in the area, there would be 150. Almost as important as the organization of the mission was the person chosen to be mission president, Harry Klein. President Klein had been the youthful administrator of the seminary and institute program of the Church in São Paulo. Born and raised in São Paulo, he had served a mission to the northeast and had developed a strong love and appreciation for the area. He arrived with energy and new ideas that were to result in growth never before seen in any part of Brazil. Milton Soares served as the first counselor in the mission presidency.

The result of the revelation and the new ideas was an explosion in the number of members. In the regions of the northeast where earlier they were baptizing seventy a month, within a year they were baptizing nine hundred. In areas where there was a small branch, there was soon a stake. By 1980 the Church organized the Recife Stake, with Milton's oldest son, Irajá, called as the pioneer stake president. Soon the stake was divided and the Olinda Stake was created. During this time Milton was asked by the Church to be in charge of chapel construction, and he spent considerable time traveling throughout the northeast. Those trips were to bring him back to the cities where several years earlier he had gone as district president. By now these small branches had become stakes.

Within months the Church had expanded into new cities. The mission was the fastest-growing area in the Church. Missionaries also went into the Sertão, where the climate and weather were harsh. They expanded throughout the Amazon region, establishing the Church in even more remote regions of the country. The Brazil Recife Mission was divided several times. In 1996 there were eight missions where there was only one in 1978. Twenty-nine stakes had been organized in the north and northeast by early 1996. Two of Brazil's first eight Area Authorities came from Recife, one being Milton's son Irajá.

Conclusion

By the 1990s Milton had been slowed by the physical complications of age. In 1994 Milton and Irene celebrated fifty years of marriage. Milton struggled with a hearing problem and was not able to do as much as he once did. He still maintained his activity in the Church and did all he could to strengthen the kingdom of God. He was often called upon to give advice to young new leaders. With Irene it was the same. She worked in her favorite organization, the Primary, and enjoyed spending time with children. They both loved to be with their grandchildren. Milton also completed a history of his life that is eight hundred pages long, recounting in great detail the many adventures of his life.

Two recent events sum up the lives of these great pioneers of the Brazilian northeast. In 1993 Elder Michael Norton returned to

Milton and Irene Soares today.

Recife to visit the family for the first time since leaving over thirty years earlier. What he found was pleasing to him. The small, hot rented room with a rented sacrament table had been replaced by over a hundred chapels in the northeast, all beautifully constructed to provide the members with all the benefits of members anywhere. The small branch with a few members had grown to over 125,000 members in the northeast. The sons and daughters of members in the northeast supply a significant percentage of the missionaries for the rest of Brazil. It was with wonderment and thanksgiving that missionary and pioneers met to discuss what had happened in the short time since they had gathered on the beautiful, warm beach at 7:00 A.M. to perform the first baptism in that region of Brazil. They also contemplated what could happen in the next thirty years!

One of those hoped-for events was to occur two years after the visit of Elder Norton. In January 1995 the First Presidency announced the construction of a holy temple in Recife. The blessing of the temple would soon be more readily available to these faithful members, who had to travel four days by bus to go to the São Paulo Temple. From rented room to temple in just over thirty years!

What about the pioneers who have watched all this take place? Irene told me during a visit in 1994 that it has not been easy to be a pioneer. That is true in any age. But when one has a testimony of the work, he or she labors for the kingdom even if he or she is the only member in the city or region. Milton and Irene realize that many others were involved in the growth, but there is still a satisfaction with what has happened. Now as they are enjoying their retirement, they can forget the work and the hard times and see the blessings. What they possibly don't realize is that thousands will praise them for the courage and faith to believe and take that first difficult step, becoming the first to be baptized and blaze the trails in northeast Brazil.

Notes

1. This chapter is largely based on earlier work I have done. I wrote a history of The Church of Jesus Christ of Latter-day Saints in Brazil in my Ph.D. dissertation in 1985 at the University of Indiana, titled "Mormonism in Brazil: Religion and Dependency in Latin America." I conducted

interviews with Milton and Irene Soares on April 22, 1982, and August 22, 1994. Transcripts of these interviews are available in the Harold B. Lee Library, Brigham Young University, Provo, Utah.

2. Michael Norton to his family, April 29, 1960. I have copies of all letters cited in this chapter.

3. Michael Norton to his family, May 11, 1960.

4. Michael Norton to his parents, May 17, 1960.

A Diplomat's Diplomat: Arwell L. Pierce and the Church in Mexico

by F. LaMond Tullis

How much difference may one individual make in the sweep of events, processes, tendencies, and global transformations that affect people's lives? A lot. Consider Arwell L. Pierce. He went to Mexico in 1942 as the newly installed president of the Mexican Mission. The mission had fallen on hard times. Fully a third of the Church's Mexican members had broken away to form their own dissident organization—what came to be known as the Third Convention (the name referring to the third in a series of meetings in which Mexican members had discussed their concerns and drawn up petitions). Relationships among members and dissident members were filled with suspicion, acrimony, and, with some, a loathing reserved especially for the very incarnation of evil. Pierce's charge: Bring the Saints back into a harmonious relationship. Through patience, self-effacement, spiritual commitment, and diplomatic tact, Pierce did that. He counselled members, dissident members, General Authorities, and even the prophet as no other had before. He got hearts to soften and extraordinary ecclesiastical decisions to be made. The reunification in 1946 made possible the Church's subsequent rapid growth in Mexico. One individual made a large difference in the history of local Mormon events. The story of Pierce's ordeal and his success ought never to be lost from our memory.

Pierce's success can be understood only in the context of his challenge. The series of events that swept the Third Convention into existence began with the Mexican civil war (1910–17) and continued through the early 1930s. The strain between Church headquarters in Utah and some of the central Mexican Saints was fueled by isolation, nationalism, pride, charismatic leaders, and insensitivity among some Anglo-Mormons. By 1936 the heat was white hot; an apparently irreversible schism was under way.

By May of 1937 the breach was absolute. The Third Convention movement was born. The Church began excommunication proceedings against all Third Convention leaders. On 6, 7, and 8 May 1937, courts were convened in San Pedro Mártir and the sentences handed down. Conventionist leaders were excommunicated for rebellion (having worked against the mission authorities), insubordination (having completely disobeyed the orders of mission authorities), and apostasy (having failed to recognize the Church's authority). The leaders went their way, along with about a third of Mexico's Mormons, some chapels, furniture, and records.

From 1942 through 1946 Arwell L. Pierce carried out a persistent, inspired crusade to undo the Third Convention and bring its members back into the fold of the faithful. The task was certainly difficult but made at least possible by the fact that most Third Conventionists refused to part ways doctrinally with the Church, or to do other than revere the prophet in Salt Lake City. So when one dissident, Margarito Bautista, challenged the Convention's leadership on a number of doctrinal points, which included his desire to incorporate polygamy and the united order into Third Convention activities, he was thrown out. Thus the Third Convention continued without Margarito Bautista, polygamy, a vision of an economic utopia, or any other doctrines radically different from those of the mainline Church.

As if to underline their intention to remain doctrinally pure, the Conventionists called themselves The Church of Jesus Christ of Latter-day Saints (Third Convention). They organized Sunday Schools, conducted sacrament meetings, established "mutual improvement associations" (MIA), and functioned very much like normal Mormon congregations. Like the mainline Church, they blessed infants, baptized children, and ordained men to the priesthood. They sent out missionaries and trained their youth in public speaking, an art especially appreciated in Mexico. They launched an ambitious building program. Donating land, labor, and capital, they constructed at least six new meetinghouses and, in accordance with Mormon custom, dedicated them to the Lord. The Third Convention also produced some religious literature.

Into this cauldron of activity stepped Arwell L. Pierce in May of 1942. He was a month short of being sixty years old when he entered Mexico as mission president. Given his age, some wondered if he would be up to the task of holding the Church together in Mexico, an undertaking that had already taxed a series of mission presidents beyond their capabilities. On the contrary, Pierce's age may in fact have worked in his favor. Mexican Mormons needed someone with patience, wisdom, insight, and compassion—characteristics frequently associated with age. Whatever the correlational logic, Pierce had those wonderful attributes, and he put them and all his other skills to work to try to salvage the Church in Mexico.

Pierce was no Mexican, either by race or by birth. Since he was not even a colonies Mormon, special arrangements had to be made for him to be president of the Mexican Mission because foreigners were prohibited from clerical activities in Mexico. Yet he was an ecclesiastically experienced man, a diplomat, and a politically sensitive leader. He developed greater propriety with respect to the society of Mexican Mormons than anyone the Church had sent to Mexico since Rey L. Pratt, a much beloved former mission president.

All this was to good avail, because Pierce's assigned task was to bring Third Conventionists back to the fold. President David O. McKay had told him that "we don't have a divided mission; we have a big family quarrel," and "you are the Abraham Lincoln who must save this union." Pierce got his inspiration not only from this mandate but from the Savior's Sermon on the Mount ("Agree with thine adversary quickly" [Matthew 5:25; 3 Nephi 12:25]) and other scriptures that he cited often (for example, Luke 6:29: "And unto him that smiteth thee on the one cheek offer also the other; and him that taketh away thy cloke forbid not to take thy coat also"). So he persuaded, loved, and gathered in the Saints and former Saints. Eventually he was able to meet with the Third Convention committee—one time for three days straight—culminating his many arguments with "the Brethren are willing to give you everything you want, but not the way you want it." Over the years the Conventionists had continued to accept the prophet, and this oft-repeated statement softened them. Pierce's success is a story of implementation of Sermon-on-the-Mount principles and an uncommon insight into winning people's hearts and minds so that they desired to do the right things for the right reasons. There is a vast difference between the art of coercion and the art of persuasion. Pierce knew everything about persuasion and consciously eschewed coercion.

But Pierce's work in Mexico was not easy. After evaluating his missionaries he concluded that they understood the gospel insufficiently and were not teaching very effectively what they did know. He immediately set up a strict regimen of work and study for them. Eventually winning their respect and admiration, Pierce worked enthusiastically and vigorously, changing procedures, establishing new policy guidelines, and generally turning the mission upside down. A dynamic leader with a sense of compelling immediacy, Pierce quickly implemented new programs and ideas.

Then he got to the Third Convention. The Convention genuinely puzzled Pierce. The more he looked into it, the more he realized that its members were vitally and energetically carrying out Church programs. The Conventionists were building chapels, sending out missionaries, and teaching Mormon doctrine strongly and faithfully. Their reasons for apostasy, he concluded, were certainly not doctrinal—yet Conventionists were outside the community of the Church. As he studied the situation he wondered how brotherhood could have decayed so completely.

Over the years the issues had become clouded, remembrances diffused or altered, and passions changed. If Pierce could not initially see the issues involved, he had no difficulty in recognizing that the Convention's return to the faith would bring great strength to the Church in Mexico. And so, slowly and painstakingly, he applied all his diplomatic skills to the task. Realizing that feelings had been hurt, he set out first to heal the wounds and then to treat the scar tissue. Although the initial response was abuse, that soon changed—first to respect, later to admiration—in part because Pierce met every travail with kindness and understanding.

He began by attending Third Convention meetings and conferences. Slowly, carefully, he introduced himself and built friendships with Third Convention members and leaders. He even tried to assist the Convention in its own programs, inviting its members to the mission home to pass on information from Salt Lake, giving advice when asked, and distributing recently translated Church literature. And he talked with Abel Páez and his wife, with Othón Espinoza, Apolonio Arzate, Julio García—principals in the Third Convention movement—and even Margarito Bautista. Always ready to listen and to see, he extended hospitality and acceptance unconditionally.

After weighing all he had heard, Pierce concluded that the Third Convention problem had been poorly handled. Given the circumstances, he even thought that some of the Convention's complaints were justified. Although having a Mexican mission president was the Third Conventionists' primary concern, they also wanted a building program for chapels as the Americans had, the same kind of Church literature the Americans had, an educational system for their children (as the American Mormons had for theirs in northern Mexico), and an opportunity for their young people to go on missions, as the Americans also did. Anything wrong with that? Yes and no, Pierce realized. He did not object to the goals, although one could legitimately wonder how programs to achieve them could possibly be funded in the 1930s. On the other hand, he saw how the Third Conventionists' methods had brought them trouble.

Pierce could not—did not—approve of the Third Convention's rebellion and withdrawal from the Church, but he did not for the most part object to the Convention's goals. He understood how its members could have reached their decision to leave the mainline Church, and because of his understanding, for the first time in nearly a decade disagreeing men were discussing the issues rather than shouting about them.

That the issues were now somewhat understandable did not nullify or simplify them. But things had changed over the years. The Church in Salt Lake appeared now to be much more committed to Mexico. It had considerably more literature in translation and additional literature forthcoming. With World War II over, the Church was developing a strong missionary program, and more missionaries would soon be called, some of them to serve in Mexico.

In the meantime, the Conventionists had generally maintained doctrinal purity, had done a lot of proselyting in central Mexico, and had promoted much interest in the Book of Mormon. Given all of these factors, reunification was possible. Certainly it was desirable. So Pierce listened, argued, lectured, sympathized, persuaded, and worked long hours. Arwell Pierce loved the gospel and he loved Mexico. He was confident that Mormonism could now make giant strides in Mexico if only the members would unite.

In time, Pierce's efforts began to pay off. The Convention recognized him as a friend, its leaders even asking him to speak in Convention conferences. He did so, carefully honoring the confidence in the initial stages by avoiding sensitive issues, speaking instead on "neutral" subjects such as prayer. He spoke of his own desire for reunification only when such talk was appropriate. In return, Third Conventionists began to visit mainline Church meetings, and Pierce characteristically asked them to sit near the front. In years past, when Conventionists visited a mainline branch, the seats would empty of mainline Mormons as Conventionists sat down. The animosity was so high that no mainline Mormon wanted to be seated even in the general vicinity of a Conventionist. But with Pierce embracing the Conventionists, the justification for continued shunning was hard to find.

It was not just soothing actions that brought the Convention around to Pierce's point of view. After they had accepted him, Pierce began engaging them in various ways. He usually took Harold Brown, his special assistant, on his speaking engagements, and often instructed Brown to give them the "word." The word was hardheaded and tough. Then Pierce would follow with his "sweet, loving, come-unto-Zion talk." Thus Brown, as the "tough man," absorbed the Third Convention's anger, and Pierce, as the "loving and understanding man," received a positive response, which he turned to bringing the Saints back into the fold.

Circumstances within the Convention itself aided Pierce's wooing of its members. Perhaps the most important was the physical condition of Abel Páez, the Third Convention's president, who had long suffered from a severe case of diabetes. As he was responsible for the spiritual welfare of over a thousand people, he worried a lot. What would happen to them after he died? Pierce could see this thought weighing heavily in Páez's mind, and he began to appeal to his sense of responsibility. Who was going to lead the people after Páez died? If the Convention was a temporary way of bringing about Mexican leadership, which was its principal impetus, how would the people get back into the Church after Páez was gone? Would future generations be deprived of the Church's blessings, and would Páez want the responsibility for that? Finally, Páez began to soften and warm up to Pierce, and he started to think with cautious enthusiasm about reunification.

Meanwhile, the mainline Church in Salt Lake City was changing. President Heber J. Grant had died and in 1945 was succeeded by George Albert Smith. This leadership change was significant: President Smith was more interested and favorable toward Mexico. Some wondered why, but most were very pleased.

George Albert Smith especially trusted David O. McKay, President of the Quorum of the Twelve Apostles and also a counselor to former President Grant. President Smith asked President McKay to continue on as a counselor in the First Presidency. This augured well for the Mexican Mission. President McKay had toured the Church's operations in Mexico extensively and happily two years earlier. Among other things, he wanted to begin an extensive building program in Mexico and so had spent time examining possible sites for chapels. While doing this, he had met, made friends with, and counseled individual Mexican Saints and had listened to their hopes and aspirations for the Church in their native land. Listening, he refrained from arguing. He accepted their proffered hospitality gracefully, even going to the home of Third Conventionist Othón Espinoza to bless his infant granddaughter. Mexican Mormons were impressed. Conventionists were overwhelmed. Through the person of David O. McKay, Salt Lake City seemed attentive to Mexico. If others were extending the olive branch of peace, why not respond in like spirit? So reasoned many Third Conventionists.

As the Church became more attractive to all the Mexican Saints, the Convention became correspondingly less so. In spite of Páez's stature, by 1945 serious leadership quarrels had developed within the Convention. Some members who had previously supported Páez began to shift their allegiance to Pierce, which was, in Pierce's way of thinking, a first step in getting them to shift their allegiance back to the mainline Church.

Well aware of this shift, Pierce kept up the initiative. He took Church literature to Apolonio Arzate to be printed—and then used the occasion to have long talks with him. He chauffeured Third Convention leaders in his car, talking all the while. He reasoned, argued, and pled—all the time and anywhere.

And Arwell Pierce was as self-effacing as he was vigorous in helping Third Conventionists to contain and to understand their own pride. This, perhaps more than any other single characteristic, enabled him to deal successfully with the Third Convention. He showed them how to deal with pridefulness. He never claimed credit for accomplishments, but always said, "Not I alone, but I with your help and with the help of the Third Conventionists together can bring to pass a great work." Never vindictive, punitive, or perceptibly worried about his own place in history, he took abuse without returning it. For that reason Conventionists remembered him as "a wise man, a very good man, very diplomatic; one who knew how to deal with people of all kinds in the world."

As Third Conventionists began to trust Pierce, his arguments rang true: "I don't understand why you want a mission president of Mexican blood," he would say. "A mission president is actually only a representative of the First Presidency of the Church. He is only in charge of the missionaries and the proselyting work. Mission presidents and missionaries only supervise branches until they are strong enough and numerous enough to be organized into a stake. What you really need here in Mexico is a stake organization, the same as the Hawaiians have. A stake is an independent unit indirectly under the supervision of the First Presidency of the Church. But we cannot have a stake in Mexico until we are more united. Let's all unite under the leadership of the First Presidency of the Church, strengthen our branches, and prepare to become a stake. We will never achieve this so long as we are divided and so few in number."

Pierce then would drive his point home relentlessly, advising his listeners that the Church would never give the Third Conventionists a Mexican mission president while they persisted in rebellion. Their cause was hopeless. And, at any rate, their goal was undesirable. If they wanted Mexican leadership, they should seek a Mexican *stake president*. And to build a stake they should rejoin the mainline Church and build the kingdom in Mexico. Mexico could rapidly achieve a stake, he affirmed, once the Third Convention returned to the Church.

Given the evolving circumstances, this argument made a lot of sense to Convention members. Moreover, Pierce supported his words with action. He got the priesthood manuals and other leadership materials translated, mimeographing some and hiring Apolonio Arzate to print others. He organized new districts under local leadership. He held leadership seminars and told the Mexican Saints that they must begin taking care of matters on their own rather than coming to the mission president with every little problem. People began to notice that Pierce was achieving the Mexicans' goals. He was, in a word, a new Rey L. Pratt, but one intent on developing local leadership not because it was required by politics of the time but because it was the right thing to do for Mexico and its members. Pierce effectively diffused the leadership issue, which was, after all, the only genuine Third Convention complaint.

Among its members the Third Convention was becoming increasingly unalluring. Aside from its internal leadership dissension, Abel Páez's health was deteriorating. Arwell Pierce was an attractive leader with an appealing idea and a program to back it. Moreover, Church authorities in Salt Lake seemed more open and favorable toward Mexico. Accordingly, for many Third Conventionists the central issue began to shift from "Should we reunite ourselves to the Church?" to "How can we reunite ourselves to the Church without losing our personal dignity?"

Pierce understood this dilemma and the role that personal dignity (*dignidad*) played in Mexican culture. A severe loss of dignity would have been so unredeemably devastating that people thereafter would not have been able to function in the Church. Strong and faithful members who also happened to be Conventionists— and their descendants—would be lost to the Church forever. Pierce energetically sought to avoid that, "even if some extraordinary measures have to be taken . . . as far as the Church is concerned." He convinced Apostles and the prophet alike that, in this case, extraordinary measures were both called for and justified.

Perhaps Arwell Pierce's crowning achievement was his initiation of an ecclesiastical review of Conventionist leaders' excommunications. This, in itself, is a dramatic part of this story, for he persuaded the First Presidency to overturn the excommunications, thereby nullifying the original disciplinary councils' ("Church courts'") decisions. In April 1946, the First Presidency changed the verdicts to disfellowshipment, a much less punitive sanction which made the Conventionist leaders' reentry into the Church much easier. This decision was no doubt influenced by President George Albert Smith's view that the Church's trouble in Mexico seemed more like a big family quarrel than apostasy. In any event, the change from excommunication to disfellowshipment meant a lot in terms of *dignidad.* Most conspicuously, Third Convention leaders did not have to be rebaptized to come back into the Church. Less obviously, it implied that the Church recognized it might have made some errors in dealing with the Third Convention episode. Mexican Saints recognized all these implications, and this change smoothed the path of reunification.

The Church made another move that allowed Convention members who had been baptized without Church-sanctioned authority to preserve their *dignidad.* Third Convention members who had never been baptized by Church-acknowledged authority were told not that they had to be rebaptized, which would ordinarily have been the case, but rather that a restitution or ratification of their former baptisms would have to be made. Rebaptism, restitution, rat-ification—the effect was the same: members were rebaptized by those holding the proper priesthood authority. But the terminology preserved *dignidad*, as did the fact that Pierce himself performed most of the rebaptisms.

Pierce tried in several other ways to help Third Convention leaders preserve their *dignidad*. One was to help them "save face." After all, he argued, Third Conventionists were not "selling out" on the idea of Mexican leadership—they were taking steps toward it. They could reason that the Third Convention had made its point and that the Brethren in Salt Lake were now listening. After the reunification, the Church in Mexico would develop rapidly, and thereafter a stake would be organized with local leaders presiding.

George Albert Smith's 1946 visit to Mexico was another impor-tant move. Pierce argued long and hard for this. When he first broached the subject with President Smith, the President turned to J. Reuben Clark, his counselor, and said: "You haven't been down there for a while; why don't you go?" President Clark responded by asking that they think about it and make the decision later. Presi-dent Clark, remembering the fracas over one of his memoranda to

Mission president Arwell L. Pierce with other Church leaders in Mexico,
about 1947. Front row (left to right): Isaías Juárez, Arwell L. Pierce, Abel Páez
and Bernabé Para. Second row (left to right): Hector Treviño, José Gracia,
and Raymundo Gómez.

Mexico nearly ten years earlier, and seeing the wisdom of President Smith's going to Mexico, joined Pierce in persuading him to go.

Mainliners and Conventionists alike were immensely proud and honored to receive the man all Mormons recognized as prophet, seer, and revelator. For President Smith's visit to the Tecalco conference, the home of the Third Convention, members spread flowers along the lane leading into the chapel and stood on each side in long lines singing "We Thank Thee, O God, for a Prophet" as the President walked along the flower-strewn path. The voiced opinion of many was that "he looks like a prophet; he acts like a prophet; he talks like a prophet; he is a prophet."

Despite his illness while in Mexico, George Albert Smith was a striking success. People pressed in from all sides wanting to shake his hand or just to be near him, and they were thrilled that he would sit at their table and share their food. Of course, many also wanted to receive him in their homes. He accepted the Mexicans' hospitality graciously, much as David O. McKay had three years earlier.

The Mexico City conference under George Albert Smith's direction saw approximately 1,200 Third Conventionists return to the fold. Tension was high as the conference began. No one was sure what President Smith might say. He might speak in a condemning tone, chastising Third Conventionists, as other Church leaders had done. He might point an accusing finger. He did none of this. His love and kindness soon dispelled the tension. Harold Brown, who translated for him on this occasion, said the tension eased and people relaxed and began to smile and respond. Brown remembered the occasion as a most extraordinary one.

The prophet spoke in both the morning and afternoon sessions, stressing the need for harmony and unity. The Third Convention choir, comprising more than eighty voices, provided the music. President Smith asked Abel Páez to speak to the congregation, and the Third Convention leader expressed his joy at being able to return to the Church and his happiness about the work that would now be accomplished. Pictures were taken, and an article of considerable length, with the pictures, was published in the *Deseret News*. Obviously, the Third Convention's return to the Church was an important and happy event to nearly everyone.

Fifteen years would pass before the new vineyard matured; the first stake for Mexican Mormons was not organized until 1961, sixty-six years after the organization of the first stake in Mexico at Colonia Juárez in 1895. And even then it was not presided over by Juárez, Parra, Hernández, or López, but by Harold Brown. Brown, a colonies Mormon like so many previous higher authorities in Mexico, was cast in the mold of Rey Pratt and Arwell Pierce. He quickly opened up leadership opportunities for his Mexican brothers. His first counselor was none other than Julio García, a former Conventionist leader. Gonzalo Zaragoza served him as second counselor and Luis Rubalcava as clerk; they were certainly Mexican enough.

Today, in 1997, Mexico has nearly 800,000 members and 150 stakes. Mexicans by birth and race preside in almost all the stakes and missions. Leadership in Mexico started to come of age in the 1930s; now it has matured.

But let us return to Mexico City in 1946, where there were a number of Anglo-Americans and Mexicans, each deeply individual, conflicting a little less in their perceptions of self, others, duty, religion, and world than they had ten years earlier. Foremost on the American side was Arwell L. Pierce, experienced president of the sorely tried but newly united Mexican Mission. Over forty-five North American missionaries filled the ranks.

On the Mexican side, there was Isaías Juárez, an astute politician and gifted leader. There was Abel Páez working forthrightly in the mission. And there were others—Julio García, Bernabé Parra, Apolonio Arzate, Guadalupe Zárraga, Narciso Sandoval, Othón Espinoza, and several Mexican missionaries, all brought together by the reunification of the Third Convention and the Church.

How much difference may one individual make in the sweep of events, processes, tendencies, and global transformations that affect people's lives? A lot.

GIUSEPPE EFISIO TARANTO:
ODYSSEY FROM SICILY TO SALT LAKE CITY

by James A. Toronto

The island of Sicily has had a colorful, turbulent, and tragic history. For twenty-five centuries Sicilians have seen a succession of foreign governments, peoples, and cultures come and go: the Phoenicians, Greeks, Carthaginians, Romans, Arabs, and Normans each in their turn invaded and subjugated Sicily. At various times it has been annexed by North African powers and cut off from Europe. In more modern times it has been ruled from Vienna, Madrid, and Constantinople, and German, French, and British powers have also exercised control over it.

In the first half of the nineteenth century, Italy as we know it today did not exist: it consisted of several monarchies and the Vatican state struggling against each other for power. Sicily was part of the Kingdom of the Two Sicilies controlled by the Franco-Spanish Bourbon family in Naples, a government the Sicilians despised and occasionally resisted in open revolt. With the unification of Italy on March 17, 1861, under King Victor Emmanuel, Sicily was finally joined politically to the Italian mainland. But the long-awaited dream of regional self-rule was not yet realized: the government in Turin (later in Rome), believing the Sicilians too backward and unsophisticated to manage their own affairs, denied them any measure of political autonomy until 1946.

The economic exploitation and mismanagement by alien governments, the destruction of invading armies over the years, and devastating earthquakes and volcanic eruptions left the island, once so fertile and productive, economically depressed and impoverished. Understandably, then, Sicilians learned to struggle for survival, to live with hardship, to receive promises of political change and economic improvement with cynicism, and to view foreigners and foreign ideas with suspicion bordering on hostility. Sicilian society, as a result, came to be a closed, conservative one—difficult for outsiders to comprehend and even more difficult to penetrate.

The years between 1800 and 1850 in particular were marked by high unemployment, low wages, severe poverty, onerous taxes, water shortages, and widespread suffering from the effects of hunger. Epidemics of malaria and cholera sometimes wiped out entire villages. Illiteracy among the population was nearly total: most Sicilians spoke one of the many local dialects but could not understand, read, or write the official language of government and scholarship. Only the educated elite at that time—a few priests, magistrates, and scholars—could communicate in the standard, "pure" Italian that originated from northern Italy and eventually became the national language spoken and written today.

Giuseppe Taranto's story unfolds, then, during a period marked by disillusionment, turbulence, and change on a wide scale in Sicily. Mundane explanations cannot fully explain why individuals seek, embrace, and make enormous sacrifices for a new religion, but against this backdrop one can more fully understand the impetus for Giuseppe's religious odyssey and appreciate the accomplishments of this Mormon pioneer from Sicily.

FROM PALERMO TO NAUVOO

Giuseppe Efisio Taranto was born June 25, 1816, in Cagliari, a fishing town on the southern shore of the island of Sardinia in the Mediterranean Sea. He was the first son and the third of seven children of Francesco Matteo Antonio Taranto and Angela Maria Fazio. His father's ancestors were a hardy and courageous people who had endured many hardships in colonizing and inhabiting the desolate but beautiful islands north of Sicily. After living a few years in Sardinia and nearby islands, the family settled in the major Sicilian seaport, Palermo, not far up the coast from Trapani, Angela Maria's hometown.

The main industries in Palermo were fishing and shipping, and Giuseppe no doubt was familiar with both at an early age. As a young man in his early twenties, he joined the Mediterranean Merchant Service, a commercial shipping company that carried goods to distant foreign ports. Later he worked as a seaman on American vessels. For the first thirty years of his life Giuseppe followed his father's footsteps and was intimately involved with the life of the sea as a fisherman and sailor. His travels with the shipping business brought him to New Orleans, where he lived and worked for a time, and subsequently to two other bustling American seaports, New York and Boston.

One time as he sailed towards New York, he became fearful that someone in the city might steal the money he had been saving for some time to take back to his family in Palermo. That night as he slept, he had a dream in which a man told him to take the money to "Mormon Brigham" and he would be blessed. When he arrived in New York, he began to inquire about "Mormon Brigham," but no one seemed to know him.[1]

From New York Giuseppe went to Boston. He apparently liked that New England city and decided to settle there for a time and to go to work for himself. He gave up his job with the Italian shipping firm and purchased a small boat of his own. He made a living by buying fruits and vegetables from the wholesale vendors in Boston and then selling them to the large ships at anchor in the harbor. It was during his stay in Boston that Giuseppe first heard the Mormon missionaries preaching the gospel as restored through Joseph Smith only a few years before. In the fall of 1843, he was baptized at the age of 27 by Elder George B. Wallace. It is likely that Giuseppe Efisio Taranto was the first native Italian and also the first Roman Catholic to join The Church of Jesus Christ of Latter-day Saints in this dispensation.

After his baptism, Giuseppe was counseled to join the other members of the Church gathering in Nauvoo. At first he declined to do so, perhaps because his fruit and vegetable business was doing well. As a seaman he had frugally saved his wages, and this money, together with his profits as a merchant, would enable him, the eldest son, to assist his poverty-stricken family in Sicily. For at least another year and a half, the new convert remained in Boston buying and selling his goods, trying to cope with a new language and culture, and learning and progressing in the Church.

During this time Giuseppe began to be called permanently by his Anglicized name, Joseph Toronto. The spelling change in the surname probably resulted from Joseph's illiteracy. He, like most Sicilians of his time, could neither read nor write the Italian dialect he spoke, and as a recently arrived immigrant he was still struggling to make sense of a new language, English. Since Joseph could not spell his name, someone else had to do it for him—someone who

Joseph Toronto

needed his name for a record of some kind and who wrote the foreign sounds as best he could while Joseph pronounced them. It could have been a commercial license, an immigration document, the title to a boat, or a baptismal certificate upon which the name *Toronto* first appeared.

Joseph might have stayed in Boston much longer were it not for a near-fatal accident he had in the spring of 1845. One day, while transporting a load of fruits and vegetables in Boston Harbor, his boat collided with a larger vessel and was capsized. He lost his cargo of goods and nearly lost his life by drowning. One of the ironies in Joseph's life is that he spent much of his life on the water and was skilled as a seaman, yet he never learned to swim. It was a terrifying and traumatic event for him, one that became a turning point in his life. This accident made him feel that he should now heed his church leaders' counsel to go to Nauvoo with the Saints. So, in the spring of 1845, he sold his boat and his business and headed to the western frontiers of the United States.

THE ITALIAN PIONEER

At the time of the Prophet Joseph Smith's martyrdom in June 1844, the Nauvoo Temple was only one story high. Less than a year later, on May 24, 1845, at 6:00 A.M., the capstone was laid amid rejoicing and shouts of hosanna from the multitude of Saints gathered to observe the long-awaited event. Joseph Toronto arrived in Nauvoo not long after the capstone-laying ceremony. Work on the interior of the temple was progressing, but persecution and financial hardships made it difficult to provide food and clothing for the workmen. Laborers were often seen working on the temple barefoot and shirtless.

When the situation became critical, Brigham Young, President of the Quorum of the Twelve, instructed those in charge of the temple funds to distribute all the remaining provisions with the promise that the Lord would in time provide them more. At Sunday services shortly thereafter, President Young announced to the assembled Saints that work on the temple would have to cease. Tithing funds were depleted, and his appeal for Saints coming from overseas to contribute their money to finish the Lord's house had not produced the hoped-for revenue. So work on the temple would have to stop, thereby jeopardizing the salvation of the Mormon people (see D&C 124:31–33).

Joseph was in attendance at that Sabbath meeting and heard Brigham Young's fervent appeal to the Church membership. The newly arrived convert from Sicily was deeply moved, and he determined to do whatever he could to help move the work along. Joseph, according to Brigham Young's account, sought an audience with the Church leader and expressed his desire to contribute all his personal savings to the Church: "Brother Joseph Toronto handed to me $2,500 in gold and said he wanted to give himself and all he had to the upbuilding of the church and kingdom of God; he said he should henceforth look to me for protection and counsel. I laid the money at the feet of the bishops."[2] Brigham Young blessed Joseph for his offering and told him that he would stand at the head of his race and that neither he nor his family would ever want for bread.[3] Many years after the event, Wilford Woodruff recorded in his journal that Brigham Young still vividly remembered and deeply appreciated Joseph's humble gesture:

> In the afternoon at a prayer circle the president spoke of a blank in the *History of the Church*, and related the following: "A few months after the martyrdom of Joseph the Prophet, in the autumn and winter of 1844 we did much hard labor on the Nauvoo temple, during which time it was difficult to get bread and other provisions for the workmen to eat. I counseled the committee who had charge of the temple funds to deal out all the flour they had, and God would give them more; and they did so; and it was but a short time before Brother Toronto came and brought me twenty-five hundred dollars in gold. The bishop and the committee met, and I met with them. . . . I opened the mouth of the bag and took hold at the bottom end, and gave it a jerk towards the bishop, and strewed the gold

across the room and said, now go and buy flour for the work-men on the temple and do not distrust the Lord any more; for we will have what we need."[4]

Other sources give more details about this episode, revealing even more about Joseph Toronto's faith and humility. The Apostles were gathered in Willard Richard's office to discuss the problem of financing work on the temple. Elder John R. Young indicated that Joseph came into the office and took off his leather money belt, which was gorged with gold coins. "He laid the money on the table, and, merely asking for a receipt, would apparently have left without further explanation, if Brigham had not detained him. The money was sorely needed, and the act was so deeply appreciated, that the humble trusting man was taken to the President's home, and became a permanent member of the family."[5]

Just how closely attached Joseph became to Brigham Young and his family can be seen from several examples. Brigham contin-ued to take a personal interest in Joseph's well-being over the years, affording him the fatherly protection and counsel he needed after giving all his earnings to the Church. Joseph was chosen to act as President Young's herdsman, driving his cattle across the plains. After settling in Salt Lake City, he was entrusted with the supervi-sion of the Young family's herds and gardens for several years, and up until his first marriage in 1853, he was commonly known as "Joseph Young." President Young had money sent to Palermo to help Joseph's family there, and his gentle prodding and encourage-ment led to Joseph's marriage to Eleanor Jones and later to Anna Catharina Johansson. In addition, John R. Young explained:

At Winter Quarters a man by the name of Majors, a gentle-man of wealth and scholarly attainments, came to Brigham and said that one of his thoroughbred mares was down from starva-tion and could not get up,—then asked if he had better not kill her. "No," replied the President, "never destroy life. Try to save her. If you can't provide for her give her to Toronto and I will tell him how to provide for her." He further arranged to have a wind-lass erected, and the mare swung up. Then sods were cut. Of them a stable was built around her, and so the animal was saved.

Afterwards I saw Brother Toronto sell a pair of her colts to Kinkaid of Salt Lake for seven hundred dollars. Moreover,

Joseph Toronto, humble, untutored Italian sailor, became, under the wise counsels of Brigham Young, a man of property, raised up an honorable family, and gave his children a good education.[6]

Because of the commitment and testimony of Joseph Toronto and others who literally gave all they had to build God's kingdom, work on the Nauvoo Temple resumed. Many Saints were thus able to receive their sacred endowments and sealings before their expulsion from Nauvoo and arduous journey across the plains.

Joseph Toronto went with Brigham Young's large company to Deseret from Winter Quarters in 1848. This division left the Elkhorn River during the first part of June. The camp journal kept by Thomas Bullock contains the following entry involving Joseph, dated June 27, written at a campsite along the Platte River some 250 miles from Winter Quarters: "At sunset the captains of companies and others met at the President's wagon to arrange about driving the cattle. Bro. Hanks and Cahoon volunteered a horse each; John Harris volunteered a driver to go with Joseph Toronto, the President's herdsman. It was left to the President to appoint buffalo hunters and the teamsters were not to leave their wagons. Much pleasantry was indulged in throughout the evening and there was some singing also."[7]

The division reached the Valley of the Great Salt Lake beginning on September 20, 1848.

A MISSION CALL TO HIS NATIVE LAND

During the year after Joseph Toronto's arrival in Salt Lake, he continued to work for Brigham Young. But his friend and mentor had other, more important plans for him. On Sunday, April 29, 1849, President Young, in conversation with his counselors and the Twelve, stated his intention "to send brother Joseph Toronto to his native country (Italy) and with him some one to start the work of gathering from that nation."[8] At the same time the Brethren were planning to send Apostles and elders to various continental European countries. It is not surprising that Brigham was interested in Italy as a prospective mission field: surely he felt, judging from the example of Joseph Toronto, that there would be other worthy people there anxious to hear the gospel. On May 10 Joseph received his first patriarchal blessing, which contained these words: "The Lord . . . hath called thee from thy native land to make of thee a messenger of salvation to thy native land even to thy brethren."[9] Three months later, on Sunday, July 22, Joseph was ordained a seventy by Elder Henry Harriman in Brigham Young's home.

In general conference the following October, during the Saturday morning session, Heber C. Kimball delivered a stirring oration on the subject of missionary work and the obligation of taking the gospel to every nation: "We want to feel for the welfare, not only of this people, but all of the inhabitants of the earth. Shall we debar one portion of the inhabitants of the world of what we have obtained? How should we feel if they had received it and would not commit it to us? We want this people to take an interest with us in bearing off the Kingdom to all the nations of the earth."[10] In the afternoon session, several motions were made and carried that certain brethren go on foreign missions. Among other calls to France, Denmark, England, and the Society Islands, it was "motioned that Lorenzo Snow and Joseph Toronto go on missions to Italy."[11] All motions carried unanimously.

The next evening, Sunday, October 7, was a memorable and inspiring occasion for the newly called missionaries as they met with the First Presidency and the Twelve to be set apart. One of the clerks, Thomas Bullock, described the evening's activities:

> The brethren who [have] been appointed to go on missions were called together in the evening, for the purpose of receiving, instructions, etc, whereupon the First Presidency proceeded to lay their hands on the quorum of the Twelve and set them apart for their respective missions.
>
> The Twelve then laid their hands on the Elders who had been appointed missions to the different nations of the Earth, and set them apart predicting their success, and the remarkable scenes that will transpire during their absence from their family. A joyful meeting was continued until 20 minutes past ten, when the meeting was dismissed, all enjoying the peaceable influence of the spirit of God and filled with faith that the Lord God of Israel would speedily work a great and glorious work on the earth.[12]

Less than two weeks later, on Friday October 19, 1849, Joseph

Toronto and Lorenzo Snow left the Salt Lake Valley in company with thirty-five other men, mostly missionaries destined for different mission fields. This was the first company of missionaries to leave the Valley to preach the gospel abroad.[13] Some were on their way to Sweden, Denmark, Scotland, and France, and others were going to the eastern United States. The group included a number of notable figures, such as John Taylor, Franklin D. Richards, Erastus Snow, Abraham O. Smoot, and Jedediah M. Grant. The hardship and toil of another trip across the plains lay ahead, as did the perils of a long ocean voyage and the uncertainties of life in a foreign land. Lorenzo Snow's own account of the journey describes his and the other men's feelings, including Joseph Toronto's, and some of the miraculous events that occurred along the way:

> Recalling the scenes of the past, my mind reverts to the 19th of October, 1849, when, in solemn silence, I left what, next to God, was dearest to my heart—my friends, my loving wife, and little children. As I pursued my journey, in company with my brethren, many conflicting feelings occupied my bosom—the gardens and fields around our beloved city were exchanged for the vast wilderness which lay spread out before us for a thousand miles. . . .
>
> Some judged our horses were too enfeebled to bear us over the mighty plain; but when the snows began to fall, winds swept our pathway, and enabled us to pass without difficulty, while, on our right and left, the country was deeply covered for hundreds of miles.
>
> One day, as we were taking our noon-tide meal, and our horses were quietly grazing on the prairies, the following scene occurred. A startling shout resounded through our little camp— *"To arms! To arms! The Indians are upon us!"* We looked, and beheld a spectacle, grand, imposing, and fearful. Two hundred warriors upon their furious steeds, painted, armed, and clothed with all the horrors of war, rushing towards us like a mighty torrent. In a moment we placed ourselves in attitude of defence. But could we expect with thirty men to withstand this powerful host? Onward came the savage band with accelerated speed, as a mighty rock, loosed from the mountain's brow, rushes impetuously downward, sweeping, overturning, and burying every thing in its course. We saw it was their intention to crush

us beneath the feet of their foaming chargers. Now, they were within a few paces, and in another moment we should be over-whelmed, when, lo! an alarm like an electric shock struck through their ranks, and stayed their career, as an avalanche, sweeping down the mountain side, stops in the midst of its course by the power of a hand unseen—the Lord had said, *"Touch not mine anointed and do my prophets no harm."*[14]

Certainly the latter half of 1849 and the early part of 1850 were joyful months for Joseph: his heart was full of gratitude to Presidents Young and Kimball for their inspiration and vision in sending missionaries to his beloved land; of anticipation and excitement at the prospect of reunion with his loved ones in Sicily after an absence of nearly ten years; of longing and enthusiasm to share the light and truth and joy of the restored gospel of Christ with his family and countrymen. It is reasonable to suppose that, during the long trip from Salt Lake to Kanesville, Iowa, Joseph had discussions with his missionary companion, Lorenzo, teaching him a few basic phrases in Italian and answering his questions about the people, culture, and religion of Italy. And surely he was comforted and encouraged by the words of his patriarchal blessing, received the previous May, informing him that he would be a "messenger of salvation" to his native land; that he would have power and the Spirit of God to work miracles, if necessary, for the salvation and protection of his people; that he would eventually have a numerous posterity; and that his name would be had in "honorable remembrance among the saints."[15]

The company of missionaries arrived in Kanesville on December 11, 1849, after a two-month journey across the plains. After resting for about two weeks, the men split up (probably to avoid arousing suspicion in this area where anti-Mormon sentiment was still strong) and took various routes to their respective mission fields. Joseph Toronto left Kanesville on December 29 along with Joseph W. Young, Peter O. Hansen, and Job Smith, journeying in Robert Caldwell's wagon to St. Louis, Missouri. At many of the places, the elders found the spirit of mobocracy rife, and sometimes they found it necessary to disguise themselves or to refrain from telling where they came from. The little party arrived safely in St. Louis early in January 1850.

After a few days' rest in St. Louis, where a thriving branch of nearly four hundred members received them warmly, the elders continued on to New Orleans, the southern seaport in which Joseph had once lived and worked. On Tuesday, February 26, 1850, Joseph Toronto and seven other missionaries sailed from New Orleans for England. Joseph joined Elder Snow in Southampton, whence they and Elder T. B. H. Stenhouse, an English convert, departed for Italy on June 15. The three missionaries traveled on board the steamboat *Wonder* to Le Havre, France, and continued overland to Paris, Lyons, and Marseilles. From Marseilles they went by boat along the seacoast to Nice, which at that time was part of Italy, and then on to Genoa, arriving there June 25, 1850. They covered the 1,200 miles from England to Italy in ten days, much more quickly than they had anticipated, having spent only three nights in a bed. These three were the first elders of the LDS Church to set foot on Italian soil as missionaries of the restored gospel of Christ.

During the weeks prior to leaving England, Elder Snow had studied and prayed to know where in Italy the Lord would have the missionaries begin their work. He had concluded, based on his conversations with Joseph Toronto, that "all was dark in Sicily, and hostile laws would exclude our efforts," and that no opening appeared in the cities of Italy. But the history of the Protestant Waldenses (in Italian called the *Valdesi* and in French the *Vaudois*) attracted his attention, and as he read and thought about the subject, "a flood of light seemed to burst upon my mind." These people lived in the mountain valleys of the Piedmont region of northwestern Italy, governed then by Sardinia. For centuries they had been bitterly persecuted and attacked by the Pope's armies but had remained steadfast in their beliefs. Having arrived in Genoa and observed firsthand the "wickedness" and "gross darkness" of the inhabitants of "Roman Catholic country," and knowing from his studies that "no other portion of Italy is governed by such favourable laws," Elder Snow soon became convinced that this Protestant people, a rose in the wilderness, should receive the first proclamation of the gospel in Italy.[16]

In accordance with that conviction, Elder Snow sent Elders Toronto and Stenhouse to observe conditions among the Waldenses and to explore prospects for missionary work among them. They left Genoa on July 1, 1850, to visit the mountain villages of the Piedmont region and less than three weeks later sent back a positive, encouraging letter. Upon receiving their report, Elder Snow was confident that the Lord had directed them to a branch of the house of Israel: "I have felt an intense desire to know the state of that province to which I had given [Elders Toronto and Stenhouse] an appointment, as I felt assured it would be the field of my mission. Now, with a heart full of gratitude, I find that an opening is presented in the valleys of Piedmont, when all other parts of Italy are closed against our efforts. I believe that the Lord has there hidden up a people amid the Alpine mountains, and it is the voice of the Spirit that I shall commence something of importance in that part of this dark nation."[17]

On July 23 Lorenzo Snow left Genoa, passing through the city of Turin, the capital of the Sardinian states, and arrived at La Tour (today called Torre Pellice) in the valley of Lucerne to rejoin his companions.

The Waldenses were indeed a remarkable people. The Lord had prepared the way for them to receive the gospel. A little more than two years before the elders' arrival in Italy, military and political events had transpired that resulted in a liberalization of law and an atmosphere of leniency unique to the Piedmont region. The king of Sardinia, on February 18, 1848, had granted these people for the first time the right to exercise their religion, to enjoy civil and political rights, and to attend schools and universities. As Lorenzo Snow observed, "Liberty is only as yet in the bud."[18] Had this relaxation of restrictions not occurred, the missionaries most assuredly would not have been allowed the freedom to travel and preach among these Protestant mountain dwellers.

Through divine intervention and inspiration, therefore, Elders Snow, Stenhouse, and Toronto were enabled to live with and teach the Waldenses. The missionaries found them to be very poor but hardworking, simple, and honest. They had few conveniences of life. Their homes were often built of stone on the steep, rugged mountainside. On holidays many still dressed in their colorful native costumes. Many aged men and women toiled up and down the mountainside with heavy loads on their backs. Their great national hero was Henri Arnaud, a pastor-warrior who had led them in the recapture of their mountain valleys from their Catholic enemies.

Shortly after coming to La Tour, Elder Snow recorded these observations: "The country in which I now found myself, bears a striking resemblance to the valley of the Great Salt Lake. . . . The Protestant inhabitants . . . number about 21,000: there are also about 5,000 Catholics. The fertile portion of these valleys are rich in their productions: but two-thirds, or more, present nothing but precipices, ravines and rocky districts. . . . The inhabitants are far too numerous, according to the nature of the soil. They are often compelled to carry mould on their backs, to form a garden amid the barren rocks." He also pointed out that French was the language generally used and understood, even though spoken imperfectly at times and mixed with local Italian dialects. Italian was understood by many people but not widely used, and there were at least five different dialects spoken in the area.[19]

The memorable events attending the labors of the Mormon missionaries among the Waldenses are well known in LDS Church history. We know from Lorenzo Snow's letters to Brigham Young, Franklin D. Richards, and Orson Hyde that the work at first was "slow and tedious"[20] and that the three elders of necessity maintained a low profile in their operations. Yet from day to day they "were always engaged forming some new acquaintance, or breaking down some ancient barrier of prejudice."[21] Elder Stenhouse wrote to his wife of their difficulties in communicating with the people and in providing food and shelter for themselves.

Joseph Toronto took leave of his missionary companions barely a month after arriving in La Tour and departed for his home in Palermo. Elder Snow explained: "During our protracted journey, the health of Elder Toronto had been considerably affected; but this salubrious clime having re-invigorated his frame, he became very anxious to visit his friends in Sicily. As I felt it proper for him to do so, he took his departure at the beginning of August."[22]

The slowness of the work during those first weeks in the mountains, Joseph's longing to see his family again and teach them the gospel, and the fact that French, not Italian, was most widely spoken and understood among the Waldenses probably contributed to Elder Snow's decision that his Italian companion's testimony and native language skills would be of greater service in Sicily. Thus Joseph was absent when, during the months of September and October 1850, some of the notable events of the Italian Mission took place: the miraculous healing of little Joseph Guy, which demonstrated the power of the priesthood to the Waldenses; the glorious meeting on the mountain overlooking La Tour in which Elders Snow, Stenhouse, and Woodard (who had arrived from England on September 18) organized the Church in Italy and dedicated that land for the preaching of the gospel; and the first convert baptisms in Piedmont. That Joseph Toronto was not present during that period is substantiated by the fact that Elder Snow's dedicatory prayer on "Mount Brigham" contained a petition to "bless Elder Toronto in Sicily, and give him influence and power to lead to salvation many of his father's house and kindred."[23]

One can only imagine the tearful embraces and the excitement in Francesco and Angela Maria's household as their eldest son unexpectedly returned home after an absence of nearly ten years. The revelation that he had left the Catholic faith and embraced a new, "foreign" religion no doubt elicited a good deal of hostility and criticism in his Sicilian neighborhood. But Joseph was undaunted in his resolve to share the joy of the gospel with those he loved most. In Boston he had intended to bring home a money belt full of gold to help his family financially; instead, having given his life's savings to build the Lord's house in Nauvoo, he brought them something even more valuable: a true message of eternal peace, happiness, and salvation.

Joseph, according to one report, was able to teach and baptize some of his relatives.[24] In general, though, few of his family members, friends, and neighbors were as enthusiastic about the good news of the restored gospel as he was. When he reported his mission in January 1853 to a gathering that included Brigham Young, Heber C. Kimball, Lorenzo Snow, and John Taylor, he commented on his reception by his Sicilian relatives, "who imagined he was very rich but on finding him poor treated him coldly."[25] Another source mentions "his severe sickness in Palermo, while preaching the gospel of Christ."[26] Clearly his missionary experience in his hometown was bittersweet. He was reunited with the people he loved but saw most of them reject the message he loved because it was spiritual, not material, in nature.

Joseph returned to the Piedmont region in the summer of 1851 and discovered that numerous Protestant Waldenses had joined the Church and were preparing to gather to Zion. He continued his missionary labors there until February 1852. On July 30, 1852, he arrived in Salt Lake City, having served honorably as a missionary for nearly three years.

THE ITALIAN PATRIARCH IN UTAH

On his return to the Great Basin, Joseph Toronto resided with and once again worked for Brigham Young. Brigham's family and the other Saints considered him an adopted son, calling him Joseph Young during this time. The prophet continued to show his concern for Joseph's welfare. When he learned that the newly returned missionary was anxious about his poor relatives in Sicily and wanted to help them, Brigham sent a letter (dated March 8, 1853) to Samuel W. Richards at the European headquarters of the Church, instructing him as follows: "I wish to pay to Joseph Toronto the sum of seven hundred dollars. Br. Toronto advanced the money for the construction of the temple in Nauvoo and a considerable amount besides. His people in Sicily are very poor and he wishes to assist them some. Enclosed are his instructions in Italian to his brother-in-law Vincenzo Corrao being at Palermo. He says that he wants you to forward the enclosed to the address with a letter from you."[27]

This episode illustrates not only the President's personal interest in Joseph's well-being but also the strong love and sense of responsibility that Joseph felt toward his family despite the vast distance separating them. Noteworthy too is the letter's implication that Joseph had written something in Italian: perhaps he had learned to write a little by 1853, or possibly another Italian convert in Utah had written down his instructions.

Brigham Young, in keeping with his custom of matchmaking among unmarried Latter-day Saint immigrants, picked a wife for Joseph: a lovely young lady from South Wales. One day President Young called Joseph in and said, in effect, "There is a nice Welsh convert named Eleanor Jones, and I think that you should marry her." Joseph, age thirty-seven, and Eleanor, age twenty-nine, were married in the fall of 1853, and a reception was given for them by Zina D. Young at the Lion House. From this marriage four children were born: Joseph Brigham, Frank, Ellen, and Jonathan J. Toronto.

One of Joseph's first endeavors after his marriage was to raise stock on Antelope Island, but due to lack of adequate pasture there he moved his herds to the Point of West Mountain, later called Garfield. He took along a young man known as Jack Toronto to work for him. This young man, one of the converts from Piedmont who had emigrated to Utah, went by that name until he married, when with gentle persuasion from Joseph Toronto he assumed his own name, which was James Bertoch. Brother Bertoch was put in charge of Joseph's and Brigham Young's cattle on Antelope Island for two years, and later he took over supervision of the Toronto ranch. Over the years Joseph continued to help the Italian Latter-day Saint immigrants from Piedmont settle in their new homeland, often giving them temporary lodging in his own home and providing them with jobs.

On his ranch Joseph raised cattle and horses and did some dry farming. There was a large cave in the mountainside that was used as a stable for horses. This cave, dedicated in later years as a Utah historical landmark and still known today as Toronto Cave, afforded him an ideal place for cattle raising. It was large enough at that time to permit haystacks to be built in front of the cave opening as a means of protecting the animals from the storms. A log cabin was also built nearby, and Joseph and his family lived there during the summer, moving back to Salt Lake City for the winter months.

While working near this ranch, Joseph had his second brush with death by drowning. His grandson, John S. Toronto, recounted this near-fatal experience:

> I am not certain of the name of the island involved in the following account. However, the island in question was connected to the mainland by a sandbar at the time of this incident. I assume this same sandbar extended from the island to an area on the south shore of the lake in the general vicinity of Black Rock near the former town of Garfield. This same sandbar served as a natural road for the movement of men and beasts to and from the island.
>
> As I recall my father telling the story, it was late one afternoon when Grandfather Toronto left the island and started for the ranch home. However, before he reached the mainland a storm of high intensity erupted. This storm brought heavy rainfall and strong winds. Whether Grandfather was afoot or horseback, I do not know. Anyway, if he was riding a horse, he apparently had to dismount and go by foot. Somehow, perhaps because of the intensity of the storm, darkness or a combination of both, he strayed from the sandbar—the one and only natural roadway to the mainland.

The next morning he was found lying on the shore of the lake. He was completely exhausted. It seems he had swallowed large amounts of salt water; his eyes were extremely irritated from the salt water, and his body and limbs were sore from having been tossed and turned by the raging waters.

Incidentally, Grandfather Toronto, from the time of his early youth and up until the time he joined the Church and moved to Nauvoo, had served in the Italian merchant marine or engaged in work that required being in open water. Yet he had never learned to swim.[28]

After nearly twenty years of marriage, Joseph and Eleanor hired a young Swedish convert, Anna Catharina Johansson, to live with them and help care for the family. In time Eleanor and Anna developed a close friendship, and because Anna had no other family to support her, Eleanor suggested that Joseph take her as a second wife. Reluctantly, and only after much persuasion from Eleanor and after Brigham Young's endorsement, Joseph agreed, and on January 22, 1872, he married Anna in the Endowment House. He was fifty-six at the time; she was thirty. From this marriage three children were born: John Charles, Rosa Anna, and Albert Toronto.

The final decade of Joseph Toronto's life was full of joy and sorrow, fulfillment and tragedy, exhilaration and despair. Within a span of five years from 1873 to 1878, three more children came into his household, bringing the total to seven. This was undoubtedly a source of great happiness to him. Two and a half years after marrying Anna, he was sealed to a third wife, a Swedish widow of about his same age, on November 9, 1874, in the Endowment House. His ranch, gardens, and fruit trees were thriving, as was the Carlgreen-Toronto Pottery Company, which supplied ZCMI and other retail establishments with flowerpots, jars, and vases.

But even as a prosperous landowner and busy father, he did not forget his relatives in Sicily. A second patriarchal blessing on July 8, 1870, contained reassuring words: "The time is not far distant when thy prayers shall be realized and thy heart shall be comforted to know of thy kindred who will accept the truth." By the end of 1875 he had received (no doubt at his own request) a second mission call to the land of his birth, and he departed for Italy in January 1876 at the age of sixty. He spent most of his time with his relatives in Sicily: his father and mother had died a few years before, and as eldest son it was his traditional duty to look after his sisters' and younger brothers' families. When he returned home a year and a half later on May 8, 1877, he brought with him fourteen of his family and friends, paying all boat and train expenses for the long journey himself. This was a costly endeavor for him, but he no doubt hoped that once they were away from negative influences in Sicily and were living among the Saints in Utah, they would join the Church.

Among the nine Taranto relatives were Joseph's older sister, Efisia Agras, a widow; his younger sister, Maria Grazia Scappatura, also a widow; Maria's four children, Antonio, Francesco, Vincenzo, and Angelina; Giuseppe Corrao, a relative of Joseph's eldest sister, Giovanna Corrao; and some cousins surnamed Adoraiddio. They were a happy, exuberant group, and the Scappatura family members were noted for their musical talents. Joseph relished the experience of at last having his American family and some of his Italian family together. In addition to the demands of his own household, he now assumed personal responsibility for the welfare and comfort of the new immigrants, trying as best he could to ease their transition into a foreign environment—a transition he himself had made successfully forty years before.

But the euphoria gradually dissipated as the weeks and months went by. The realities of adjusting to a strange culture, a puzzling language, and a harsh climate began to take their toll. Many of the Sicilians were discouraged and disappointed with conditions in Utah, finding them very different from their native land. One family returned to Italy, while another moved to California, where the climate was more to their liking. Maria Grazia Scappatura elected to stay in Salt Lake City with her children, and the federal census records of 1880 indicate that Efisia Agras became a permanent resident of Joseph's household, along with his three wives, three of his sons, and one of his daughters. Ultimately only one or two of his Italian relatives joined the Church in America—a severe disappointment to a man of such deep faith and conviction. Worry and distress about his relatives eventually resulted in a nervous breakdown and related illness that lingered for the next six years.

Life went on, however, and there were as always many gratifying, joyful events and activities to divert his mind from such concerns. Association with his wives and children and service in the

Church continued to be a constant source of comfort and happiness to him. In February 1878, less than a year after Joseph's return to Utah, another son, Albert—his last child—was born. Joseph also loved gardening and had brought back from Sicily roots from which he could grow figs, lemons, oranges, almonds, English walnuts, bamboo cane, and some tropical fruits. However, the climate proved too cold for the tropical fruits and only a few of them grew. He was an expert horticulturist, having one of the finest fruit gardens in the city, and he derived much pleasure and satisfaction from planting and landscaping his yard. The block he owned on First Avenue from A to B Streets was surrounded by a rock wall, over which grapevines trailed. The garden was laid out after the fashion of the terraced gardens he had seen on the mountain slopes of Sicily and northern Italy. He planted one of the first peach orchards in Salt Lake City. His fig trees were bent while young so that they could be covered in winter with straw and soil to prevent freezing. Many a slip was taken from the original tree.

It is often true that great men and women must pass through great adversity and sorrow. So it was in the life of Joseph Toronto, the irony being that the most disheartening, painful trials for him seemed to be reserved for the final years of a lifetime marked by unfaltering devotion and a succession of generally happy, rewarding experiences. In May of 1865 his little girl, Ellen, passed away. She was four years old and his only daughter at the time. In August 1877, three months after returning from his second mission to Italy, Joseph was saddened by the passing of his beloved friend and benefactor, Brigham Young. In February 1879, with his health already in a serious state of decline due to anxiety about his Sicilian relatives, Joseph suffered another heartbreaking setback: five-year-old John Charles, his first child by Anna, died after a tragic accident at the Toronto ranch. Tragedy struck again four years later when Joseph's second-oldest son, Frank, was killed after being thrown from a horse. His death was particularly grievous because Frank was the only married child at that time and left behind a wife, Rose Hannah, and two young sons.

The combined effect of the untimely death of several children and of the distressing turn of events with his Italian family proved too much for Joseph's fragile health to bear. On Friday July 6, 1883, just four months after Frank's death, Joseph Toronto died at his home in Salt Lake City. He was sixty-seven. His obituary that appeared in the *Deseret Evening News* stated: "While many people know a great deal of good about Brother Toronto, we do not think there is anyone who can truthfully say anything bad about him."[29]

THE LEGACY OF JOSEPH TORONTO

Joseph Toronto's life is a testament to the manner in which the Lord guides, blesses, and nurtures his children here on earth and keeps his promises to them. It also illustrates the tremendous influence—both spiritual and temporal—that one righteous, steadfast individual can have in the lives of future generations. The untutored sailor from Sicily could not have fully envisioned the far-reaching impact of his decisions to embrace a new faith in Boston, move to Nauvoo, and give his life's savings to the Church. Brigham Young's promise that Joseph would stand at the head of the Italian race and that his family would never want for bread was comforting, as was his patriarchal blessing that spoke of his becoming eventually a "messenger of salvation" to his family and of having a numerous posterity and a name held in "honorable remembrance among the saints." But certainly he, like most people, could not foresee the profound implications of righteous decisions and marvelous promises such as these in shaping the quality of life and affecting the destinies of men and women yet to be born.

While most of these promises were fulfilled by the time of his death in 1883, some were not. He and his family had indeed become prosperous, respected members of the Church and community, but with only four children and two grandchildren alive then, prospects for a numerous posterity were not very encouraging, and his success in bringing salvation to his family, despite his valiant efforts, had been minimal and extremely disappointing.

But the Lord's timetable for the realization of prophecies and promised blessings is frequently not the same as man's. His is eternal and merciful in scope; ours is finite and often shortsighted and impatient. The lives of Joseph Toronto's descendants have continued through the years to be blessed spiritually and temporally as a result of his faith and courage. Now, more than one hundred years after Joseph's death and with the advantage of hindsight, it is clear that the rest of the Lord's promises to him have literally been fulfilled. His posterity surpassed "numerous" long ago. In 1996

Joseph's direct descendants numbered more than three hundred, including seven children, seventeen grandchildren, fifty-four great-grandchildren, and 153 great-great-grandchildren. As for becoming a "messenger of salvation" to his family and people, this blessing has been realized in several ways: Joseph himself has no doubt continued his missionary labors for the past century on the other side of the veil; extensive genealogy and temple work performed by descendants of Joseph have made the ordinances of salvation available to literally thousands of his Italian relatives in the spirit world; the descendants of those first Italian converts from Piedmont are multitudinous in the Church today, many having served as missionaries in Italy; and finally, Joseph's own posterity has included a great number of missionaries and Church leaders who have worked with the Italian people in Italy and other parts of the world.

Joseph Toronto's life illustrates the pattern of spiritual seeking, religious conversion, migration and resettlement in Zion, and valiant missionary service that characterized the lives of hundreds of new members in the post-Nauvoo period of LDS church history. His physical and spiritual odyssey from Sicily to Salt Lake City profoundly altered his life and the lives of his descendants. Leonard J. Arrington, former Church historian, summed up the transforming impact of these religious experiences on the lives of early pioneers like Joseph: "Brigham Young was the most dramatic example of what happened to all the pioneers: of the Lord taking the small of the earth and making them mighty. . . . The restored gospel put his sights on something outside himself and expanded him as a husband, father, and man. His experiences and the spirit of the Lord made him over. . . . The challenges sharpened his powers, belief gave him confidence, and these things he could have found only in Mormonism."[30] The ancient proverb wisely says: "Children's children are the crown of old men; and the glory of children are their fathers" (Proverbs 17:6). This interrelationship of blessings between parents and posterity was never more clearly demonstrated than in the life story of Giuseppe Efisio Taranto, the Italian pioneer and patriarch. He won the promise of blessings to his posterity forever, and his posterity have continued to reap those blessings and to bring honor to his name.

Notes

1. As recounted by John R. Young, who was Brigham Young's nephew and knew Joseph Toronto in Nauvoo and in Salt Lake City. See John R. Young, *Memoirs of John R. Young* (Salt Lake City: Deseret News, 1920), p. 47.

2. *History of the Church* 7:433.

3. Joseph Toronto was illiterate and therefore left no personal written account of his life. He did, however, recount his experiences to family members, who recorded them and passed them on to subsequent generations. Some of the details included here are based on these family records and on interviews with Joseph's children.

4. Quoted in B. H. Roberts, *A Comprehensive History of the Church* 2:472.

5. Young, *Memoirs*, p. 47.

6. Young, *Memoirs*, p. 48.

7. Journal History of The Church of Jesus Christ of Latter-day Saints, 27 June 1848, Historical Department, The Church of Jesus Christ of Latter-day Saints, Salt Lake City, Utah.

8. Journal History, 29 April 1849.

9. In Alan F. Toronto, Maria T. Moody, James A. Toronto, *Joseph Toronto: Italian Pioneer and Patriarch* (Toronto Family Organization, 1983), Appendix B, p. 56.

10. Journal History, 6 October 1849.

11. Journal History, 6 October 1849.

12. Journal History, 7 October 1849.

13. See Journal History, 19 October 1849.

14. Lorenzo Snow, *The Italian Mission* (London: W. Aubrey, 1851), pp. 5–6. See also Eliza R. Snow Smith, *Biography and Family Record of Lorenzo Snow* (Salt Lake City: Deseret News Co., 1884), pp. 110–115.

15. In *Toronto*, Appendix B, p. 56.

16. Snow, *Italian Mission*, pp. 8–11.

17. *Italian Mission*, p. 10.

18. *Italian Mission*, p. 18.

19. See *Italian Mission*, p. 13.

20. *Italian Mission*, p. 20.

21. *Italian Mission*, p. 23.

22. *Italian Mission*, p. 13.

23. *Italian Mission*, p. 16.

24. "Joseph Toronto: The Italian Pioneer," manuscript of TV program broadcast on KVTV in Salt Lake City, November 21, 1954, p. 4. In author's possession.

25. Journal History, 2 January 1853. The meeting in which Joseph spoke was held in the Bowery, the structure used for large gatherings before the Tabernacle was completed.

26. Daniel B. Richards, *The Scriptural Allegory* (Salt Lake City: Magazine Printing Company, 1931), p. 9.

27. Letterbooks, Brigham Young Papers, LDS Church Archives, Salt Lake City.

28. John S. Toronto, unpublished manuscript in author's possession.

29. *Deseret Evening News*, July 6, 1883, p. 3.

30. Leonard J. Arrington, "Brigham Young," in *The Presidents of the Church,* ed. Leonard J. Arrington (Salt Lake City: Deseret Book Co., 1986), p. 71.

In God's Hands in Divided Germany

by Wolfgang Zander

God's ways and purposes often remain long hidden from us and are difficult to understand. Sometimes our trust in him is put to a difficult test. In my family, however, the words of Paul have proven to be true: "And we know that all things work together for good to them that love God" (Romans 8:28).

It was directly before Christmas of 1944. We lived at that time on a military air base on the outskirts of Koenigsberg in East Prussia. The chaos of the final months of World War II was fully evident in the surrounding area, with a foreboding sense of doom. My father, Max Zander, who had been deferred from serving in the war because of a long-standing critical illness, received a new summons for military duty. Within two days he was to report to the eastern front in Silesia.

He recognized immediately that he could not leave his family alone in this threatened area. As a result of rather dramatic circumstances, we succeeded in traveling by train without incident to my grandparents' home in Wolgast, hundreds of kilometers to the west. Shortly thereafter, hundreds of thousands of fleeing inhabitants drowned, froze to death, or died of hunger. Those who survived lived like animals for several years in the ruins of Koenigsberg, until they were deported to what was left of Germany. East Prussia had been annexed by the Soviet Union, with intervening territory awarded to Poland.

Even my father succeeded, thanks to an unexpected assignment that turned out to be a blessing in disguise, in leaving the Russian front and moving to the west and falling into eventual British captivity. He was released soon thereafter in connection with a new

Translated by D. Brent Smith

flare-up of his illness and was thus already reunited with his family in autumn 1945 at the time many of his former comrades were arriving in Siberian work camps, where they would languish for many years. He could not have survived such a camp in his poor state of health. So it was that what we then considered to be our great misfortune was, I strongly believe, the way in which our family was saved.

Wolgast was at that time a small town with about seven thousand inhabitants near the Baltic coast of Mecklenburg-Western Pomerania. My father, who was a native of Wolgast, succeeded in finding employment as the gardener for a Lutheran cemetery. In the following months, he had a great deal of contact with a former school friend, who was intensively involved in the study of religious questions but who, as a result of family pressure, remained an uncommitted seeker.

In the autumn of 1946 this friend mentioned for the first time the Mormons, of whom we had never heard anything before. He spoke of their strong faith and special spiritual strength, the difficult challenges they faced as pioneers, and the Book of Mormon, and he mentioned a missionary who had just arrived at the home of the only Mormon family in the town. This was the Skibbe family, whose youngest children had not been baptized because of the chaos associated with the war. This missionary was Walter Krause, who is known to all of the Saints in East Germany.

My father was deeply impressed with the Book of Mormon and wanted in particular to get to know Brother Krause. At this point my father's friend sought to stifle my father's interest out of fear of gossip spreading in this small town in which everyone knew each other. But it was already too late.

In the subsequent weeks we had many intensive encounters with Walter Krause. Relatives and friends sought to keep us from pursuing this "disastrous, false course." In this connection, they were as much concerned about protecting their own "good reputation" as they were about our family's welfare.

My knowledge of the conditions in areas in which there are large concentrations of Latter-day Saints is limited to one visit to the United States, but I can imagine that my father's situation was roughly comparable to that of a Mormon meetinghouse custodian in southern Utah who converts to Catholicism. In Wolgast, with its purely Lutheran population, even a conversion to Catholicism would have resulted in notoriety and malicious gossip. My father understood very well the consequences of his conversion: necessary changes in our way of life, the loss of his job, and his essentially being banned from society.

Brother Walter Krause was, however, an extremely zealous and gifted missionary. While I cannot attest to the accuracy of reports of his activities in distant parts of Mecklenburg, I do know that he dedicated himself with a passion to the restored gospel and was a true friend and supporter of all earnest investigators of the Church. And his efforts bore fruit.

On December 14, 1946, my father was baptized in the ice-covered Peene River. He was, with the exception of the Skibbe family, the first convert in Wolgast. Neither he nor Brother Krause was healthy, and so my father hesitated at the thought of being immersed in ice-cold water. However, Walter Krause stated, in essence: "If you have faith, the water will not harm you. And if you don't have faith, then you won't need to be baptized in summer, either!"

I have since gotten to know Walter Krause and again and again have found him to be energetic and consequential, inspiring and unwilling to compromise his strong beliefs—engaging himself sometimes to the point of exhaustion, expecting his family as well as branch members to be ready to sacrifice, though not as much as he himself was prepared to give. He can seem harsh and on edge as well as warmhearted and sympathetic, and at the same time personally unassuming and extremely unpretentious. He is a true pioneer of our religion. Up until today, fifty years after my first encounter with him, he is among all the Saints the one that I most revere and love as a second father. His courage in facing difficult challenges has always touched me, as has the complete trust in the strength of the priesthood of those he baptized. It hardly needs to be mentioned that my father did not even catch a cold. I, just having turned thirteen, understood intuitively that there was something very special about this church.

When my father left to be baptized, only my mother knew where he was going. It was her birthday, and my parents wanted on this day to avoid any arguments among our relatives about the Church. My mother accepted her husband's decision. She was overwhelmed, however, by the doubts expressed on all sides, even as she defended him from the slander of others. Only after it happened did all who were close to us find out about the baptism. Their bitter recriminations thus had no real impact. It would take decades for their scorn and insults to be replaced by a certain degree of acceptance.

My grandparents on my father's side were deeply religious but were trapped in the narrowness of their views. They belonged within the Lutheran church to a strongly pietistic Protestant regional organization that had its own meeting rooms and its own preacher. When my father presented them with a Book of Mormon shortly after his baptism so that they could themselves become convinced of its contents and spirit, my grandmother burned it on the advice of their preacher.

Apart from such painful experiences, we learned very soon how the Lord took care of us. This was the time of great hunger right after the war. With great appreciation during these years of need, we received relief packages sent by American Church members in connection with the Church welfare program. Only one who lived through such a period can imagine what it is like to be always hungry and insufficiently clothed. Some of the special types of food and clothing received had never been seen by our children and youth in their lifetimes. Our own children today regard such recollections as fairy tales from another world. We members of the postwar generation still regard the disposal of leftover food to be a sin, since in many areas of the world there is still dire need.

My parents' concern about a livelihood was soon relieved. My father received a position that was a much better match to his training and qualifications. As a result, we had to leave our beloved branch in Wolgast and move to Prenzlau, a county seat about one hundred kilometers north of Berlin. Prenzlau was, in the final days of the war, almost fully destroyed as a result of the insanity of fanatical Nazis. Here there was a small branch also belonging to the Mecklenburg District, so we did not lose contact with the members in Wolgast. Later my father was for many years the president of the Prenzlau Branch.

I have a vivid memory of my first visit to a Church meeting in Wolgast. I stole glances in every direction to see whether I would be recognized by anyone I knew on our way to meet in the Skibbe home or later in rented meeting rooms facing the market square. For me, as a thirteen-year-old, attending such a meeting was adventurous, even conspiratorial.

Strong belief in God and daily prayer were taught to us children by our mother. Often she sang while working, singing mostly well-known Christian songs. Some of these songs with their simple messages remain with me today. As a child, I already had a great deal of interest in religion and listened with great enthusiasm to gospel discussions among adults. For my age, I judged myself to be still very naive, almost too serious and at the same time extremely insecure and therefore quite impressionable. I was often taken advantage of by those I trusted, placing me, as one not yet fully developed, into spiritual predicaments.

So it was that every Sunday for a year and a half I attended three different services. In the morning I attended Mormon Sunday School where my father took us. Following this, I walked to the children's meeting in the Lutheran church, which was important to my mother, and in the afternoon I went to the children's hour at the regional Protestant organization, which pleased my grandparents. In each case I was a welcome and eager participant.

This also caused some difficulty for all sides. Just as soon as I learned something of interest in one of these places, I would bring it to the other group in the form of a question to the teacher. I thus had, for example, heated discussions with my Lutheran minister as a result of my questions on baptism, the Trinity, priesthood, and modern-day revelation. Then his answers became questions that I would ask of the teachers and leaders of the restored Church of Jesus Christ.

After the Lutheran minister and the leader of the children's group in the regional Protestant organization learned the source of the unwelcome questions I was asking, they countered by filling my young soul with doubt and fears about, for example, the origin of the Book of Mormon (though they had no interest in its contents), about the alleged immoral way of life of the Mormons in connection with polygamy, or about the practice of "conjuring of spirits" (here they were referring to proxy baptisms for the dead).

Although all of this brought distress and turmoil, in the end it contributed to my having to thoroughly come to grips with the gospel and recognize its truth. It was my great luck to encounter leaders and teachers in our church who took a youth posing critical questions seriously and who responded with patience and sincere answers to every uncomfortable question asked them. As they were able over time to help me satisfy my understanding, the Lord was able to plant in my heart gradually, but with ever-increasing intensity, a strong testimony of the restoration of his church.

In the end I only needed the courage to admit this myself and testify of it to others. From this point forward, I pressed my mother—with the strong support of my father—to thoroughly investigate the teachings of the Church. This took its time because she was much more dependent on the opinions of others than was my father.

Finally, on July 31, 1948, this was achieved: my mother, my sister, and I, with several other new converts, were baptized in an inlet of the Peene River. My entire family belonged at last to the Church. For me, at that time almost fifteen, this was a profound and unforgettable experience that has carried me through crises and disappointments.

There have been many critical moments and times in my life. Walter Krause said thoughtfully to Aaronic Priesthood holders once, "Everyone who becomes an elder and wants to diligently serve the Lord will also feel of the power of Satan, who tries in any way possible to destroy Zion." I have never forgotten this admonition, but I have learned that God's power is always stronger than that of the wicked one and that He can in miraculous ways be close to us when we are in extreme danger.

Three times I have owed my life to such miraculous help. In the first instance, towards the end of the war, I stood at an unprotected window as a grenade was thrown at the roof framework diagonally below me on the other side of a narrow street. The house I was in suffered great damage as a result of the impact of the explosion and flying debris. I was not even touched by splinters of glass from my window; against all expectation they all fell outward! An invisible wall of protection must have shielded me.

Barely a year later, and before we learned about the Church, I suffered a complicated skull fracture. My body reared up under the severe brain convulsions, and the chief surgeon gave my parents no more hope. My father implored him to nevertheless attempt an operation. I am convinced that the doctor, who later was incredulous at my complete recovery, was not only guided by his own capabilities but by the power of the Lord who responded to ardent prayers even though we were not able at that time to call upon the healing powers of the priesthood.

Ten years later, while hiking in the mountains I was placed in great danger when a large boulder was dislodged as a result of some frivolity. It all happened so fast that I could not move out of the way when I recognized the danger. At the last moment, the boulder changed its course and flew by directly next to me into the valley below. I have thus felt a number of times that I was receiving the gift of a new life.

Much was expected of us youth in the Mecklenburg branches. We foraged for kindling material (at that time very difficult to obtain) and often cleaned the meeting rooms. Sacrament meetings every Sunday were a particular challenge for us. Walter Krause did not approve of preparing sacrament meeting talks far in advance; he specifically wanted the Spirit of the Lord to be able to spontaneously manifest itself. So he expected us to have studied the scriptures intensively and to be ready at any time to be called upon to speak. The earliest he specified who was to speak was during the prayer meeting before the sacrament meeting. We deacons and teachers sat at the beginning of the meeting in the front row and waited nervously to see who he would call upon to speak. Only when an older brother was announced did we feel safe.

I recall only one exception to this practice, and that was in connection with my first talk. I was told a full hour before the meeting that I would speak. As much as I must have been frightened, I did not dare turn down such an assignment issued by our priesthood leaders. They inspired our trust by providing worthy examples of spiritual leadership. I can remember today the topic of my first talk: "Lay not up for yourselves treasures upon earth, where moth and rust doth corrupt" (Matthew 6:19).

There were some very ordinary people who joined the Church back then in Mecklenburg. Through the influence of strong spiritual leadership, they often grew much beyond their own capabilities and demonstrated spiritual strengths that hardly anyone would have expected of them, themselves least of all. Perhaps my memory is subject to some youthful bias here, but I have retained those sacrament talks and class discussions among my spiritual memories more than many later ones.

This strict spiritual instruction helped me a great deal later on. I really grew to know and love the scriptures, and they have become constant companions and counselors to me in many situations in life. Perhaps it was good for us that, living at that time in the Soviet-occupied part of Germany, we had for our use almost no other religious materials than the four standard works.

Hilde and Max Zander (center) in 1956 with their children,
Wolfgang, age twenty-three (left), and Brigitte, age twenty (right).

Personally, I was influenced most by the New Testament—even though the Book of Mormon and the Doctrine and Covenants often inspired and strengthened me. In the New Testament I encountered Christ not only as the Son of God deserving my awe, but also as a human being full of warmth and loving sympathy who occasionally had to admonish and call other individuals to repentance but who could also provide wonderful comfort and lift the downtrodden. Peter was only one such example of a person whose life was changed by Christ, but for me he is one of the most impressive.

This love and mercy of Jesus have often overwhelmed me and given me the unextinguishable hope, despite my many faults and shortcomings, of being accepted by him. I can best express this feeling with the words of a hymn:

> I stand all amazed at the love Jesus offers me,
> Confused at the grace that so fully he proffers me.
> I tremble to know that for me he was crucified,
> That for me, a sinner, he suffered, he bled and died.
> Oh, it is wonderful that he should care for me
> Enough to die for me!
> Oh, it is wonderful, wonderful to me!

An ever-recurring subject of countless discussions among Church members in East Germany was the soon-to-come Millennium and the gathering of Israel. This topic always resulted in a great deal of debate and fascination. We loved to fantasize how through the Lord's power we would be able to quickly leave the Communist part of Germany and enter into Zion before the Lord would come again and appear there.

All of the older members were caught up in these thoughts. This went so far that Walter Krause strongly urged us youth not to study intellectual subjects or pursue studies at a higher education level but instead to pursue simple manual professions. He reminded us about the Mormon pioneers, who because of strong persecution had to build new homes and then leave them several times over the course of a few years before they found peace from their enemies in the wilderness of the Rocky Mountains. At that time, he contended, the Lord needed workers who could use their hands to build the covered wagons and guide the oxcarts, not people with a higher education. With gleaming eyes, we young people listened to such narrations, and we felt ourselves, in our fantasies, to be the heirs of the Israelites of old who had been led by Moses toward the promised land.

My mother, however, who had lived through two world wars and experienced privation and unemployment during the world economic crisis, insisted that I complete my university qualifying examinations to have the chance for a "better" occupation. In retrospect, I must be thankful that she was so insistent back then. Brother Krause has changed his views on this topic over the course of time. His son Helaman completed studies in the natural science field some fifteen years later.

In expecting the imminent end of the world, the Saints at that time in East Germany were not the only ones to have had false conceptions. Paul and the other Apostles expected the Lord's return to take place quite soon, and it appears that even Joseph Smith did not think that it would be very long until it happened (see D&C 130:14–17).

My father did not have an easy time as president of the small Prenzlau Branch. That was mostly because my mother often withdrew into herself with regard to the Church. She would blame the whole Church for some personal differences she had with members, and that of course could have a major impact in such a small branch. For years she attended the Lutheran church on Sundays while my father was presiding over the meetings in the branch. My father died at age sixty-six in 1973 in Stuttgart. Until his death he remained a convinced Latter-day Saint. My mother in the last years before her death in 1975 attended Church meetings regularly and also participated in temple sessions. My parents and I were sealed to one another without my sister, however, who became less active after her marriage outside the Church.

The Communist youth organization was the sole organization authorized to conduct youth activities in East Germany. Walter Krause, however, was able to organize unofficial events that became for us youth the highlight of our Church activity in the Mecklenburg District. For example, every year there was a youth camp on the Baltic Sea coast and an end-of-the-year get-together on New Year's Eve that was both cheerful and reflective.

Our district conferences also were events we would not forget. Often we youth rode our bicycles to the conferences in Neubrandenburg. To stay overnight in this heavily demolished city we had to stay either with members or in mass accommodations at the branch meetinghouse. These conferences lasted two or three days and included a cultural activity. In between the individual meetings, one could often see Brother Krause putting together a large pot of pea soup. He had learned as a result of many years of want that it is important to strengthen not only the mind but also the body.

From age seventeen on, I had great difficulties at school and later at the university. I was considered to be politically unreliable and was only allowed to enroll because my father, in recognition of his experiments in cultivating plants, had received special authorization that would allow his children to attend schools of higher learning.

Particularly repulsive to me was the despicable falsification of history that we were forced to accept and even celebrate, as well as the ever-present spiritual dictatorship of the Communist Party with its militant atheism. Originally I wanted to study to become a teacher but then began to fear that this would result in political problems. However, at the university I was forced after all to become a teacher. Here again I had to recognize God's direction. A profession as a scientist would have required much work with a microscope, which because of my defective eyes would have been a great problem for me.

At the completion of my university studies in Rostock, I experienced yet another small miracle. I was originally slated to be assigned to a very remote secondary school where I would have hardly had an opportunity to attend church regularly. When the most politically active student failed his exams, I received his position in Rostock, so I was able to remain in my own branch with my friends in the Church.

Two years later my difficulties had indeed become intolerable. One day, three particularly politically active students appeared at my home and reproached me with the charge that I was leading astray their colleagues who were not yet firm in their Communistic development. They claimed that as a result of this deportment, I was no longer fit to be a teacher. That night I was unable to sleep. Quite often people in my neighborhood were picked up by the secret police, and they sometimes vanished without a trace. One individual who returned after an absence of months never said anything about his experience, as if it had been expunged from his memory, so great was his fear of further consequences.

Following intensive prayer, I stood before my students the next morning and with great mental strain expressed my convictions. I told them that I did not have the intention of dissuading them from their Communistic materialist worldview but that I was confident that they as adult individuals could develop their own convictions. That was, of course, the opposite of what was expected of teachers in the East German state. I ended with the words: "You may go now to the school authorities and inform them as to what has happened. Then, as a result, I will no longer be your teacher."

Then I left the classroom. After about ten minutes, some students came to me with the request that I stay at least four weeks through the completion of their university qualification exams. For them this was almost as dangerous as it was for me, but even the three young Communists held their silence.

On the day of the exams, a final episode took place. The party secretary of the school requested that I give an unfavorable grade to a student who had done extremely well on the just-completed exam, so that it would be easier to block his pursuit of higher education. His father had been arrested three months previously, and his family had not been informed as to his whereabouts. As I repeatedly refused this request as unjust, I was myself threatened. I fled that same evening, June 20, 1958, to West Berlin. Three years later, after the Berlin Wall was built, I would no longer have been able to easily cross the border.

As my university degrees were not recognized in West Germany, I had to take additional course work at the University of Tuebingen. I belonged at that time to the small Reutlingen Branch in the Stuttgart Stake. In 1961 I was called from this branch to serve a mission in the South German Mission. In East Germany, missionary service had been very limited. An attempt to marry had fallen through, and I was already twenty-eight years old. I could not afford to wait much longer and still be accepted as a secondary schoolteacher in the educational system. For this reason I served for only fifteen months as a missionary. I believe, however, that they were just as effective as the two years served by most others. I was already more mature and not only knew the language but, thanks to Walter Krause's instruction, also had a thorough knowledge of the gospel. I was thus able to work at full strength from the first day of my mission.

Each missionary has special experiences. My most memorable one took place only five weeks after the beginning of my mission in Stuttgart. Our district leader needed to work with my senior companion and therefore sent me out with a brand-new missionary to establish initial contact with a woman who was a referral. I did not like the memorized missionary discussions with the predetermined sequence of questions and answers, though I had learned them obediently as was at that time required of us. As my companion knew almost no German, we had planned in advance exactly what he should say.

The young woman and her boyfriend received us. Just as we sought to enter into a dialogue, she said in a lightly mocking tone: "I can hardly wait to see which of your six discussions with Mr. Brown [this was the fictional investigator in the discussions] you will want to give us today. I have already received them. One of my acquaintances [a stake sister missionary, as I found out later] gave them to me to read. I find them indeed somewhat comical."

I was shocked! I felt deeply offended to see the missionaries and the Church shamed. My companion could not help me at all because he did not understand what had happened. Silently I prayed to the Lord for help and began to defend the missionaries. I described how they were called, their devotion, and their difficulty in dealing with a foreign language. They do not deserve to be mocked, I added, when in today's world most young people do not make such sacrifices for their convictions.

Then I asked her about her own principles and goals in life. I did not accept empty answers but wanted her to recognize her own immaturity and superficiality instead of making fun of others. Finally, I told both of them how my own faith and the Church had influenced me.

As we bid farewell after an hour and a half, I asked myself whether we had wasted our time, and I felt very weak. Then she said, to my great surprise: "When will you come again? You have deeply impressed me." Eight weeks later she was baptized, though not by me. For many years she has lived in the United States as the mother of a large Mormon family. "Man thinks, but God directs" is a German proverb applicable to this experience.

Missionary work can, however, take place in a quite different manner and even without our being aware of it. I experienced this again just a short time ago. I was asked by the two missionaries assigned to the neighboring ward in Stuttgart about a certain young man who up until a few weeks before had been one of my students. "He will be baptized today," the missionaries said, beaming. As I reacted with astonishment, finding this hard to believe, they added, "He only let us in because he knew you and knew that you were a Mormon." How easily he could have slammed the door on the missionaries with the response, "I don't want to get to know any more Mormons. One of them, my teacher, is enough for me."

In 1963 I first met my wife, who was at that time investigating the Church. Missionaries came to me often at that time when they encountered difficulties in not being able to recognize or resolve problems faced by their earnest investigators. Such was the case with Hanne Lotte Lingenauer. She had received all of the discussions and found many of the principles of the gospel to be convincing, but the missionaries had not taken into account that she—like many people following the terrible wars and atrocities in Germany—did not really believe in God. Only when this foundation was laid was she ready to be baptized.

Yet another quite unnecessary hurdle also had to be overcome. One week before her scheduled baptismal date, another sister was baptized. Three times she had to return in her clinging wet dress to the baptismal font until she had been completely immersed. This shocked my future wife so much that it required a great turnaround before she finally agreed to be baptized. I later observed in many instances how negligence or limited appreciation of an individual's

Wolfgang Zander (far left) with his daughter, Susanne (far right), on a 1987 visit to Walter and Edith Krause in Prenzlau, East Germany.

cultural idiosyncrasies could cause one to turn back from a path already embarked upon.

On November 21, 1964, exactly one year after my wife's baptism, we were married. We would have liked to do this months earlier, but we wanted to wait until we could seal our marriage covenants in the temple. We knew that for our future life together we would need not only mutual love and respect but also the Lord's blessing.

My wife has been a loving companion, full of faith, who has always stood loyally at my side through good and difficult days. Our two sons and our daughter have served missions in England and in New York, and they have all married in the temple. We have thus been able to let them leave our nest and to trust them unto the Lord. Good friends have thus far accompanied us on our way through life with trust, understanding, and energetic support. In them we have also recognized the blessings of God.

Through his humility and readiness to believe, my father took the step on that icy December day in 1946 that has led to the conversion of numerous others, initially in his own family but also as a result of his son and three grandchildren fulfilling missions. Walter Krause was one of the true and faithful pioneers that God used as an instrument to help bring this to pass. As amazing as have been the paths of our lives, including many experiences that remain unmentioned here, God's hands have always been there, guiding and blessing us.

ANTHON H. LUND:
GENTLE DANISH APOSTLE

by Bruce A. Van Orden

Anthon Henrik Lund (pronounced "Ahn-tone Hen-rick Loon" in his native land) was a different kind of pioneer than many others described in this volume. He was a sterling representative of thousands of souls converted to the restored gospel in nineteenth-century Europe and gathered to the mountain Zion in America. Brother Lund never forgot his European roots. Many times he returned to Europe to carry on his lifetime quest to proclaim the gospel to all the world with no respect of persons.[1]

Anthon was born in Aalborg, Denmark, on 15 May 1844, the year of the death of the Prophet Joseph Smith. Aalborg was the fourth-largest Danish city and had about forty-five thousand inhabitants at that time. Aalborg is located on the mainland (or Jutland) of Denmark about forty-five miles south of the northern tip of Denmark and about twenty-five miles west of the Baltic Sea.

When Anthon was three and a half, his mother, Anne Kirstine Anderson, became seriously ill and passed away. A few months later his father, Henrik Lund, was drafted into the Danish army to fight in the war with Prussia over the disputed provinces of Slesvig and Holstein. The lad was placed in the care of his Grandmother Anderson, who proffered him tender care mixed with strict Danish discipline. Anthon rarely saw his father during his sixteen years before he emigrated to Zion.

Anthon, a precocious child, was placed in a private school at age four. When he later entered the public schools, his industry and intellect allowed him to jump over a few grades. He took private tutoring in English and became a master of that language. He also studied German and French. Anthon was recognized as the brightest student in his school. He spent all his pocket change he could get his hands on to purchase new books. Anthon's most irresistible desire was to study the Holy Bible. In his youth he read the entire book, much of it out loud to his grandmother.

In 1850, when Anthon was only six, Elder Erastus Snow of the Twelve Apostles arrived in Denmark to open the Scandinavian Mission. While Mormon missionaries to Denmark were frequently persecuted by Lutheran priests and many citizens, they nevertheless were able to stay in the country, baptize converts, and establish branches and conferences (the name for a group of branches in that time period). This same advantage was not available in the 1850s in the other Scandinavian countries of Sweden, Norway, and Iceland, where no religious freedom existed. The reason why elders in Denmark were able to carry forward their work was simply that the new Danish king, Frederick VII, was forced by the National Liberal movement during the revolution of 1848 to 1849 to sign a new constitution that, among other things, guaranteed religious liberty. Elder Snow quickly learned that he and his elders would have protection under the law and acceptance by at least some of the Danish people if they carried a copy of the constitution with them along with their scriptures and other teaching materials.

One of the early Aalborg converts to Mormonism was Anthon's uncle, Jens Anderson. Aalborg was the first city after Copenhagen to which Elder Erastus Snow sent missionaries. This northern Jutland vicinity became the stronghold for the Church in Denmark. Jens shared his newfound treasure with as many of his family as would listen, including his mother, Anthon's grandmother. In 1853 Jens was among the first Danish immigrants to the Utah Zion. Before he left, he baptized his mother. Anthon Lund, nine years old, looked on with curiosity. In his grandmother's home he came in constant contact with Mormon literature, including the Danish Book of Mormon that had been published in 1851. The Danish translation was the first edition translated from English in Church history. Anthon read eagerly, whether in Danish or English, and mastered whatever he could of Latter-day Saint doctrines and history. He cherished the new truths highly and compared the restored gospel to clear daylight and old Christianity to the uncertain flare of the northern lights of the darkened sky.

However, Anthon chose not to be baptized at that time. In the 1850s the new Danish converts were socially ostracized. The spirit of meanness spread even to the schoolboys, so that the Saints were not allowed to send their sons to attend public schools. (No girls attended public schools in Denmark at that time.) Anthon's peers knew of his interest in Mormonism. Sometimes the boys threatened to "baptize" him in one of the local ponds or to beat him. But his father's younger brother, who was three years older than Anthon and at the same school, would not allow anyone to abuse his nephew. Actually Anthon won over most of the boys as friends by his willingness to help them with their studies. The schoolteachers also respected his intellect and tried to help him. The school's principal became Anthon's mentor, and when he learned of the lad's sincerity in studying Mormon doctrines, he said: "I thought you were persuaded by others, but I see you are thoroughly convinced of the truth of Mormonism. Follow your honest convictions, my boy. I would not hinder you from obeying the dictates of your conscience." This schoolmaster bestowed the coveted title of *dux*, meaning the first of the class, upon Anthon as he graduated at age twelve, three years younger than most of the others.

Except for his grandmother, Anthon's relatives were opposed to his interest in the LDS Church and wanted him to go on to the collegiate school. Most of his teachers also urged him to reject Mormonism and to proceed with specialized intellectual training, for which they were convinced he was especially suited. For a few weeks during his last year at the public school, Anthon was tormented within as he struggled with his decision whether to be baptized a Mormon or not. But the Holy Spirit won him over. He cherished and was greatly influenced by the profound teachings of the local priesthood leaders: Christian D. Fjelsted, who presided over the Aalborg Conference, and Christian A. Madsen, who oversaw Aalborg and several other conferences. Both of these men would remain close associates with Anthon in the ministry after they all gathered to Zion. Brother Fjelsted would become a member of the First Council of the Seventy, and Brother Madsen would be bishop of the Gunnison Ward in Sanpete County. Anthon Lund submitted to baptism on his twelfth birthday, 15 May 1856.

The local members were pleased with Anthon's decision, and they became his family. Brother and Sister Madsen took him in and helped him with his studies of English. Brother Fjelsted called Anthon to the ministry when he was but thirteen. His mission was to distribute tracts, help the elders hold meetings, and teach emigrating Saints to speak English. When he made his first report to a mission conference, Elder Fjelsted lifted him onto a table so he could be seen. Anthon carried with him copies of the *Millennial Star* published in Liverpool, England, by the president of the European Mission. He read articles from them to the Danish Saints, translating them as he spoke. The members were delighted and strengthened in their faith. He used the "Answers to Objections" printed in the paper to meet arguments of the Lutheran ministers, who were then publishing in Danish the same falsehoods about Mormons that had flooded America and England.

During the more than four years he served as a missionary, Anthon labored without purse or scrip throughout the Aalborg vicinity. One trait Anthon always showed was kindness. In many locations, other elders met persecution but Anthon succeeded in making friends. Nearly all his listeners were awestruck that this mere boy could be so spellbinding in his delivery. Anthon succeeded in baptizing scores of people who later emigrated to Zion. One of the more common things Anthon did from week to week was to hold English classes for those Saints scheduled to emigrate that particular season. From night to night he stayed in the homes of the various members.

Anthon, of course, had to face some fierce opposition to his work. One day he was out inviting people to a meeting for that evening. He invited the woman of one house to attend. When she learned that it was to be a "Mormon meeting," she became enraged, picked up her fire tongs, and flew at him. "I will give you a Mormon meeting," she screamed. Realizing that discretion was the better part of valor, Anthon ran out of the house, but the woman raced after him and called for her husband to shoot the young man. She made such a disturbance that the neighbors came running to see what was the matter. One of them explained to Anthon many years later in Ephraim, Utah: "I became curious to learn something about the Mormons and went to the meeting. I heard you speak and was convinced of the truth."

Anthon kept a journal of his early missionary experiences. Some of the entries were in Danish, others in English. On the last day of 1860, he penned, "I thank you my Father in Heaven that this year is finished, and thou has kept me faithful, and I pray thee, give me power in my body and strengthen my mind, that I may be faithful in the next year and to the End of days. Amen."[2]

In 1862, when he was eighteen, Anthon received permission to emigrate to what would become his "mountain home" in Utah. His company went to Hamburg, Germany, and boarded the German flag square-rigger ship *Franklin* that had been chartered by the Church's Perpetual Emigrating Fund Company (PEF) agents. Anthon's mentor, Brother Christian Madsen, was the captain of the Mormon company consisting of 413 Danish Saints. The disease of measles came aboard the ship and ravished the Latter-day Saint children. The captain of the ship insisted that only a doctor could distribute medicine, so the Saints voted Anthon Lund "physician" of the company. He received a medicine chest and a book in English describing the common diseases and their cures. Throughout the voyage Anthon hardly had a moment to himself for rest as he cared diligently for his brothers and sisters in the gospel. Unfortunately, sleeping quarters were of the rudest sort, and the passengers between decks had only 160 bunks to share. Measles and chicken pox claimed forty-eight lives.

Sadly, the company had further difficulties after arriving in the United States. First they were quarantined for a few days on ship. Fourteen more deaths took place as they crossed the plains.[3] One year earlier Church officials had initiated the Church Trains system wherein the PEF would provide all the wagons, animals, teamsters, and food from Florence, Nebraska, which was located on the Missouri River, to Salt Lake City. Anthon's company arrived in Salt Lake on 24 September 1862.

Most new arrivals from Denmark gravitated to Sanpete County in central Utah. Such communities as Manti, Ephraim, Mt. Pleasant, Fairview, Gunnison, Moroni, and Fountain Green were filled with Jensens, Lauritsens, Nielsens, Pedersens, Olsens, Johnsons, Andersons, Petersons, and the like from Denmark, Sweden, and Norway. This was the only county in all of Zion where the majority of residents were not of British lineage. Sanpete was known as "Little Scandinavia." Brigham Young urged all Scandinavians to learn English and gain American citizenship, but in the Sanpete towns the old country tongues still were often used. If nothing else, strong accents flooded the air. Anthon settled in Mt. Pleasant at the home of John Barton, where he taught the children in the home. He took on all kinds of jobs—digging potatoes, working on threshing machines, working in a harness shop, and manufacturing shoes. But he was discouraged. He missed his books more than anything else. He finally found a discarded astronomy book and whiled away his free hours locating the constellations of stars and the planets. In 1864 he undertook a mission as a teamster to go to the Missouri River and help gather a new company of Scandinavian Saints.

When he returned, Anthon accepted a call from Brigham Young, along with other young men and women, to learn telegraphy so that the Church would have skilled people to run the new Deseret Telegraph Company then being established throughout the territory. He developed a lifelong friendship with another student, John Henry Smith, with whom he would have many refreshing experiences in the ministry. Together they would one day serve in the apostleship and also the First Presidency. When he returned to Sanpete, Anthon assumed the directorship of the telegraph office in Mt. Pleasant. He also opened a photography studio. Photography had just reached Utah.

Later in the 1860s Anthon took on other responsibilities. In 1865 he helped start the first children's Sunday School in the city as part of the Deseret Sunday School Union as created by Elder George Q. Cannon of the Quorum of the Twelve. When the first cooperative stores were established under the umbrella of ZCMI (Zion's Cooperative Mercantile Institution), Anthon was appointed secretary of the Mt. Pleasant Co-op. He was also elected a member of the city council.

But there was one problem. He could find no wife in Mt. Pleasant. The older elders of the village tended to take all the available younger women as additional wives in this era of plural marriage, known then as celestial marriage throughout Zion. But here was Anthon Lund, twenty-six years old in 1870 and still not married. Anthon had an important friend in Ephraim who looked out for him: the stake president of the Sanpete Stake, Canute Peterson, an immigrant from Norway who had converted to the Church in the United States. President Peterson introduced Anthon to the third daughter of his first marriage, Sarah Ann, who was seventeen. A romance soon developed between these two young people. The Petersons and Anthon journeyed by horse and buggy in late April and early May 1870 to the Endowment House in Salt Lake City, where Anthon and "Sanie" were endowed and then sealed in eternal marriage by Daniel H. Wells of the First Presidency. Anthon took up residency with his bride in Ephraim. Anthon and Sanie nurtured a truly loving relationship throughout their lives together. They would have nine children, two of whom would die as children. Anthon never married plurally.

Anthon's close relationship with his father-in-law continued. In 1871 Canute Peterson was called as the new president of the Scandinavian Mission. He requested that his son-in-law Anthon Lund be called to accompany him to mission headquarters in Copenhagen to serve as business manager of the mission. It was entirely not unusual for young men in that era to accept and fulfill a mission not many months after their marriage ceremony. This duo of Peterson and Lund proved to be a dynamic force for good in the Scandinavian Mission for over a year. Baptismal statistics rose, and the number of emigrants from the mission went up higher than they had been since the mid-1860s.[4] Each emigration season, which lasted from February to July, Brother Lund made all the arrangements for the Scandinavian Saints to lodge for a night near the mission office and to gain passage to America. At this point in time, the Saints arriving in New York could travel all the way by rail to Ogden, Utah. This was definitely safer and faster, but it was just as expensive. Anthon was constantly working long hours to keep up the necessary bookkeeping. He also handled all the business for the mission publication the *Scandinavian Star*, wrote some of the articles, and translated many materials from English to Danish for the benefit of the Saints. The Norwegian and Swedish Saints could read these same articles because of the similarities of the languages.

While on this mission, Anthon missed Sanie very much. He yearned to see her and, of course, his new son, Anthony Canute, who was born 25 February 1871, just a few weeks before Anthon left on his mission. On his birthday in 1871, he reminisced in his journal about his fifteen years as a member of the Lord's true church on the earth. Then he confided, "Towards evening I commenced a letter to my wife—How I long to see her and my son." The next month he conducted a marriage of two young Danish converts and wrote: "I find it the greatest blessing that man can enjoy to have a good sweet dispositioned wife—Thinking of her who is my companion and now so far away may be nursing him who is the pledge of our love I feel to pray God bless you my pure-hearted wife and may you and my boy enjoy good health till the time when we shall meet. I did not go to bed but had a busy time of it settling up [the emigration business]."[5]

While on his mission, Elder Lund took opportunity to visit all of his relatives on both his father's and his mother's sides in Aalborg. The reunions were joyous, and he got caught up on family news.

But Anthon was saddened that none of them desired to accept the restored gospel. Regarding a favorite aunt, he wrote in his journal: "Poor Aunt why can't you believe the truth. She was always so kind and good and is a general favorite among the saints and sinners." He also acknowledged, "I feel my true relations are among the saints."[6]

Anthon returned from his mission in the fall of 1872. His reunion was sweet with Sanie and little Anthony. The family settled down to solidarity and growth. Over the next eleven years, until Anthon went again to serve in the Scandinavian Mission, their family grew steadily with the births of Henry in 1873, Sarah in 1875 (who died after only nine months), Herbert in 1877, Canute in 1879, and Othniel in 1882. Anthon H. Lund served diligently in the local Church programs and gained invaluable experience and wisdom that would later provide the bedrock for his apostolic ministry. President Peterson, who had returned to his presidency of the Sanpete Stake, called Anthon to the stake high council in 1874 and to be stake clerk as well in 1877. In 1878 he became superintendent of the Sunday School programs in Ephraim, a calling he dearly loved. On the temporal level, Anthon assumed the directorship of the Ephraim Church Co-op in 1873 and reestablished his photography business. It was generally conceded that the Ephraim Co-op was the most successful in Sanpete County.

In 1883 Brother Lund was called to fill a third mission in Scandinavia. Again he left his family at home without him. This type of sacrifice was not considered unusual in Zion in the nineteenth century. For the first year of his third mission in his beloved Scandinavia, he served as office manager in Copenhagen under President Christian D. Fjelsted, who to this point in time was the most well-known and beloved son of Scandinavia in the LDS Church. Anthon translated numerous key doctrinal items into Danish, including speeches of the prophet, President John Taylor, and of Book of Mormon commentator George Reynolds. In March 1884 Anthon learned that he would succeed Fjelsted as Scandinavian Mission president. He served over a year in this capacity. His presidency required frequent visits to Sweden and Norway as well as throughout the Danish conferences. He made detailed entries in his journal regarding his daily responsibilities and how he strived to help individuals. He realized that each soul was precious in God's sight. He conducted numerous councils for Church members in transgression.

President Lund always labored to help the transgressor get on the road of repentance and forgiveness.[7]

Before Brother Lund returned from his mission in 1884, the Church hierarchy arranged for Anthon to be on the ballot for the Utah Territorial Legislature, representing Sanpete County. The political party favored by Latter-day Saints at this time was the People's Party, organized in 1875 in response to the Liberal Party that had been created in 1872 to represent the political interests of disenchanted Mormons and of Gentiles in Utah. Starting in 1870 the United States federal government in all three branches—executive, legislative, and judicial—had waged the anti-polygamy crusade against the Mormons to dismantle what they labeled "polygamic theocracy." The U.S. president pressed for harsh legislation against the Church, appointed strong anti-polygamy and anti-church-state governors and judges, and threatened military intervention in Utah affairs. The Congress passed a series of new laws making it easier for Mormon polygamists to be arrested, convicted, and jailed. The U.S. Supreme Court ruled that all these new laws were constitutional and that Mormon polygamy was obnoxious and could not be justified as approved "practice of religion" under the Constitution. In 1882 Congress had passed the Edmunds Act, which threatened the arrest of all polygamists. Thus, President John Taylor and his brethren looked for men to serve in the Utah legislature such as Anthon H. Lund who were not polygamists and who would not be arrested.

Anthon Lund served in the territorial legislature for two four-year terms. He sincerely strived for the improvement of education in Utah. The federal government had mandated by law that the territorial superintendency of education be taken out of the hands of Church officials. Anthon Lund helped oversee a smooth transition. He introduced legislation to establish the Ogden Reform School for delinquent boys. His greatest contribution was overseeing the process of creating the Utah State Agricultural College (USAC) in Logan, Utah. Years later one of Utah's greatest educators, Dr. John A. Widtsoe, who at one time served as president of USAC, remarked, "It was President Lund's conception and his diligent labor that led to the founding of the Agricultural college, the result, as he often told me, of his observation of agricultural education in Europe, especially in Denmark."[8]

Why Anthon Lund never entered plural marriage is not entirely discernable. It is certain he loved his eternal companion, Sanie, very dearly and had no desire to share his affections with other wives. Quite likely also, as the anti-polygamy crusade worsened from the point of view of the Latter-day Saints, his priesthood leaders, including his father-in-law, Canute Peterson, counseled him to remain monogamous to have more freedom of action in local and territorial affairs. Certainly his monogamous status came in handy for the Church as a whole from 1888 to 1890 when the screws of federal pressure had tightened to their most uncomfortable point.

The Manti Temple, the magnificent hilltop, sandstone structure built to the glory of God, was finished in 1888. Residents from all over Sanpete County, including Anthon, had sacrificed time and treasure and had consecrated skills to complete it, even during the duress of having many polygamous husbands either in hiding or in the territorial penitentiary. The Lund family in Ephraim lived only five miles from Temple Hill. All faithful central Utah Saints who were free to walk about without threat of arrest gathered in May 1888 for the glorious dedication. Just weeks before the dedication, Anthon Lund learned that he was to be the vice president of the Manti Temple under Elder Daniel H. Wells, the first temple president. Anthon was thoroughly devoted to this work of love in the house of the Lord. He came to be totally dedicated to family exaltation and to the redemption of as much of the human race as possible through the assistance of eternal temple ordinances of endowments and sealings. In due course Elder Lund would preside over both the Manti and Salt Lake Temples and be president of the Genealogical Society of Utah. In all these capacities he had further opportunity to promote the cause of his fellow Scandinavians, both the living and the dead.

The LDS Church was in desperate straits in 1888. President John Taylor had died in exile a year earlier. Nearly all the Apostles, including the senior Apostle, Wilford Woodruff, were still in hiding from federal marshals. George Q. Cannon, President Woodruff's chief adviser, was free after serving his time in prison. He was sent to Washington, D.C., to try to lobby the federal government for relief. He learned that relief would be forthcoming only if the Church was willing to compromise on polygamy and church-state domination. As an act of compromise, the Church tore down the Salt Lake Endowment House, where the bulk of plural marriages had been performed, and ceased promoting plural marriage in any

public sermons. Another highly symbolic act took place in October
general conference of 1889 when the new First Presidency, comprised of Wilford Woodruff, George Q. Cannon, and Joseph F.
Smith, called monogamous Anthon H. Lund to fill a vacancy in the
apostleship. Elder Lund was the first nonpolygamous Apostle to be
called during the entire Utah period of Church history. He was also
the first Scandinavian to be called to the holy apostleship. All of
Sanpete County and all Scandinavian descendants throughout Zion
could not have been more pleased.

Elder Anthon H. Lund continued to reside in Ephraim and to
serve in the Manti Temple presidency. He succeeded the temple
president in 1891 and was called that same year to be part of the
Church's newly created Board of Education. Anthon made frequent
trips to and from Salt Lake City on the Denver and Rio Grande
Western Railway system in order to attend important quorum and
board leadership meetings.

During his temple service, Elder Lund wrote a poignant piece
in his journal in May 1890: "Little Othniel [my eight-year-old son]
came to the Temple with his Grandpa [Canute Peterson] to be baptized. Thomas Higgs baptized him. I confirmed him. Prests. Peterson and P. B. Maiben were witnesses. This is my marriage day. 20
years ago I took Sanie to wife and she has proven a faithful, sacri-
ficing wife who has done all in her power to make my home a
home indeed. God bless her and help her to bear life's trials
patiently, and give me wisdom to make her happy."[9]

One of Anthon and Sanie's severest trials came later that year in
December when their eleven-year-old son Canute, stricken with
diphtheria, died in his father's arms. The household was quarantined. For days Sanie could not be comforted at the loss of her dear
boy, not even when Anthon tried to reason with her. Finally, after
Christmas, their oldest son, Tony, a faithful young man of nineteen,
was able to turn her around by explaining the glorious work
Canute was doing in the world of departed spirits. Anthon was
most grateful for such a wonderful son as Tony.[10]

In his position as a member of the Board of Education, Elder
Lund proposed a program that would have long-lasting effects in
Latter-day Saint culture. By the late 1880s the Utah system of public
schools had become entirely secularized in the same pattern as the
rest of the United States. Yet Church officials were anxious that the
children of the Saints not be denied weekday religious devotional

and education opportunities. Elder Lund suggested that the children could go directly to the Latter-day Saint chapels following their school day and receive an hour's worth of instruction, including singing, prayer, and scripture study. Thus was born in 1890 the Church's Religion Class program. Elder Lund served as the first general superintendent. The program took a great deal of effort to administer, especially in the early times, since each ward in Zion had to be motivated to call a capable superintendency and teachers.[11]

In May 1894 the First Presidency called Anthon H. Lund to preside over the European and British Missions. Since 1850, when Elder Franklin D. Richards of the Twelve was called to both posts, the presidency of both missions was held by one man, usually a General Authority. Actually the European Mission was an umbrella organization to which all the various missions in Europe belonged. Having an Apostle in such a position with all the necessary keys to direct this vital work a long distance from Zion seemed always to be prudent. Every Apostle was expected to take his turn in presiding over these missions for two or three years at a time. It was not uncommon for an Apostle to have two or even three terms as European Mission president. One major advantage in a mission of this kind was that the Apostle took one of his wives and some of his children with him. In Elder Lund's case, he had but one wife and, at this point, five dependent children. Anthon and Sanie's last three children since his Scandinavian Mission presidency of 1883 to 1884 were August William (born in 1886), George Cannon (1891), and Eva Anna (1893). Upon his arrival in Liverpool, President Lund wrote for the mission periodical that he now edited, the *Millennial Star*. "In contemplating the great and onerous responsibility of the work before me, I feel, more than ever before, a distrust in my own abilities, and my entire and absolute dependence upon the Lord for aid and assistance to perform the duties now assigned me."[12]

As president of both the British and European Missions, Anthon spent considerable time traveling from conference to conference encouraging the elders and the members. His linguistic abilities made him more effective in communicating with the Saints on the continent than any of his apostolic predecessors had been. His soul was filled with joy and gratitude for his testimony of Christ and his redeeming gospel but also with sadness that only a few "strangers," as investigators of the gospel were then called, were willing to be baptized. The halcyon days of success in the British Mission had long been over, and hosts of prejudices, traditions, and police restrictions kept the various European missions from prospering as well.[13] Missionaries in the 1890s used two main methods: distributing tracts from door to door hoping to make appointments to come back and teach the gospel, and inviting the public to preaching meetings held outdoors in the summer and occasionally in rented halls in colder weather. Neither method produced many teaching opportunities; usually people spoke with the elders, if at all, merely out of curiosity, not with deep and abiding interest in their religion—or in any religion, for that matter. The age of science in Europe was marked by deepening apathy toward institutionalized Christian religion and the Bible. At the end of his presidency in 1896, President Lund challenged the missionaries: "Study the best ways and methods of reaching the hearts of men with the convincing truths of the Gospel, and let your best endeavors be directed to building up the kingdom of God. Be pure in thought, prudent in your sayings, and wise in your actions."[14]

One of President Lund's missionaries, who became his chief aid, Elder Nephi L. Morris, later commented on his experiences traveling throughout Europe with his president: "This gospel dispensation has not produced a nobler or more Christ-like man than Anthon H. Lund. In spirit he was as sweet and pure as a child; in temperament as charming and affectionate as a woman; in character 'his strength was as the strength of ten because his heart was pure;' in companionship he was as enjoyable as a devoted kinsman because he carried a merry heart that bubbled with gentle mirth and a refined humor." Elder Morris also reported that President Lund sought out the best of European culture by visits to museums and educational institutions.[15]

When he returned to Utah, Elder Lund continued to reside in Ephraim. He threw himself back into his labors, having been reappointed superintendent of Religion Classes and a director of both ZCMI and Zion's Saving Bank. He took frequent assignments to visit the wards and stakes of Zion to instruct priesthood leaders and attend their regular or special conference sessions. Many of his assignments, naturally, were to the Saints in Sanpete County, where he was always nobly received.

In 1897 the First Presidency called Elder Lund to another mission, this time for a few months to the Mediterranean area to oversee the expansion of the Turkish Mission and to determine whether there should be a local gathering place for the Saints of that mission. The Turkish Empire, also known as the Ottoman Empire, at that time consisted of present-day Turkey, Anatolia, and all of the eastern ridge of the Mediterranean, or Near East, region that is now Israel, Palestine, Lebanon, Iraq, and Syria. The Ottoman Empire refused its subjects the right to emigrate to the United States. The Turkish Mission had existed since its founding in 1889 by European Mission elders Jacob Spori and Ferdinand Hintze. Turkish Mission elders over the first decade had succeeded in establishing branches in Aintab (today Gaziantep) and Zara in the Turkish portion of Armenia in the large city of Aleppo in Syria that had a sizable Armenian population, and in the coastal city of Haifa, Palestine. The elders had preached the gospel only to Christians and never to Muslims, for it was absolutely forbidden among Muslims to pay any heed whatsoever to any form of Christianity.

Missionaries had met with relatively good success among the Armenians, whose forefathers had become Christians as early as the second century A.D. Some attempts had been made in Damascus to preach to Arab Christians but with virtually no success at that time. In Haifa elders had brought a few Arab Christians into the fold, but the majority of their success was from among a group of German Christians known as Templers who had immigrated to the Holy Land to await the second coming of the Savior.

Elder Lund was accompanied on his six-month mission by Brother Ferdinand Hintze, one of the cofounders of the Turkish Mission. Elder Hintze knew Turkish as well as his native German and could serve as an interpreter among the Saints and "strangers" they would visit. Elder Lund thoroughly enjoyed visiting the Armenian Saints in Aintab and Aleppo and hearing their hearty *hosh geldinis* (welcome) as they happily greeted an Apostle of the Lord. Elder Lund and Elder Hintze also took many opportunities to preach the gospel to interested investigators. Demonstrating that he was perfectly willing to adapt to local cultural traditions, Elder Lund reported in the *Millennial Star* the following missionary setting in Aintab:

> Our room was crowded from morning till night with people who either wanted to learn our principles, or show us that we were wrong. It was an interesting sight to see them sit Turkish

fashion on the carpet, most times as many as thirty at once, with Brother Hintze in the middle. They would ply him with questions, and listen to the answers he gave them. The Armenians are very earnest in their discussion, and when this became very animated, to me, who did not understand the language, it also sounded as if a quarrel was going on; but that was not the case. They would all at once become quiet and listen to a passage of scripture read to them. Some would smile approvingly, showing that they were convinced, others would raise fresh objections, and so it would continue for hours. A missionary to be successful in Turkey must be gifted with conversational powers.[16]

Seventeen of these individuals submitted themselves to the brethren for baptism within four days of their arrival in Aintab. They fashioned a baptismal font out of a basin of hewn rocks with flowing water, enclosed in a courtyard.

Sadly, however, Elder Lund witnessed considerable persecution of the Latter-day Saints by other Armenian Christians in Aintab. An American Mission Society professor published a number of anti-Mormon broadsides that were widely distributed. The Sunday meetings of the Saints were interrupted by huge rocks thrown into their midst. One hit Elder Lund in the leg.

When the brethren went to Haifa and other parts of Palestine, they were accompanied by three other elders from the mission. They traveled together for protection from Bedouin robbers. They even enlisted the aid of a government soldier as they walked from one community to another. South of Mount Carmel they looked for potential sites for a gathering spot for the Latter-day Saints. In their hearts they felt that such a gathering place in the Holy Land, where the Savior of the world had once walked and taught, would be an important precursor to the Lord's second coming. A potential spot was chosen, but circumstances in subsequent years never proved pleasing for the establishment of a Mormon community in the Near East. The brethren visited Jerusalem also. As Andrew Jenson reports, while they were there "the first baptisms by divine authority in this dispensation at Jerusalem, Palestine, took place in Mary's Well, where Elder Ferdinand F. Hintze baptized Geo. Vezerian and Geo. Nadgarian, two Armenians from Asia Minor. They were both confirmed the same day, the first-named by Apostle Anthon H. Lund and the latter by Elder Hintze."[17]

*President Heber J. Grant (center) with First Counselor Anthon H. Lund (right)
and Second Counselor Charles W. Penrose (left).*

Back in Zion, Elder Lund moved to Salt Lake City in 1898. Following the death of Elder Franklin D. Richards, Elder Lund assumed the dual role formerly held by Elder Richards of Church historian and president of the Genealogical Society of Utah. These two callings were in addition to the superintendency of Religion Classes and membership on the General Church Board of Education.

A singular honor came to this "Apostle of Scandinavia," as he was often known, in October 1901 when Joseph F. Smith, the successor to President Lorenzo Snow, called Anthon to be his Second Counselor in the First Presidency. Brother Lund remains the youngest person (fifty-seven) to be called to the First Presidency in the twentieth century. He became First Counselor in 1910 following the death of President John R. Winder. He continued in this position throughout the remainder of President Joseph F. Smith's life. During this span he continued to serve in the key executive positions in history, genealogy, Board of Education, and Religion Classes. In 1918 President Heber J. Grant called Anthon H. Lund to be his First Counselor, in which position he remained until his death in 1921.

As a Counselor for twenty years, President Lund helped issue official doctrinal statements, epistles, and special messages from the Presidency to leaders and the Church membership. When he died, President Lund was second in apostolic seniority to President Grant.

In 1909 President Lund, accompanied by Sanie and their daughter Eva, made a tour of each of the European missions. This was a rare privilege for the Saints in each Scandinavian country as well as Germany, Holland, and Britain to be taught by a member of the First Presidency. This was President Lund's sixth separate assignment in Europe.

In 1910, under President Lund's tutelage, the Church began publishing the *Utah Genealogical Magazine* to motivate members to research their genealogies and to provide ideas to assist them. President Lund's chief assistant in this endeavor was Elder Joseph Fielding Smith, newly called to the Twelve and son of President Joseph F. Smith. The next year President Smith released himself as president of the Salt Lake Temple and called his First Counselor, Anthon H. Lund, to assume this responsibility. This duty occupied most of his time during the week. He enjoyed presiding over this priceless work of saving souls. In one of his conference talks he declared: "The work done by the Genealogical Society cannot be classed as an auxiliary. It is a basic part of the work of the Church. Take away the power of the priesthood to seal for time and eternity husbands, wives, and children; take away the binding power of the families of the nations, past, present, and future; and the bringing to the dead the ordinances of the gospel; and you will take away the means of a perfect salvation for us all."[18]

Anthon H. Lund was eulogized for his sterling character at the time of his passing in March 1921. The president of the University of Utah and future Apostle John A. Widtsoe said: "President Lund was a cultured man. He had cast behind him many of the disturbing fears of life. He knew that out of contention comes chaos. He knew that peace builds up, and warfare destroys. He knew that love serves humanity as the sun warms the earth. His vision was clear, his gaze steady, his trust unfaltering and his methods of a character to make men feel easy and happy."[19]

Elder Orson F. Whitney of the Twelve, referring to his "gentle" mentor, Brother Lund, declared: "Gentility does not consist in wearing costly clothing, nor merely in a show of polite manners. It is kindness of heart, chivalry of soul. A real gentleman is considerate of others, a friend to the friendless, a champion of the oppressed, mindful of the aged and infirm, tender towards women and children, treating all men fairly, respectful to authority, and reverential towards God."[20]

Charles W. Penrose, who served for a decade with Anthon Lund in the First Presidency and before that in many intimate capacities, observed: "He was really the idol of the Scandinavian people and after being more closely associated with him in later years and being in his society, I knew that he was beloved, not to say idolized perhaps, by people of all races and countries that came to the presidency for advice and for help on many occasions. . . . [T]he poorest of the poor, no matter what country they came from, . . . could come to him and he would listen to their tales of woe and give them advice and counsel and comfort and send them away rejoicing."[21]

The prophet of God, President Heber J. Grant, concluded that his soul mate Anthon H. Lund had epitomized the declarations of priesthood power emanating from Liberty Jail more perfectly than any man he had ever known: "No power or influence can or ought to be maintained by virtue of the priesthood, only by persuasion, by long-suffering, by gentleness and meekness, and by love unfeigned; by kindness, and pure knowledge, which shall greatly enlarge the soul" (D&C 121:41–42).[22]

Anthon H. Lund, originally from Aalborg, Denmark, but at ease throughout Europe and in the Middle East and beloved in all of Zion, was from a different era. But we can still all learn from his pure goodness and reach out to all souls everywhere, regardless of their culture, ethnicity, color, creed, or nation. Had he lived in this glorious time of reaching out to more than 150 nations, he surely would have shown the way in his love and respect for all the human race.

Notes

1. I have gathered the bulk of the general biographical material on Anthon H. Lund from the lengthy sketch on him in the *Juvenile Instructor* that was part of a series of biographies on all the Apostles in 1900. See "Lives of Our Leaders—The Apostles. Anthon H. Lund," in *Juvenile Instruc-*

tor 35 (1 November 1900): 705–13. Janne M. Sjodahl, a *Deseret News* writer and fellow Scandinavian, wrote this piece. Andrew Jenson drew from Sjodahl's sketch to prepare his piece on Anthon H. Lund in his *LDS Biographical Encyclopedia*. I have added my own interpretations and additions based on my own studies of the Church in Denmark, emigrating Mormons, Sanpete County, and plural marriage. The *Millennial Star* provided numerous comments by or about Elder Lund that were helpful.

2. Anthon Henrik Lund, Diaries 1860–1921, 31 December 1860, Archives Division, Church Historical Department, The Church of Jesus Christ of Latter-day Saints, Salt Lake City, Utah.

3. Details about the *Franklin*, the company captained by Christian Madsen, and their journeys and misadventures are recorded in Conway B. Sonne, *Ships, Saints, and Mariners: A Maritime Encyclopedia of Mormon Migration 1830–1890* (Salt Lake City: University of Utah Press, 1987), pp. 78–79, and Conway B. Sonne, *Saints on the Seas: A Maritime History of Mormon Migration 1830–1890* (Salt Lake City: University of Utah Press, 1983), p. 54.

4. See Marius A. Christensen, "History of the Danish Mission of The Church of Jesus Christ of Latter-day Saints 1850–1964" (master's thesis, Brigham Young University, 1966), p. 210.

5. Lund, Diaries, 15 May 1871 and 20 June 1871.

6. Ibid., 10 August 1871.

7. Ibid., 1883–1884.

8. In Janne M. Sjodahl, comp., *In Memoriam: Anthon Henrik Lund* (Salt Lake City: 1921), pp. 24–25.

9. Lund, Diaries, 2 May 1890.

10. See ibid., December 1890.

11. See D. Michael Quinn, "Utah's Educational Innovation: LDS Religion Classes, 1890–1929," *Utah Historical Quarterly* 43 (Fall 1975): 379–89.

12. *Millennial Star* 55 (19 June 1893): 404.

13. See Bruce A. Van Orden, "The Decline in Convert Baptisms and Member Emigration from the British Mission after 1870," *BYU Studies* 27 (Spring 1987): 97–105.

14. *Millennial Star* 58 (23 July 1896): 473.

15. In Sjodahl, *In Memoriam: Anthon Henrik Lund*, pp. 21–22.

16. *Millennial Star* 60 (21 April 1898): 242.

17. Andrew Jenson, *Church Chronology* (Salt Lake City: Deseret News, 1899), p. 219.

18. As quoted by Archibald F. Bennett, a later leader of the Genealogical Society of Utah, in a speech given to seminary and institute faculty at Brigham Young University, 2 July 1958. All of this is cited in Boyd K. Packer, *The Holy Temple* (Salt Lake City: Bookcraft, 1980), p. 207.

19. In Sjodahl, *In Memoriam: Anthon Henrik Lund*, p. 25.

20. In ibid., pp. 37–38.
21. In ibid., pp. 41–42.
22. See ibid., pp. 41–42.

Japanese Pioneers:
Masao and Hisako Watabe

by Masakazu Watabe

Grandma, you are the pioneer heritage I always admired; the strength, courage, wisdom, and love; I will love you forever," wrote my second daughter, Paulette, to send my mother to the spirit world after the completion of her life on January 22, 1996. Although there are no deserts to cross in Japan, no oxen to pull, nor cows to milk in twentieth-century Tokyo, the story of my father, Masao, and my mother, Hisako, resembles that of the early Mormon pioneers. The legacies they leave behind are continued by their faithful descendants, just as pioneer legacies are alive among Latter-day Saints all over the world.

My parents served in various capacities in the early history of the Church in Japan. Masao served as the first native branch president in Sendai from 1951 until 1957, when he left there to become a full-time translator for the Church at the mission home in Tokyo. He translated many Church materials with Brother Tatsui Sato, who translated the standard works into Japanese. This itself is quite an accomplishment because Masao taught himself English after the war when he was over thirty years of age. After moving to Yokohama, he was immediately called to serve as the first counselor in the branch, then as the district high councilor, and thereafter as the genealogy chairman of the whole mission in Japan. When the first stake in Tokyo was organized in 1970, he was called to serve in the stake mission presidency. In 1971 he was set apart as the first patriarch in Asia by Elder LeGrand Richards.

My parents were the first native Japanese couple to be called to serve in the Hawaii Visitors' Center, from 1978 to 1980. Masao was also ordained a sealer in the Hawaii Temple by President Spencer W. Kimball. When the Tokyo Temple was completed in 1980, they were again among a few native couples called to serve as temple missionaries in the first temple in Asia. When the next temple in Asia, the Taipei Temple, was dedicated in 1984, they were called to serve there as temple missionaries as well, and Masao was called as the first counselor to the first temple presidency under President John Clifford. They served there as missionary couples three terms until 1990. After they returned, they served in the Provo Temple as ordinance workers and Masao was again called to serve as a patriarch in the Brigham Young University Fourth Stake, where many Saints from Asia attend.

However, I feel their Church callings and assignments are not that important in relation to the pioneering legacies that they have left for us. The way they accepted the gospel; the fact that they kept their faith during such an infant stage of the Church in Japan; and the efforts they have made to pattern their lives in accordance with the gospel they embraced are the things I consider to be of greatest importance. In order to understand their faithfulness and steadfastness, we must go back to see under what circumstances they came to this earth and the context in which the gospel was planted in their lives.

MASAO WATABE BEFORE MARRIAGE

Masao Watabe was born on June 6, 1914, at Keikanzan, a small town in South Manchuria, China. His father, Senji, participated in the Japanese-Russian War during 1904 and 1905. After the war, Senji returned to his native land, Fukushima Prefecture, in the northern part of Japan. His ancestors were farmers, and it was tradition that the first son inherit most of the family property and land after the father's death. Unfortunately, Masao's father was the third son and couldn't expect to receive an inheritance, so he decided to emigrate to a new place of opportunity, the United States. However, since he lacked sufficient funds, he went instead to Manchuria, where he was employed by the South Manchurian Railroad Company.

After a few years a marriage was arranged, and Kon Takano came from Senji's native land of Japan to be married to him. Masao was the second son of twelve children. He was apparently an excellent student, and his oldest brother, Masaaki, told me once that Masao could have and should have gone to the Imperial University of Tokyo. Instead he worked at the Manchurian Central Bank after high school in 1932 to earn money for his younger brother's education. After working one year, he enrolled in a college in Harbin to study Russian to prepare to become a diplomat. He had been interested in religion ever since he was young and was affiliated with one of the Shintoist sects. He was also a devout nationalist while he was a college student. Thus, his dream was to work for and to devote his life to his divine country, Japan. In one of his classes at Harbin he became very good friends with Masashi Watanabe, who was also studying Russian and shared similar views and beliefs.

Hisako Watabe Before Marriage

My mother, Hisako Watanabe Watabe, was the third child of Gengoro and Chikae Watanabe, born on April 1, 1921, in Tokyo. Gengoro was a colonel in the Imperial Army and was an army attaché in charge of accounting sent to the Japanese embassy in Tenshin, Manchuria. On May 7, 1925, when Hisako was barely four, her mother, Chikae, passed away during the flu epidemic. My mother's oldest sister, Chieko Ohta, told me about their mother's death in more detail than even my mother knew. Chieko remembers vividly how their mother passed on calling my mother's name, "Hisa-chan, Hisa-chan," before dying.

My mother had no recollection of her birth mother but always loved and missed her. She was not treated very well by her stepmother, Toku, for very understandable reasons—the maid that came with Chikae when she married Gengoro took care of my mother very dearly until Gengoro remarried. When the stepmother came, the maid was let go and my mother treated and talked to her stepmother as just another maid. In addition, when my mother was nine, her half brother Tadashi was born (in 1930) and then Kazuko (1932), Akira (1934), and Makoto (1938). Naturally, Hisako's stepmother favored her own children. My mother's father, Gengoro, was transferred back to Japan, and the family moved around a lot. Hisako went to elementary schools in Tokyo, Osaka, Himeji, Kurume, and then finally moved back to Hoten, Manchuria, in 1933 when Gengoro became an instructor at an imperial military officers academy there. She entered the Hoten Naniwa Women's High School in 1933. Four days after she graduated from the high school in 1938, she married Masao Watabe, who was studying Russian in Harbin as a future diplomat. Hisako married at the young age of sixteen for a very significant reason. Her older brother, Masashi,

*Masao and Hisako Watabe on their
wedding day, March 20, 1938.*

whom she loved very much, was the best friend of Masao at
Harbin. But when he died of tuberculosis in 1936, Gengoro asked
Masao to marry Hisako to smooth family life with his second wife.

EARLY YEARS OF MARRIAGE

My mother lived with Masao's family in Ryojun, Manchuria, for
a while after their marriage. Their first son, Masahisa, was born in
1940 during this time. The family moved back to Tokyo because
Masao was transferred to the main office of the Japanese foreign
ministry from the embassy in Peking. However, World War II broke
out, and Masao was drafted; Hisako evacuated to her husband's
hometown of Fukushima with Masahisa and Masaji, who was only
two months old. After the war, Masao was transferred to the U.S.-
Japan Liaison Office (a new name for the Ministry of Foreign Affairs
during the Occupation period) in Sendai. The postwar baby
boomer, Masakazu, joined their family in Sendai in 1947.

Masao was very much troubled, at the time, with the outcome
of the war. The country he wanted to devote his life to was

defeated in the war and many of his close friends had sacrificed their lives for their country. Many questions bothered his spirit. "Why was I not taken in the war for my country? Why was Japan— the chosen nation, in Shintoist belief—defeated in the war?" He began teaching Chinese at night at the Tohoku Foreign Language School and there he came in contact with a Catholic father who was teaching English. Masao asked many questions concerning Christianity and he began to have more hope about life through the influence of this Catholic father. In fact, this father invited him to become a Catholic and to help him establish an orphanage in Sendai. Masao soon discovered that the Catholic father was more interested in establishing a place of worship than in the orphans themselves. With this revelation, coupled with the transfer of the Catholic father to Germany, he discontinued attendance at the Catholic Church.

Following this, Masao began to attend the Methodist Church, which he was introduced to by a Methodist minister and his wife. They also invited him to accept Christ through baptism into their church. My father kept holding off because he had several unanswered questions. Meanwhile, one of his students at night school mentioned that two American missionaries had started boarding at his house. My father asked the student to bring them to the school so he could meet them. They came and invited him to attend their first meeting in Sendai on the following Sunday. My father went there instead of the Methodist service and received a pamphlet, *Joseph Smith Tells His Own Story*. The following is his own account of what happened:

> As I read the booklet I felt so inspired that I couldn't sleep, so I continued to read until dawn. I was surprised to learn that the Prophet Joseph Smith saw the living God, our Heavenly Father, and his Son, Jesus Christ. At first I couldn't believe it, but something enlightened my mind and aroused a desire within me to know more about this incident and to search out facts to see if they were really true. I started reading the Book of Mormon. When I found the following scripture in First Nephi my heart was filled with joy:
>
> "Yea, even my father spake much concerning the Gentiles, and also concerning the house of Israel, that they should be compared like unto an olive-tree, whose branches should be

broken off and should be scattered upon all the face of the earth.

"Wherefore, he said it must needs be that we should be led with one accord into the land of promise, unto the fulfilling of the word of the Lord, that we should be scattered upon all the face of the earth.

"And after the house of Israel should be scattered they should be gathered together again; or, in fine, after the Gentiles had received the fulness of the Gospel, the natural branches of the olive-tree, or the remnants of the house of Israel, should be grafted in, or come to the knowledge of the true Messiah, their Lord and their Redeemer." (1 Nephi 10:12–14.)

I was impressed because in those days I had joined the United Nations Association and had known that the olive tree is symbolized on the United Nations flag, each leaf representing a member nation. I found in this scripture an exact analogy of the United Nations flag. It seemed to me the goals and purposes for which I had aimed through participation in the United Nations Association had become clearer. I gradually realized my true purpose was here in the Book of Mormon.

Also, when I learned about temple work and about baptism for the dead and the saving of our ancestors, principles that I couldn't find in any other religion, my joy and gratitude were beyond expression. Many of my relatives and friends had been killed in battle, but now I could be an agent of salvation for them through genealogical work and temple ordinances.

I quit attending the Methodist Church and began to attend the Mormon meetings regularly. The more Mormon doctrine I studied the more my testimony was strengthened. I felt that finally I had found the complete truth I had been seeking for a long time, and I made up my mind to be baptized into the true Church of Jesus Christ.[1]

On a cold November 6, 1949, in the river Hirose, my father was baptized by Elder Hugh Lynn Oldham, thereby becoming the first convert in the city of Sendai. Shortly after he received the Melchizedek Priesthood, he served as a branch president in Sendai from 1951 until 1957, when we moved to Yokohama. After his conversion to the gospel, he was not interested in his government position anymore. Actually, understanding the gospel more fully would have helped him to live in the world better, but at that time he felt his conversion and faith in Christ were much more important than anything else, including his position in the government. In addition, since the end of the war, he began losing that sense of mission with regard to the Japanese government that he had felt previously. He quit his prestigious job in the diplomatic service because the lifestyle required by his church conflicted with the lifestyle he had led as a diplomat. He thought telling others to live the Word of Wisdom was much more important than keeping his job and acquiescing with his colleagues in violating the Lord's laws. My father was completely satisfied with his decision. But for my mother it was a complete shock and a serious trial.

Hisako Watabe's Acceptance of the Gospel

Heavenly Father reveals his truth in many ways, and testimonies are gained and expressed through different means. Some gain it through dramatic spiritual experiences and others after quiet yet constant and faithful application of the principles of the gospel throughout their lives. Unlike my father's swift and dramatic conversion to the Church, my mother's was the latter type of conversion— through dedicated practice of the gospel throughout her life. The teachings of the Mormon church must have been totally foreign to my mother at first. According to my older brother, Masaji, my mother even thought seriously of leaving my father when he joined the Church.

She came from a very prestigious and elite family, and her marriage at such a young age was specifically arranged, by her father, to be to a promising future government officer and a close friend of her deceased brother. This was an assurance to her father that he could entrust her to him and that she would not have to go through difficulties in life. But now she faced an unknown future with a choice to make. Should she leave this visionary man who became almost fanatic about a small, unknown, foreign church to the extent that he gave up his position in the government and a secure future, or should she accept the gospel and stay with him? Nine months after his baptism, on July 4, 1950, my mother decided to experiment and plant the gospel of Jesus Christ in her life. However, nurturing the seed was not very easy for her; she knew so little about the gospel. There were no others she could go to to ask about the gospel or the Church, nor any books or texts written in Japanese that she could read to obtain information. The war-torn city was not any comfort to my mother. Since my father had some marketable skills, he was able to teach and translate and make ends meet. We had a small farm outside of Sendai with a vegetable garden, pear orchard, chickens, and goats that our family took care of.

While my father was the branch president, I don't recall going to church together with him. My mother would take us—by then, five small children—to church every Sunday on a train. We would walk twenty minutes to the train station closest to our house and get off the train one station before the station closest to the church because this would save a considerable amount of money for the six of us. My sisters were so small that my mother had to carry one or sometimes two children, one in front and the other on her back, as we walked at least thirty minutes each way from the station to the church. This was not easy for a woman who was raised in a home with a maid. I can see why my mother thought of leaving her visionary husband who was completely immersed in the teachings of Christ. Yet, my mother endured. The Lord was good to our family during this time of hardship. The little branch grew to be like a family to us, and we really enjoyed the close association with each other and the wonderful missionaries that were sent to our branch. During this time, we had visitors such as Elder Harold B. Lee, whose visit I distinctly remember. Of course, I had no idea what significance his visit had or what kind of man he was. Yet the Spirit must have been very strong; I still remember him clearly, attending our small conference, and I also remember the testimony I bore even though I was only seven years old.

MOVE TO YOKOHAMA

When the Church needed a full-time translator to translate some materials into Japanese, my father must have felt that it was a call from the Lord and he immediately accepted the offer. But it meant that we had to make a major move. In this modern age, it takes a few hours to go from Sendai to Yokohama, but at that time it meant travelling all day on a train to go to Tokyo, then several hours from Tokyo to Yokohama. We had to sell our farm and take all our essential belongings to a small house in the city. I am sure my mother was wondering what the future was going to bring to our family, but she chose to follow her husband just as Sariah had followed Lehi. We said good-bye to our wonderful and close friends in Sendai, some of whom, by the way, came to see my mother in Utah when they found out that she was seriously ill. Others also came all the way from Sendai and other places in Japan to her funeral in Utah.

My mother's adversities did not end with separation from her friends. The salary that my father earned was insufficient for a family of six growing children. The economic growth of Japan was keeping the nation's inflation rate high. I am sure that the mission home budget was not very much either; my father was not one to demand a higher salary. I remember him scolding my mother and telling her not to complain, because he was being paid out of the tithing funds of the Church. We, all boys, have worked since we were young. In the United States, a young person's taking on a part-time job is considered normal and is encouraged, but in Japan it meant poverty and was an extremely humiliating experience, particularly for the parents because it indicated that they did not have the means and abilities to provide for their children. Eventually, my mother, too, had to work; she sold life insurance. Looking back, I think it was a great blessing to us because we learned to enjoy work. I still remember the happy, beaming smile on my mother's face when I bought the first refrigerator for our family out of the money I saved from tutoring young students while I was in high school.

But my mother's financial trials were nothing compared to the challenges she faced with us growing up in the Church. Ironically, just as in the case of the early Mormon pioneer women, the greater challenges came because of the gospel. They made us stretch, become strong, and grow to be worthy of greater blessings, though at the time we could not see the Lord's purpose, as things seemed so hard to bear.

One of the missionaries we met in a branch in Tokyo soon after we moved somehow felt that it was his mission in life to bring my brothers and me to study in Zion. He had just come to Japan on a mission and did not speak a word of Japanese; we did not speak a word of English. He never was assigned to Yokohama, but we used to see him often in conferences and other district meetings, and he would often visit our home in Yokohama. There were several other missionaries who talked about inviting us to come to the States with them, but they were not as determined as this missionary, John D.

Chase. In fact, since I have come to the States, he has shown me the entries in his missionary journal in which he wrote about us when we first met in Tokyo and about his spiritual experience in which he felt strongly that it was his mission in life to bring us to the States to study.

Although my oldest brother, Masahisa, was studying English and wanted to go to the States, my other older brother, Masaji, and I never wanted to go to America. My mother, who had devoted her life to her family, was not eager to send her children to a country that seemed so far away at that time. America, to us, was the end of the world, an unknown country on the other side of the ocean. It took my brothers a whole month to cross the ocean by boat. We had no telephone in our house; even if we had had access to a phone, to make a call would have meant a substantial amount of my father's meager salary. We had a silent understanding that a phone call or a telegram meant serious news such as death. To see her sons leave one by one to the country of a former enemy, a country which seemed so far away, must have been almost unbearable to her. Once they were gone, they seemed to have gone forever. My mother must have felt that the Church was taking not only her stable future but also her own sons. I saw my mother in tears, hanging on to the colorful paper tapes thrown by my brother from the deck of the ship that took him to an unknown country.

Since I knew how much my mother grieved when the other two brothers left for the States, I was determined to stay in Japan and succeed in Japanese society. To do this I was determined to go to a prominent Japanese national university and secure my future. Somehow I was blessed in being accepted into a national university with a national scholarship. I remember seeing my mother's relief to see me pass the test. However, the missionary that felt that we ought to come to the States again insisted that I should follow my brothers. He was even ready to come to Japan to persuade me to go if I did not live up to the promise I made with him once when he was in Japan that I would come to the U.S. I had many arguments with my father as to what to do. He felt it was the Lord's will for me to go to the States. I felt I should stay in Japan. Obviously, my mother wanted me to stay because I was the last of the three oldest boys and she depended on me considerably, but she continued to advise me to follow His will. My father told me that I had come to the age when I must go to Heavenly Father on my own to make a decision, which I did, and decided to leave home. My mother wrote several poems and gave them to me as I left home. They described her pains in being a mother and yet relying on the Lord for understanding and comfort.

> So this child in his heart
> has chosen the hard way
> over the way of ease—
> And I must understand,
> I must bear silently the pain of parting.

> My thoughts are
> on the time just ahead
> when he must leave me—
> Yet still I say
> nothing.

> The words we shared,
> the things we did,
> these
> will only be beautiful
> when he is gone.

> Today again
> my time is spent in vain,
> my only moment of delight
> when I see my children
> gathered around the table.

> Relying on God
> to show me
> the way,
> I will go on working,
> as long as I have strength.

> I think of long ago,
> when I was a child,
> and my mother sang to me;
> fifty years have passed,
> gone as in a dream,
> and here I am, a mother myself.

How grateful I am to my mother.
I think of long ago, of that third child,
who caused me so much trouble—the one who now
leaves me in shock, leaves me on a long journey.
How grateful I am to mothers.

—Hisako Watabe, April 21, 1966

Although my father is the one that has received the most attention as one of the first to embrace the gospel and the one who has
had so many callings in the Church, from being a branch president
to the first patriarch in Asia, it is my mother's faithfulness and obedience that influenced us children. We, who were born and raised
in a non-Christian country where education, science, and physical
proof and reasoning are much more important than emotion and
abstract concepts such as faith and belief, needed a person such as
my mother to nurture our seeds of faith. In her testimonies and
talks I do not remember her ever talking about anything supernat-
ural or of a so-called "spiritual experience." She would say a testimony is expressed by living what you believe. In fact, she never
was one to stand up voluntarily to express her testimony. Yet she
continued to live faithful to the gospel and to serve in whatever
calling she received, such as Relief Society president, teacher in various organizations, a stake missionary, etc. Heavenly Father blessed
her abundantly and let her know that the gospel is true as she practiced it in her life.

Two years after I came to Brigham Young University, in the
summer of 1968, we three boys and John Chase saved money from
our part-time jobs and summer work, and invited our whole family
to come to the States so that we could be sealed in the temple and
tour Church historical sights. Imagine the joy we all felt in the Salt
Lake Temple when President Harold B. Lee sealed our family for
eternity. I remember him telling us that heaven was smiling on us.
My mother spoke at my farewell at the end of that summer trip
before my departure to Brazil on a mission and said that she had
always been a nearsighted person not only physically but also spiritually, and had never known that the Lord had these blessings in store
for her as a result of her painful yet faithful obedience to his will.

After our grand reunion in the States, our family was again scattered all around the world, but this time with the assurance that we

were sealed together forever. My oldest brother, Masahisa, was working in Los Angeles with his wife and two children after his mission in Japan and graduation from BYU with a master's in accounting. Next oldest, Masaji, was completing his master's in math at BYU after his mission in Japan. I was off on my mission in Brazil, and two younger sisters, Seiko and Yasuko, and my youngest brother, Masasue, all headed back to Japan with my parents. My mother wrote me while I was in Brazil that it did not matter where we were as long as we were walking toward the same direction, looking at the same star.

Masao and Hisako Watabe in front of the Tokyo Temple.

Eventually, my youngest brother, Masasue, also served a mission in Japan, and all six children were married in the temple to wonderful spouses who are committed to the gospel.

After we all grew up, my parents devoted their lives to missionary work and temple work. As mentioned earlier, they served in the Hawaii, Tokyo, and Taiwan temples. My parents loved the people and all the missionaries that they worked with, which is the reason they decided to extend their mission until May of 1990. I had to go to Taiwan to literally take them away from the work they so enjoyed.

The Lord has blessed our family with many marvelous manifestations of his hand in our lives. I will share only one for each of my parents. My father, ever since he joined the Church in Sendai in 1949, has been a gung-ho missionary. He used to embarrass me all the time by talking to any stranger he met on the bus or train about the restored gospel of Jesus Christ. When I was teaching one beautiful Japanese family in Brazil, I could not commit them to baptism. But in a fireside we held for all the Japanese members and investigators we were teaching then, I discovered that the father of the family, Mr. Taizo Sato, had received a tract and invitation to the Church when he was in Sendai, Japan. I knew, when he was talking, that it must have been my father. He was able to recognize my father from the family picture I showed him, and it was indeed my father who gave him the tract back in Sendai, Japan, fifteen years prior to that. I will never forget what he said in tears after I baptized the whole family: "Heavenly Father loves me and he did not forget me."

Interestingly enough, not too long ago we hosted a young medical doctor from Brazil, Marilia Ogawa, who was not a member of the Church. She stayed with us for a while and went to BYU to study immunology. While she was there she joined the Church and later went on a mission to Brazil. After her mission, she went back to her home ward in São Paulo for the first time, and there she found Brother and Sister Sato and their daughter and her children. Now my oldest daughter, Michelle, is serving a mission in São Paulo, and she is enjoying her association with these wonderful Saints. She jokes about the people who won't hear their message and says that she'll send her children later to finish the work. I don't think my parents ever dreamt that their decision to join the Church would ever produce this type of intertwining of eternal friends and families in the gospel.

And these associations are not limited to this earth only, as our beloved mother, who went before us to the spirit world, taught us. About two weeks before her passing, our family got together for our niece's wedding. After her reception in Salt Lake City, we all gathered in my mother's room to sing a couple of hymns for her because she enjoyed our singing. After we sang her favorites, "There is Beauty All Around" and "I Am a Child of God," everyone left. When I was helping my mother prepare to go to bed, she said, "Angels were standing all around when you were all singing for me. . . , many, many angels." Hearing this from my mother, I do not doubt whatsoever the reality of the angels she saw. As I mentioned, she was not a visionary person and was totally coherent until almost the last day. A few days before she died, she kept calling, "Mother, Mother." I am sure her mother was one of the angels that was anxiously waiting for her to come to the spirit world.

On the day she passed away, we received a letter from Michelle, from her mission field in Brazil, dated December 7, saying that she had a dream about Grandma. On the day of the funeral, after the services there was another letter from her dated January 17. The following is the first part of her letter:

Beloved Family!

One challenge for you, Dad and Mom . . . How are you? I haven't heard from you for quite some time. I hope everything is all right! This morning I read an article about the spirit world that was written by Heber Q. Hale of Boise, Idaho. He had a dream in which he saw the spirit world, the missionary work there, the vicarious work there, and the relatives and friends there. He described what they are doing there, and everything there is well organized. They have teachers there teaching the gospel, people with work and responsibilities and callings, depending on their degrees. . . . He also said that people there are waiting for the people from the earth. They were being prevented from coming to the spirit world because the people on the earth would not let them go. If the people on the earth could see the spirit world, they would not stop others from going. As I read this article, I began thinking about Grandma and that we probably are preventing her from going to the spirit world and we should let her leave already. They are waiting for her with festivities and with a great reception, and her friends on the other side are waiting for her. They do not quite understand why we here have fear of the word "death" so much, because in reality we shouldn't. It comforted me so much, to know more about the spirit world.

Little did she know that four days later, her grandma started to have great pains, and Masaji, Masasue, my father, and I blessed her about eleven o'clock that night. We all took turns giving her blessings. All three children thanked her for all she had done for us and blessed her that she could go to the next world where her loved ones were waiting. Masaji especially asked Heavenly Father not to let her suffer any longer and pleaded with him to take her to his presence. The next morning about four-thirty, I was awakened by my father's call, and shortly thereafter, she took her last breath. When I told her, "Mom, thank you," she did not say a word, but had a tear in her eye as she left. It is interesting that her devotion to the gospel through actions was blessed with such a powerful heavenly manifestation of the spirit world and that passing on to the next world is part of our loving Heavenly Father's plan.

She truly lived up to what she sang in her poem:

> Relying on God
> to show me
> the way,
> I will go on working,
> as long as I have strength.

I am sure my father will continue to bear testimony of Christ and the truthfulness of this gospel, and so will many that have been privileged to come to the gospel through these faithful and devoted pioneers, Masao and Hisako Watabe.

Notes

1. "Masao Watabe's Story," in Spencer J. Palmer, *The Expanding Church* (Salt Lake City: Deseret Book Co., 1978), pp. 174–75.

A HINDU FINDS THE RESTORED GOSPEL: MY CONVERSION STORY

by Ketan Patel

As I reflect on how I came across the doctrine of The Church of Jesus Christ of Latter-day Saints and the events which led to my conversion, I am reminded that as members of the human family, we each have our own individual identity. Our individual identity is made up of our life's experiences, our cultural and religious backgrounds, the environments we are exposed to, and of course the political and social arenas we live in. Given this reality, I am also reminded of the fact that we are accountable for the choices that we make. And in this life or the life that comes after, we are each given the opportunity to hear and accept the gospel of Jesus Christ.

I was born in Uganda, Africa, in 1969 during the political turmoil of the Idi Amin regime. When I was very young, it was a very tumultuous time for my family. Having refused to hand over his assets to the government, my father was taken as a prisoner to a labor camp. During the course of a day he was tortured and beaten and was then taken to the jungle and was left for dead along with others. Fortunately he had enough strength left in him and was able to make it out of the jungle. There were others who were not so fortunate. He presumed that many of his friends and their families, as well as others who had been taken to the labor camps, were executed. My father was able to make it back to our home and was nursed back to health by my mother. Within a matter of days we fled the country. We took what we could; however, we had to leave our assets behind, for they had been seized by the government.

During this time, the British government was offering asylum to Ugandan citizens, and my father knew that this was our only hope and our only way out of Uganda. It was a very dangerous journey fleeing the country. My father knew very well that if on his way to the airport the guerilla soldiers found out he was a survivor of one of their labor camps, he would be executed immediately. He knew that the authorities would especially be on the lookout at the airport for anyone who had been a "political prisoner." It was because of this uncertainty that my father decided to leave by himself and go to England, while my mother would take my sister and me to India. We were all fortunate enough to make it out of the country without incident, and within a matter of months we were all together again in England.

I do not know why in life some are spared and others are not. I do not know why some are brought into the afflictions and sufferings of tyranny and others are not. What I do know is that our Heavenly Father is fully aware of all the things that will happen to his children from the beginning. And with this foreknowledge he brings about his righteous purposes. I have no doubt that he is fully aware of all the trials and tribulations that each of his children will go through in life, and in his infinite wisdom, justice and mercy are satisfied. I recognize the guiding hand of God that preserved us.

England was very good to us, and we prospered while we were there. However, the prospects of a better life in America convinced my father that such an opportunity should not be missed, and in 1976 we arrived in New York City. Growing up in New York City was quite an interesting and unique experience. During the twelve years that I lived there I was exposed to many diverse cultures and religions from all over the world. Many of my friends and colleagues came from diverse backgrounds, and each had a unique history. I shall always be grateful for having the opportunity to come to know and understand the many diversities that exist among our Heavenly Father's children.

I was raised in the Hindu culture and faith, and like many of my friends, I worshipped in the religion I was raised in; and it did not matter as to whether or not I agreed with this way of life, only that I was strict in obeying the social, cultural, and religious heritage I came from. I bear no resentment to any religion or culture. Tradition can be a sad thing, however, for when it is not flexible, it leaves no room for agency or seeking out individual identity. I often wonder how many people reject the gospel because of social, cultural, and religious pressures, with the truth not being permitted to stand for itself nor even given a chance. When the truth is rejected as a result of such norms, we all have cause to mourn.

As the years went by, I was becoming quite the American. I fell in love with America and immersed myself in all that it had to offer. I readily admit that this was not always a good thing; however, it allowed me to truly come to know who I am and not have it dictated to me. The full realization of that would come many years later. This was the cause of much contention between my family and me because I was breaking away from all their traditions. This situation continued and heightened well into my high school and college years. In 1988, during my first year in college, my father decided to go into business for himself and moved us to South Carolina. Unfortunately, about a year later, things were not going so well for my father's business, and as he was given the opportunity to return and work for his former employer, he decided to do so and moved the family back up north. However, I decided to stay in South Carolina and continue my education.

Looking back, I feel a certain sadness and sense of regret when I think about the experiences I had growing up in New York City. For me it was such a worldly place. I felt no need or desire to try to find a path to God. I felt that all that life had to offer and all the things I wanted out of this life could be obtained and achieved through my own efforts. As hard as it is to admit, I saw no need to turn to Deity or God or any sort of ethereal medium to guide me on this journey we call life. I always wish I had had the gospel in my life back then; however, I firmly believe that there is a time and season appointed for all things. And when we are ready, the gospel is brought before us to accept or reject.

As my academic pursuits continued in college, I found myself relying on the understanding, knowledge, and wisdom of man. Given my upbringing, I never saw any need for God in my life and I never believed in any core religious concepts. I never claimed allegiance to nor had faith or conviction in any specific established religion. Indeed, I suppose one could say that my "faith" was in "the arm of flesh." I truly marvelled at the accumulated knowledge and understanding that mankind had gathered, and I felt that as science, technology, and inventions progressed, answers to many, if not all, of life's questions could be found. Of course this "intellectual" attitude left very little room for God in my life or to even attempt a path which could lead to God.

However, as time went on, I began to question the many precepts put forth by modern science and many other areas of secular thinking. I began to question the order in nature, in the universe, and in many other things. I began to realize that there was an order in the physical world. From the microscopic to the macroscopic and everything in between, life had order. I realized that this order was no accident and that there was purpose behind it. I grew tired of hearing or seeing the word *theory* in every explanation put forth by men trying to explain the extensive magnitude of this order. I felt there had to be something more out there to explain this order.

As I began to question and ponder this impasse I had come to, I started thinking about the existence of God and began to pursue, at a very academic level, an understanding of God and, if there was such a being, how one could find a path to him. I had many diverse religions I could choose from. Notwithstanding my Hindu background, I chose Christianity, because I was partial to it, and began to read the Bible. I cannot help but be reminded of the words of the prophet Alma, who wrote: "And all things denote there is a God; yea, even the earth, and all things that are upon the face of it, yea, and its motion, yea, and also all the planets which move in their regular form do witness that there is a Supreme Creator" (Alma 30:44). Indeed I am grateful for having had my eyes opened to such truth in my life.

As I continued in my pursuits to try to read the Bible in an attempt to try to find answers to my questions, a spiritual awakening was happening within me, though I did not realize it at the time. A certain change started to take place, and I started believing what I was reading. However, I was confronted with another problem: What is truth? And given the many beliefs within Christendom, which one was the right one, if there was such a thing? Though my pursuits were only academic, I felt that if God truly did have a church here on earth, surely he would have a direct guiding hand in its function, and I saw none of that in the many faiths I was acquainted with. By saying this, I do not intend disrespect for any of the religions of the world.

At the same time, a close friend who had converted to The Church of Jesus Christ of Latter-day Saints suggested that I meet with the missionaries from this new-found faith. I agreed and decided to meet with these missionaries, if for nothing else than to perhaps learn of another religion. As one who had little or no experience in faith and things of the Spirit, I had a very hard time accepting what I was being taught. Having become acquainted with the Bible and believing it was an ancient record, I did not believe that God spoke with people today. The Bible seemed to be a finished record and it spoke as if there were nothing more needed. I found it difficult to accept the Joseph Smith story, for I did not believe that God spoke to people in modern times. I did not believe there was a need for God to speak to anyone, because I believed all that we needed was given to us in the Bible—at least that was the impression I had at the time. I had what could be construed as a "that was then, this is now" mentality, and since I had no interest in converting, I decided to no longer meet with the missionaries.

I have often reflected on those meetings I had with those two elders and recognize that I was perhaps being prepared to accept the fulness of the gospel at a later time, for I know now that I certainly was not ready then. The truth can often seem to be strange and unusual, given a world that refuses to open its heart and mind to the simplicity of the gospel and insists on raging on in its own traditions and understanding. How much better the world would be if people would realize that God is not a twentieth-century man, but he is the same yesterday, today, and forever! After this experience I continued in reading the Bible and began to put forth efforts in trying to apply some of the teachings of Jesus Christ in my life. This progressive effort was the beginning of my understanding of faith and things pertaining to the Spirit. Sometime later, this same colleague who had converted to the Church left his home state of Utah and came to stay with me in South Carolina. One day as I was browsing through his bookshelf, I came across a book titled *Jesus the Christ*, by James E. Talmage. I opened the book to a certain page and began to read. The words immediately sparked my intellectual curiosity and they caught my eye. I inquired about the book and he told me it was written by an Apostle of the Church. I asked if I could borrow the book. He agreed and I proceeded to read at every opportunity I could.

I found the book to be a very intriguing and interesting piece of work. As I was reading, I came to realize that the author was writing with authority and personal knowledge. He wrote as if he personally knew Jesus Christ, and although I had read some of Christ's teachings in the Bible, the book opened up a world of understanding regarding these teachings, and I truly came to understand who Jesus Christ is. After I finished reading the book, I realized it left quite an impression on me. I could not deny the feelings I had while reading the book, and I began to educate myself with respect to Latter-day Saint theology. This had to be put on hold, however, due to unforeseen circumstances.

There was a recession during this time, and because of severe economic hardship my LDS friend and I decided that we would move to his former home state of Utah to pursue a better life. It was during this period of adversity that I had resolved to pray, hoping that whoever was listening would guide me out of my present situation. I shall ever be grateful to my Heavenly Father for giving me the opportunity to come across a book like *Jesus the Christ.* I believe and know that this book had such a profound effect on me, that it caused me to turn to God at a most desperate time in my life.

After our move in June 1992 to Ogden, Utah, I was fortunate to have two elders living next door to me, and, being missionaries, they were quite persistent in trying to teach me the gospel. I had said no to them, for I had become desensitized to things of the Spirit. My only focus was on trying to get my life back to normal again. However, one day I bumped into these two elders and I felt impressed to ask them to teach me about their faith. My interest here was to continue my understanding of Latter-day Saint theology and not to convert. We met for quite some time, for I had many questions. To my great surprise and joy, they had the answers I was looking for. These answers had such a resounding finality to them, that there was no question that what I was being taught was truth. After we finished, I agreed to meet with them again the next day and looked forward to our next meeting. That night I decided to "test the waters" a little and began to read parts of the Book of Mormon. I then knelt down and asked God what he would have me do and how I was to proceed. I met with the elders the next day, and as we were finishing up, I decided to be baptized and I knew it was the right thing to do. I don't know how this decision came to be, for I felt little or no spiritual manifestations. I only knew that it was the right thing to do. Of that, I have no doubt. I was baptized the following week, July 29, 1992, and it was one of the most joyous experiences I have ever had in my life.

I informed my family as to what had transpired, and of course, to no surprise, they were quite distraught at my decision. I had broken all their traditions and had done the unthinkable. They encouraged me to return and live with them, thinking I had come under the influence of some unscrupulous persons. But how could I? I could not deny what I knew to be truth, nor did I dare. They could not understand the peace and happiness I had found. In their eyes, I had abandoned them. They thought I was being quite selfish, and given their traditions and ways, they cut me off from them. It was quite a difficult time for me, but my strength and my faith were in the Lord and I knew he would guide me and bless me. The Savior taught, "And every one that hath forsaken houses, or brethren, or sisters, or father, or mother, or wife, or children, or lands, for my name's sake, shall receive an hundredfold, and shall inherit everlasting life" (Matthew 19:29). Indeed! Since then, my parents have softened their stance and in fact have been somewhat receptive to the gospel. As for the rest of my family, recently some of them have been open-minded about the gospel and have been receptive to the path I have chosen.

The tears that have followed since I came into the waters of baptism have been accompanied with much joy and happiness. Peace and contentment have been the daily norm. True, I have had many interesting challenges and I have my faults, but the presence of the Father, the Christ, and the Holy Spirit is always near. After all, in the school of life it is the gospel that brings harmony and balance into our lives and gives a path that leads to the strait and narrow way. Life is not static, but is dynamic. Adjusting to the everyday volatility of this world can be done only in and through Christ, whereby we obtain that "brightness of hope" that we all need.

I have had the opportunity to be ordained to both priesthoods. I was endowed in the holy temple on August 20, 1993. I received all these blessings with the realization and holy conviction that they will allow me to return to live with my Heavenly Father. They afford me the opportunities to grow temporally and spiritually and to draw closer to him. I cannot express enough the deep love and gratitude that I have for my Heavenly Father and his Son, Jesus Christ. They have blessed me with tremendous opportunities to receive the requisite ordinances, that I may enter into exaltation. I testify that these ordinances are necessary for our temporal and spiritual salvation.

The holy temple is a piece of the celestial kingdom here on this earth. It is here that we are taught from on high and receive more enlightenment with regard to the gospel. The temple helps us focus our lives on Christ and gives us the means to overcome the world.

Ketan Patel

Through the temple we subject ourselves to the Spirit, that we may stay on that path that leads to perfection. I have received blessings tenfold, both seen and unseen, from on high because of the temple. I testify that the temple and the work done therein are true. Temple work is revealed religion and offers mankind the gateway to the kingdom of God. What great blessings and joy are to be had in the temple!

Of the many opporunities I have had to serve in the Church, the one that I have been involved in with the most is stake missionary work. The gospel is the fruit that everyone wants and needs. We are all children of our Heavenly Father, and as such all those whom we come across in our daily lives are brothers and sisters. It is our responsibility to get them "back home." The Lord has taught, "And if it so be that you should labor all your days in crying repentance unto this people, and bring, save it be one soul unto me, how great shall be your joy with him in the kingdom of my Father!" (D&C 18:15.) Indeed! I testify that I have tasted of such joy in influencing someone to accept the gospel and come into the waters of baptism. I love missionary work! What a privilege it is to labor in the Lord's vineyard. What great spiritual experiences are had when we open our mouths and "shout" with exceedingly great joy the restored gospel to our brothers and sisters.

I believe that the transformation any Hindu would have to make to embrace the gospel would be to overcome religious and cultural traditions. I believe that the heritage most Hindus come from is very interwoven in the fabric of their everyday living. This cultural and religious heritage has been around for hundreds of years, and most Hindus do not know any other way to think, act, or behave. Because of this, there is very little room left to seek out and find individual identity, and little room to exercise agency. These traditions are so very strongly held that within Hindu society as a whole there is rarely ever an attempt to step outside the bounds of these religious and social norms; most Hindus would probably never even consider such a step, for fear of losing their family ties and all that they hold dear.

The gospel of Jesus Christ teaches that we are all individuals and that each of us is unique. The gospel teaches that we are all children of our Heavenly Father and that we can have a one-on-one relationship with him. The gospel teaches individual agency and the right to make choices without having them dictated to us. Through the plan of salvation we understand where we came from, why we are here, and where we are going. Such teaching overshadows any prior cultural or religious heritage that any of us may have had, and enlightens our minds and hearts to the truth, which is encompassed within the gospel of Jesus Christ. The gospel and the plan of salvation empower the children of God to raise themselves to their highest potential and return to the presence of our Father in Heaven. The gospel dispels all cultural and religious heritage, for it is above them. Both the gospel and the truth are of divine origin and as such must take precedence over all other things. The truth is what matters the most. It sets us free from the bondage of religious and cultural heritage and provides the path that leads to life eternal.

My conversion to The Church of Jesus Christ of Latter-day Saints was truly a pioneer experience for me. I say this because, having been raised up until the age of sixteen in the Hindu culture and faith, I was not really exposed to the gospel of Jesus Christ, which was initially very alien to me, as it is to most Hindus. Furthermore, I was the first person in my family line (which goes back many generations) to join the Church or, for that matter, to even convert to another non-Hindu religion. It is practically unheard of for a Hindu to convert to Christianity (at least in my experience), let alone to become a Mormon! Like the pioneers of old, I feel I have sacrificed and have been willing to sacrifice all that I have for the kingdom of God, which is The Church of Jesus Christ of Latter-day Saints. In joining the Church, I risked losing my connection to my family, but I knew I had felt the Spirit testify to me that the gospel had been restored, that it was the only true path to God, and that The Church of Jesus Christ of Latter-day Saints was the only true church on the earth. I then realized that that meant more to me than what my family held dear, but more important, I knew that

God was pleased with me. I knew I had done what he would have me do. And who can ask for more than that? Who can ask for more than a witness from God himself that these things are true? And who dares to question God and what he reveals to man, or to put the traditions of men above him?

With this special privilege of having membership in the kingdom, I feel that I can help other Hindus make the transformation to see the light and receive their own personal testimonies of the restored gospel. I believe I can do this by being an example and sharing my testimony that I know that these things are all true and by letting them know of the peace and happiness and joy I have found. I would like to show other Hindus that the gospel truly does make us free and that the traditions of religion and culture can be overcome through faith and by recognizing the divine origins of this work. What Hindus need to realize is not what may be lost should they convert and receive their own spiritual witness, but what can be achieved and realized through the fulness of the gospel. By this I mean that the gospel gives us the realization of who we really are and what our ultimate destiny can be should we abide by its teachings. It needs to be understood that this truth existed from the very beginning of the world and that throughout the ages it has been lost or has been turned into other philosophies or religions. I believe I can help Hindus make this transformation by showing them that I have done it!

My patriarchal blessing states that I am to do the genealogy work for my ancestors, as I am the first member of the Church in my family line. I rejoice in this, for my Father in Heaven has provided a way for my kindred dead also to receive all the blessings of eternal life and exaltation. The plan of salvation is perfect! It provides a way for all to accept or reject the gospel of Jesus Christ. I look forward with great hope as I do this work for my ancestors. I pray that they may also come unto Christ and be perfected in him!

The gospel has taught me that life is simple and that true happiness and peace in this life come from living the principles of the gospel and from being obedient to the commandments of God. I have come to know that the beginning of wisdom is recognizing one's own nothingness before God and one's own complete reliance on him. I testify that this work is true. I know that The Church of Jesus Christ of Latter-day Saints is the ancient faith restored to the earth. I know that Joseph Smith was and is a prophet of God. I bear witness of the divinity of the Book of Mormon. I have read it and studied it out in my mind, and I testify that it is the word of God. I have felt the guiding hand of God in my life, and I testify that God lives and that Jesus is the Christ. I would implore all those who come across this great work to open their hearts and minds and let the Spirit of the Lord work upon them, that they themselves may know that these things are true. To those who seek truth and to those who have it the Lord has counseled:

> Fear not to do good, my sons, for whatsoever ye sow, that shall ye also reap; therefore, if ye sow good ye shall also reap good for your reward.
>
> Therefore, fear not, little flock; do good; let earth and hell combine against you, for if ye are built upon my rock, they cannot prevail.
>
> Behold, I do not condemn you; go your ways and sin no more; perform with soberness the work which I have commanded you.
>
> Look unto me in every thought; doubt not, fear not.
>
> Behold the wounds which pierced my side, and also the prints of the nails in my hands and feet; be faithful, keep my commandments, and ye shall inherit the kingdom of heaven. Amen. (D&C 6:33–37.)

I pray that we may all be diligent and have strength of character to give heed to such wisdom and counsel as given by the Lord, in the hope that we may truly come unto Christ.

EMMANUEL ABU KISSI: A GOSPEL PIONEER IN GHANA

by E. Dale LeBaron

Perspiring profusely in the humid African heat, I interviewed Dr. Emmanuel Abu Kissi on May 12, 1988, outside the Deseret Hospital that he administers in Accra, Ghana. Brother Kissi, then a counselor in the Ghana Accra Mission Presidency, was among the first Africans to join the Church following the revelation now known as Official Declaration—2 in the Doctrine and Covenants.

Emmanuel Kissi grew up in a close-knit family of twelve children in the little village of Abomosu in the eastern region of Ghana. His father had a large farm that provided much work and sustained the family. Emmanuel went to school in Abomosu, but on the weekends he went to the farm, where there was plenty of food. He yearned for Friday evening to come so he could rush to the farm. His father was a successful farmer, and each weekend they carried enough food for the coming week on their heads back to their home. Brother Kissi recalled: "We worked hard. When we went to the farm, my father would give us a contract. We would each be given a portion of the farm to clear for the day's work, so we would all weed and clear the land. At the end of the day, we would harvest what we needed and go back home."[1]

They would return home on Sunday in time to go to the local Presbyterian church, where Emmanuel's father served as senior presbyter. His father would conduct the meetings and take care of other church matters before returning to the farm Sunday evenings with family members who were not attending school. Brother Kissi observed, "There was a very strong religious influence in our home."

At the age of nine, Emmanuel volunteered to live with his blind grandmother because other family members declined. This experience, which lasted five years, impacted his young life. "We would always walk very close," he recalled. "I held her hand. Sometimes she had a stick and I held one end of the stick. Because of this everyone used to call me 'the old lady's walking stick.'"

This service of love bonded him closely to his grandmother and affected his future choice of a career. "This is one of the reasons I decided to go into medicine," he said. "I felt so moved that people who are unable to do things for themselves need somebody to care for them. . . . That influenced me so much. I had a desire to help. . . . I realized that medicine was one of the best ways one could help mankind."

In 1953, when Emmanuel was fourteen years old, he left home to attend an Anglican boarding high school in Cape Coast, Ghana. After seven years of study, he qualified to go to the University of Ghana at Legon to study medicine. After graduating as a medical doctor, he began practicing medicine in Kumasi, Ghana, where he met Benedicta Elizabeth Banfo, his future wife. Brother Kissi related the following about their budding relationship:

> I came out of medical school at about thirty years old and thought it was about time to marry. While still in medical school, I didn't have the financial means to do so. Now I had my education, and the next thing was to find a companion in life.
>
> My wife was one of the nurses who worked on the ward in the hospital in Kumasi where I started working as one of a first batch of newly qualified medical doctors from Ghana. I invited her to my home one evening to a program the medical association was having. When she came, I was rushing to leave, so I asked her to have anything at the house she liked—to take the key, and I would come back and collect it. She says that impressed her very much that I had trusted my whole house in her hands. She thought I would be generous in life. So we soon after got married.

In 1974, Brother Kissi came back to Accra to study surgery. Two years later he received a scholarship to further his surgical studies in London, England. He had never been outside of Ghana. In addition to wanting to further his skills as a surgeon, Brother Kissi had yet another deep desire for going to London. He was searching for answers to religious questions and for spiritual

strength that he had not yet found, although he had actively participated in churches throughout his lifetime. He remembered:

> I felt that the churches were empty even though Christianity
> is not empty. I felt that there must be something more than
> what they were teaching us. So I made up my mind that there
> must be something more that I hadn't found yet. I had read the
> Bible several times from Genesis to Revelation. I did that for a
> long time with still the same emptiness. I desired to know more
> and to find a church that would satisfy my idea of what it really
> should be like. I felt that London was the center of civilization
> and the center of the Lord. If I go to London and find no such
> thing, then I will forget about it. It doesn't exist.

After completing his studies in London, Brother Kissi moved
with his wife to Manchester, England, where he worked at a hospital. During this period Sister Kissi suffered from severe depression,
and for about one year she was unable to work much of the time.
Believing that the depression was caused from her not having their
children with them, Brother Kissi sent her back to Ghana to visit
with her family and to bring her children back to England. After she
returned, however, she was still depressed, and often she remained
in the house and wept instead of working. One day while their children were in school, Sister Kissi had a life-changing experience that
she described as follows:

> When two young men rang the bell, I accepted them in
> since they told me they were missionaries. We sat down and
> they started telling me about Joseph Smith, then the teachings. I
> was convinced. When they got up to go I told them: "Young
> men, I have a problem. I've been trying to sleep, but even
> when I visit my doctor and take medicine, I can't sleep." They
> asked, "Do you mind if we anoint and bless you?" I said, "You
> are most welcome." I sat on a chair, and they put some oil on
> my forehead, and the two of them blessed me. Since that day I
> became perfectly well.[2]

Brother Kissi observed: "She was back to her normal health again.
She had an immediate, instant testimony."
Sister Kissi phoned her husband and told him of her healing.

She urged her husband to listen to the missionaries. Although extremely busy at the hospital, Brother Kissi relented and met with them. He related: "The missionaries said that their church was the only true Church of Christ on the earth today. 'Nonsense,' I said. 'If you didn't think your church was true, you wouldn't be in it. Everybody thinks their church is true. That's why they belong to it.' I told them not to make superior statements like that."

However, Brother Kissi was impressed that these young men could answer his questions so readily and with such understanding. As they told him about the Book of Mormon, Brother Kissi eagerly responded: "Don't tell me about the book. Give me one to read. If you have read it and understand it, I suppose that if I read it, I would understand it too. When I have read it, then we can discuss it."

Reading the Book of Mormon made a deep impression on Brother Kissi. "I read it and loved it," he said. "The Spirit gave me clear understanding." He then received the missionary discussions while also reading *A Marvelous Work and a Wonder* by Elder LeGrand Richards and *Jesus the Christ* by Elder James E. Talmage. He observed: "I was impressed with *Jesus the Christ* by James Talmage. As soon as I completed it, a feeling entered my heart. I knew it was true. I made up my mind right then to ask the missionaries for baptism."

Brother Kissi felt he could relate to the Prophet Joseph Smith's search for truth. He said: "Joseph Smith's story was similar to my situation. He had the same problems with churches that I had. I just put myself in his place and found myself enjoying every bit of his experience. It wasn't difficult for me to understand him. The answers came, and nobody told me them. I simply knew that the things the missionaries were talking about were true. All my questions were satisfied, and I was now ready for baptism."

Brother Kissi soon discovered that learning and growing in the gospel is a continual process. He observed, "One must thirst for knowledge and understanding, and there's no end to the thirst."

One issue that soon surfaced was the Church's former policy of withholding priesthood ordinations and temple blessings from Africans and those of African descent. The Kissis joined the Church in 1979, a year after the revelation to President Spencer W. Kimball and the members of the First Presidency and the Quorum of the Twelve recorded as Official Declaration—2. The nurses with whom Sister Kissi worked asked her how she, being black, could expect to

Dr. Kissi in front of his Deseret Hospital.

be a Latter-day Saint. Mormons, according to popular perception, considered black people inferior. Sister Kissi discussed the matter with her husband, who said: "When I have problems like that, I go to the scriptures, so I wasn't worried. I have no problem with the issue."

Following the completion of his training as a specialist in surgery, Brother Kissi practiced medicine briefly in England before contemplating returning to his homeland. Because of the poverty in Ghana, many could not afford to pay for medical treatment; hence, many physicians there made less than taxi drivers. Brother Kissi was urged to stay in England, and he was offered an excellent position. However, his response was, "The British people *want* me, but my people *need* me."[3]

In 1979 the Kissi family returned to Ghana, where Dr. Kissi began practicing medicine. Three years later, he and his wife, who was a nurse, opened a private clinic that they named Deseret Hospital. This venture did not prove to be as financially rewarding as most other private clinics in Ghana. One reason was that Dr. Kissi would not perform abortions. Although performing abortions is technically illegal in Ghana, the practice was very lucrative for many other doctors who perform them.

Describing the impact of the poverty that exists in Ghana, Dr. Kissi told of a mother and two children who came to his clinic during a famine in 1983. They were suffering from severe malnutrition, so in addition to treating them he gave the mother a basket of food. He explained: "When I filled her basket with food, she knelt down over the basket to thank me for the food. I almost cried. . . . There is so much poverty—so many people who are unable to have the basic necessities of life. That hurts me. That's why we spend so much time with patients who can't afford to pay. I see so much suffering in my country. I don't want to leave Ghana. Maybe the one or two people I could save will be worth the stay."[4]

Brother Kissi had an even greater reason for returning to Ghana than to practice medicine among his own people. He stated, "Before I joined the Church, I was anxious to return to Ghana because I knew my people would need my medical skills. But after I joined, I knew they needed my testimony of the gospel even more."[5]

Upon Brother and Sister Kissi's return to Ghana, one of their top priorities was to live near a branch of the Church, as they understood that the Church had been established in Ghana since they had left. Dr. Kissi immediately began working at a hospital in Accra, but he had not yet located the Church or the members. One day as he was visiting patients in the hospital he noticed a woman reading the Doctrine and Covenants. He asked her if she was a Church member, and she introduced herself as Sister Sampson-Davis of the Accra Branch. She told him: "Oh, we've heard all about you. We've been looking for you!"[6] The Kissi family immediately became involved in the Church, and within the next ten years Brother Kissi served as a branch president, district president, and counselor to the mission president.

In addition to his professional and Church service, Brother Kissi was also in great demand for serving in the community. He noted, "Whenever I attend a meeting for an election, I am invited to run for an office. I have done more than my share of community work."

Brother and Sister Kissi have seven children, one of whom they adopted. Following the death of Sister Kissi's older sister, they followed the African tradition and helped care for her four children and later adopted one of them. Brother Kissi explained: "In Ghana, when a woman dies in a family, her immediate younger sister is responsible for taking up the reins of the administration of the deceased sister. All the sister's children become your children. So when my wife's elder sister died, my wife automatically became the successor of her sister. We took one of the four children and have legally adopted him."

In 1981 Elder David B. Haight of the Council of the Twelve Apostles dedicated Ghana for the preaching of the gospel. Brother Kissi remembered, "We hadn't had rain for a long time. It rained that day for the first time in many months, and we knew a man of God was there. Elder Haight has been watching my footsteps all the time."

Brother and Sister Kissi later had the opportunity to travel to the United States, where Brother Kissi gave lectures. While there they had a chance to receive their eternal temple ordinances. Brother Kissi said:

> Going to the temple is, of course, the highest spiritual experience one could encounter. My wife and I were sealed by Elder David B. Haight in the Salt Lake Temple, then we went to other temples. When you go into the temple, you forget that the world exists. You forget, that is, until you come out and say, "Oh, the world is still around after all." The feeling of the temple is different; you are in a different place.
>
> Before I went to the temple, I had a dream, which I told to my wife. I was in a beautiful room. We went to the Jordan River Temple and went into the celestial room there. The atmosphere was exactly what I had seen in the dream. It was an exciting situation.

Ten years after the Church was established in Ghana in 1979, a major temporary setback occurred. The LDS Church was banned as an acceptable denomination in Ghana.

Brother Kissi had observed for some time during the 1980s that there was a growing opposition to the Church by religious leaders who felt threatened by the Church's growth. False charges were made regarding the Church's doctrines and practices. Accusations were made that the Church was a front for the U.S. Central Intelligence Agency (CIA). Brother Kissi reported:

> The Ghanaian public was excited about the Church for good and bad, and with the rapid growth of the Church came also an

escalation of the persecution of the Church. Nearly all the Mormon converts were originally of other Christian faiths, so the growth of the Church in effect resulted in reduction in numbers of all other churches. There was evidently great concern among leaders of these other churches who realized that the LDS Church was growing rapidly at their expense. Much deceit was employed to dissuade Ghanaians from joining with the LDS.[7]

In spite of the opposition, back in 1988 Brother Kissi predicted: "People are making frantic, strenuous efforts to make sure the Church doesn't cover the ground that it should. I think that the Church will in time experience geometric growth, rapid increase in membership." About one year after Brother Kissi made the above statement, on 14 June 1989, the Ghanaian government ordered the Church banned from any operation and ordered all expatriate missionaries to leave the country within seven days.

This ban on the Church came as a complete surprise, even though the announcement referred to "repeated warnings." The anti-Mormon film *The God Makers,* was shown over Ghanaian national television twice prior to the announcement.

With the announcement of this ban, the floodgates opened with a barrage of accusations and lies in the press. Under the headline, "The Axe Has Fallen," a Ghanaian newspaper reported:

> The axe has fallen mightily on two apparently powerful religious sects—The Church of Jesus Christ of Latter Day Saints (Mormons) and the Jehovah Witnesses. Two others, the Sampa Church of Ekwankrom and Jesus of Dzorwulu, both of which have acted in devious obscurantism, have also not been spared the corrective axe.
>
> The Government has found it necessary to disband these churches because they have continually misconducted themselves in ways [detrimental] to the public good, and also have by their activities been observed to be inimical to the sovereignty of the country.
>
> The Mormons, for instance have preached and perpetrated racial discrimination, for they have propagandized the falsity that the black people are "inferior" and are "cursed" by God.[8]

After describing charges made against the Church, this editorial concluded, "Most importantly we must be sure that religion does not escalate into another nightmare in the parallel of the Jonestown tragedy."[9] In one Ghanaian newspaper, under the headline, "I Was Bathed with Water from Dead Body," one young man told of being "lured" into the Mormon Church and going to "the Temple at Tesano" where "cuts were thus made" on his body and "some ointment with ashes was used to treat the wounds." He falsely described being "bathed with water drained from the body of a dead man around midnight" and then being "made to stand in a circle of candles and incense" with people chanting around him until he had "fulfilled all my days of purification." He then added that he feared that he would be killed for defecting from the faith.[10] Others, claiming to be former Church members, described "secret initiations and ceremonies" performed in our temples which involved demonic worship, the slaughter of animals, and the sprinkling of blood.[11]

The First Presidency assigned Brother Kissi to be the acting mission president during this critical and difficult time. One government official stated that the Mormons would never return to Ghana. But local Saints viewed this as a trial of their faith. They were filled with hope as they fasted and prayed for the ban to be rescinded. During the next eighteen months, with little contact or support from the Church, Brother Kissi provided inspired leadership over the Saints and wisely represented the Church in negotiating concerns with the government and community. He succeeded in protecting the Church's properties.

During this ban, the Church meetinghouses were locked with guards posted at them. Members were not allowed to meet together except in their homes, and then only with family members. Families without a priesthood holder were allowed to join with other families, but there were not to be any large group meetings. "You could not sing loudly, or you would be picked up," reported Stephen Abu of Abomosu. Some members, including Brother Abu, were arrested and imprisoned for administering to the sick and other activities that were perceived to be in violation of the ban. Others were evicted by landlords or otherwise persecuted during "the Freeze."[12]

Brother Kissi described some of the blessings that came to the Saints during this period of trial: "Faith promoting talks were given at these meetings. Members who were [too] shy to speak at Church got involved in these family units and [this] strengthened their testimonies. Elder J. W. B. Johnson, now stake patriarch, and his wife were full-time couple missionaries. He continued to tour the mission, talking with and encouraging the Saints."[13]

Brother Kissi also "travelled extensively to visit and encourage members to be patient and wait on the Lord." He noted the overall result of this time of testing: "This long period of deliberate threats and lyings that buffeted the Church caused some to lose their testimonies and to look back. The Church, as it were, had been placed in the refiner's crucible. The chaff perished but the gold was refined."[14]

Eventually some of the larger churches in Ghana, particularly the Roman Catholic church, charged the government with violating religious freedom by imposing the ban. This, along with external pressures, brought an end to "the Freeze."

The ban lasted from June 14, 1989, to November 30, 1990. John Buah, who served as a counselor to two mission presidents in Ghana, noted that "after the Freeze, good people wanted to know more about the Church." Curious to discover if what they had heard about the Mormons was true, many asked their Latter-day Saint friends or neighbors. Some accepted invitations to learn about the gospel and were baptized.[15]

A tribute to the leadership of Brother Kissi and to the faith of the Ghanaian Church members is that in less than five months after the ban was lifted, the first two stakes in Ghana were organized. On April 21, 1991, Elder Boyd K. Packer and Elder James E. Faust of the Council of the Twelve Apostles created the Accra Ghana Stake and the Cape Coast Ghana Stake. Elder Kissi was called as the Regional Representative for Ghana. In more recent years Elder Kissi has been called to prepare sacred temple ordinance materials for his fellow Ghanaians.

Emmanuel Abu Kissi, one of the great pioneers of The Church of Jesus Christ of Latter-day Saints in Ghana, gave the following message to his future posterity:

> I have found the truth. I have found it. I think of the story of the Samaritan woman who met Jesus by the well of Jacob. After talking, she was satisfied that Jesus was a great man, so she rushed to the town and made noise, saying, "Come, come, and see the man who told me everything I did in my life. Might this be the Messiah?"

That is my message: I have found the Messiah. I have found the fulness of the true gospel of Jesus Christ. My message is that people should search it out themselves and prove if this is not that true gospel, in its fulness.

The Church is so true, I don't think I have words to convey the message. We should stick to the Church and hold on to everything it brings us.

Notes

1. Unless otherwise stated, all quotations are from an interview by the author with Dr. Emmanuel Abu Kissi at his medical clinic, Deseret Hospital, in Accra, Ghana, on May 12, 1988.

2. Interview by the author with Benedicta E. Kissi at Deseret Hospital, Accra, Ghana, on May 12, 1988.

3. See Carla Brimhall, " 'They Need Me,' " *Church News*, November 23, 1986, p. 5.

4. See Reed L. Clegg, "Friends of West Africa: An Opportunity for Service," *Dialogue: A Journal of Mormon Thought*, Spring 1986, pp. 94–104.

5. See Joseph Walker, "Doctor Takes Skills, Gospel Back to Ghana," *Church News*, July 4, 1981, p. 10.

6. See ibid., p. 10.

7. Emmanuel Kissi to E. Dale LeBaron, January 6, 1996; letter in author's possession.

8. *Weekly Spectator*, June 17, 1989.

9. Ibid. The Jonestown massacre, which took place in Guyana in South America, was a mass suicide of followers of a religious sect that originated in the United States.

10. *The Watchman*, a Ghanaian newspaper, no. 19/93.

11. Emmanuel Kissi to E. Dale LeBaron, January 6, 1996.

12. See Don L. Searle, "Ghana: A Household of Faith," *Ensign*, March 1996, p. 38.

13. Emmanuel Kissi to E. Dale LeBaron, January 6, 1996.

14. Ibid.

15. See Searle, "Ghana: A Household of Faith," p. 39.

CONTRIBUTORS

Bruce A. Van Orden is professor of Church History and Doctrine at Brigham Young University, with a specialty in teaching and researching the international Church. He is author of *Building Zion: The Latter-day Saints in Europe.*

D. Brent Smith is chief, International and Interagency Affairs, National Environmental Satellite, Data, and Information Service, Washington, D.C. He has researched and written about the LDS Church in Germany, where he served as a missionary.

Everett Smith, Jr., is tax director, ICON Health and Fitness Inc., Salt Lake City. He was an early missionary in the former Yugoslavia.

Nathan C. Draper is a graduate of Brigham Young University in International Relations. He has traveled and researched extensively in Thailand, where he served his mission.

Mark L. Grover is chief Latin American studies librarian in the Harold B. Lee Library, Brigham Young University. He has compiled numerous oral histories of Mormon leaders throughout Mexico, Central America, South America, Spain, and Portugal. He wrote his Ph.D. dissertation at Indiana University on the LDS Church in Brazil.

E. Dale LeBaron is professor of Church History and Doctrine at Brigham Young University and a historian of the LDS Church in Africa. He is author of *"All Are Alike unto God."*

Kahlile Mehr is a collection development specialist at the Family History Library, Salt Lake City. He has degrees in Russian, library science, and history. He has traveled extensively in Russia, and has written articles on the history of the LDS Church in Hungary, Czechoslovakia, Russia, and Bulgaria.

Hermann Mössner is a retired municipal utilities manager living in Stuttgart-Weilimdorf, Germany. He served as the first president of the Stuttgart Stake.

Spencer J. Palmer is professor emeritus of Church History and Doctrine at Brigham Young University. He has served as a mission president in Korea and as president of the Seoul Korea Temple. He is co-compiler of *The Korean Saints.*

Ketan Patel was born of Hindu parentage in Uganda. He immigrated to the United States with his family and became acquainted with the LDS Church in South Carolina.

James A. Toronto is a descendant of Giuseppe Taranto. He is associate professor of Church History and Doctrine at Brigham Young University and is currently serving as director of the Brigham Young University Center at Amman, Jordan. A specialist on Islam, he served his mission in Italy.

F. LaMond Tullis is professor of Political Science at Brigham Young University, with a speciality in Latin American issues. He is author of *Mormons in Mexico.*

Masakazu Watabe is professor of Asian and Near Eastern Languages at Brigham Young University. He is the son of Masao and Hisako Watabe, the subjects of his biography.

Dennis A. Wright is associate professor of Church History and Doctrine at Brigham Young University. He spent most of his earlier Church Educational System teaching career in Canada and is a historian of the LDS Canadian experience.

Wolfgang Zander has recently retired as a German secondary school instructor. His family joined the Church in East Germany after World War II through the efforts of East German LDS pioneer Walter Krause.

INDEX